Blue Collar & Beyond:

Resumes for
Skilled Trades & Services

Yana Parker

Ten Speed Press
Berkeley, California

Acknowledgments

I would like to acknowledge with deep appreciation the contributions of many job hunters and resume writers who provided examples of blue collar resumes to broaden the scope of this collection—especially resume writers **Jenny Mish** and **Susan Ireland**, as well as **Roving Resume Writers** and the **Dislocated Workers Project**, who together account for over half the resumes in this book. Dislocated Workers Project is based in Portland, Oregon and Roving Resume Writers are volunteers who write resumes for homeless job-hunters in the San Francisco Bay area.

Jenny Mish and Susan Ireland, both independent professional resume writers, also helped me put this book together, applying their organizational and editorial expertise as well as tireless effort for "the big push" to complete this project.

Once again, Ten Speed's incomparable copyeditor, Jackie Wan, kept me on the straight-and-narrow, always looking out for the needs and interests of the readers, to be sure the material would be as clear and useful as possible. For this I thank her.

—Yana Parker, January 1995

Note: The author names printed at the bottom of the resumes are generally professional resume writers (except where they are the job hunters themselves) and those writers' full addresses appear on page 192.

Ten Speed Press
Box 7123
Berkeley, California 94707

Cover design by Fifth Street Design Associates
Text design and composition by Jeff Brandenburg
Illustrations and cover art by Akiko Shurtleff

Library of Congress Cataloging-in-Publication Data

Parker, Yana.
    Blue collar & beyond : resumes for skilled trades &
services / Yana Parker.
       p.   cm.
    Includes index.
    ISBN 0-89815-689-0 : $8.95
    1. Résumés (Employment) 2. Blue collar workers. I. Title.
II. Title: Blue collar and beyond.
HF5383.P348   1995
808'.06665—dc20

94-41828
CIP

Table of Contents

INTRODUCTION

Why a Blue-collar Resume Book?

Good resumes for "blue-collar" jobs are really no different from good resumes for "white-collar" or "pink-collar" or "NO-collar" jobs. **So why a separate book?** For several reasons:

1. **Blue-collar workers have been largely left out of the existing books on resume writing,** which focus most of their attention on white-collar workers—administrators, educators, managers, office support staff. That is not surprising because **in the PAST, blue-collar workers usually didn't need or use resumes.** They got their jobs by directly applying in person at the job site. That's still a great way to job hunt, *BUT. . .*

2. Now times have changed, and **employers in ALL fields, blue collar included, have started demanding resumes** as a way to screen out some of the applicants. This screening-by-resume helps them cut down on the time and expense of interviewing by eliminating applicants who aren't fully qualified.

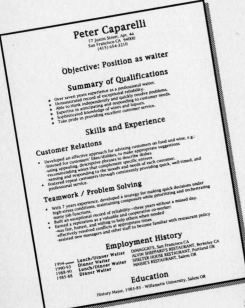

3. **Blue-collar workers often have no experience writing resumes.** Therefore, some who ARE qualified may actually NOT get interviewed for the job just because they didn't submit an **impressive resume**.

4. **Counselors and agencies are having difficulty helping blue-collar workers write resumes because:**

   - they're having to write blue-collar resumes for the first time, with little training and few good examples from which to learn;

   - their job-hunting clients often can't describe their work experience in words that would impress an employer;

   - their clients may have work-history problems that don't look great on a resume. And some counselors aren't yet skilled in designing resumes that play DOWN problem areas and play UP the unique skills and assets of blue-collar workers.

SO . . . The examples and problem-solving sections in this book show how blue-collar workers in particular can produce a *damn good* resume and hopefully get a shot at a job they might otherwise have missed out on.

About These Resume Examples

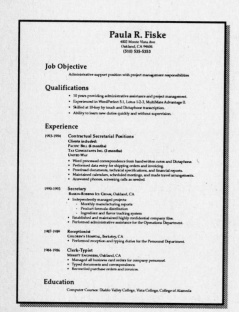

All of these resumes were written for real job seekers, although some names have been changed. You will notice that they were written by many different people—including unemployed job hunters, professional resume writers around the country, associates of Damn Good Resume Service, and author Yana Parker (that's me). The source of each resume is printed at the bottom of the page.

The writers of these resumes were all generally guided by the concepts of good resume writing as presented in my book, *The Damn Good Resume Guide.* Yet **how different the resumes look!** Clearly the concepts have been applied in a variety of ways. And with varying degrees of success. There is much diversity here—in style, content, and sophistication—and that is good, since **resumes ideally should be as individualized as the people for whom they speak.**

These resumes are not perfect! Hopefully I haven't let a misspelling or a typo slip through; even so, **these resumes are not flawless models.** Blue-collar resume examples are in such short supply that I loosened up a bit on my stringent standards when it came to fancy language and fancy word processing, and tended to overlook cosmetic imperfections such as misaligned words and all those punctuation deviations that drive good copy editors up the wall. (Oh, I *know* I will have words with my copy editor over THAT decision! But I'm sure I'll prevail!) Instead, I looked for overall effectiveness. The key question was always whether or not a resume would help someone get a job.

I selected these resumes with the help of another professional resume writer, Jenny Mish of Higher Powered Resumes (Tempe, Arizona) who is a fine writer and a good judge of these things.

Whatever its faults, this collection of resumes does provide a rich and rare source of ideas and options for blue-collar workers to express their skills and competence in an effective and appropriate way.

I hope that readers will NOT copy large portions of the resume examples they find here. And I hope they will NOT conclude that any of these resumes constitutes "The One Right Way" to write that particular category of resume. Instead, I hope they will be **inspired by the variety of approaches, and comforted by the simplicity** and directness of some of the resumes.

About the Rest of the Book

BEFORE you get to the main section with all the resume examples, you'll find **"A Crash Course in Resume Writing"** which provides **instructions** on how to write a good resume "from scratch" by applying the same **basic concepts** used in all these resume examples.

FOLLOWING the main section of resume examples you'll find the **"Resume Clinic"** which provides **creative solutions to some of the common problems** faced by all job hunters, and especially blue-collar workers, when creating their resume.

What Does Blue Collar Mean?

Back in the 1940s, when the term *blue collar* first came into popular use, it generally referred to a job where you'd need to wear protective clothing—work that required manual labor and tools of the trade. And that blue-collar work was probably done outdoors or in a factory setting. Blue collar was further defined by what it was NOT: it was *not* a desk job where a dress shirt and tie were the appropriate uniform.

Now the nation's employment scene has dramatically changed, and **the emphasis has shifted from *products* to *services*.** It's not so easy anymore to categorize occupations by what people wear to work. Fifty years later we're still using the term "blue collar," but the distinction between what IS and what ISN'T blue collar has gotten VERY fuzzy. Is it still a useful term? I think it IS. But rather than waste time splitting hairs—Is a chef a blue-collar worker? How about the person who bags fries at the local fast-food shop?—I decided to define blue-collar work VERY loosely as **any job that does not <u>require</u> a college education,** and I included jobs that blue-collar workers typically MOVE UP TO with experience and training, such as supervisor, foreman, or quality controller. I expect that this b-r-o-a-d definition won't make *everybody* happy, but what counts is: Does this book help you write a resume for a blue-collar job, *however* you choose to define it? If it helps, that's all that matters to me!

A Personal Note

I would like to say that I care a great deal about the struggle of ALL of us workers to find and keep good jobs. I believe that everybody needs and deserves a working role in the society where they can apply their unique talents to work that is satisfying to them, and through which they can support themselves in dignity. It is a great satisfaction to me when my work contributes to other workers' success.

—*Yana Parker, January 1995*

A CRASH COURSE IN

"DAMN GOOD"

RESUME WRITING

The people who wrote the resumes in this collection of blue-collar examples were inspired and guided by the principles of good resume writing described in my book *The Damn Good Resume Guide*. You may want to use those same guidelines in writing YOUR resume, so I've outlined them below.

As I've noted in the Introduction, **good resumes for blue-collar jobs are really no different from good resumes for any other-collar jobs.** But workers in the trades may have a tougher time writing resumes because they haven't had much experience at it, and thus haven't learned to describe their skills and abilities in writing. It isn't really a mysterious process, though. Anybody can do it. Try this straightforward, step-by-step process, and I think you'll be pleasantly surprised at the results.

First, here's a quick-and-easy summary:

What is a Good Resume?

A good resume is a **self-marketing tool**—a kind of personal advertisement—that shows off your job skills and their value to a future employer, and the main purpose of a resume is to **help get you a job interview**.

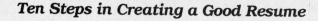

Ten Steps in Creating a Good Resume

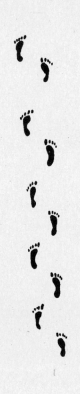

1. **Choose a job target** (also called a job objective).

2. **Find out what skills, knowledge, and experience are needed** to do that kind of work.

3. **Make a list of your two, three, or four strongest skills or abilities** that make you a good candidate for that target job.

4. **For each key skill, think of several accomplishments** from your past work history (paid or unpaid) to illustrate that skill.

5. **Describe each accomplishment** in a simple, powerful action statement that emphasizes results that benefited your employer.

6. **Make a list of the past jobs you've held, in chronological order.** Include any unpaid work that fills a gap or shows you have the skills for the job.

7. **Make a list of your training and education** that's related to the new job you want.

8. **Choose a resume format that fits your situation,** either chronological or functional.

9. **Arrange your action statements** according to the format you chose.

10. **Summarize your key points at the top of the resume.**

▶ In REAL-LIFE resume writing, we DO skip around. So *don't worry if YOUR resume comes together in some other sequence!* (As long as you *do #1 and #2 first!*)

The Biggest Hazard to Avoid

The main reasons people DON'T write effective resumes are that they trip over Steps #1, #2, and #5:

- **They don't choose a clear job target or they don't find out what's required in the new job.** *Already they're off to a bad start!*

- **They describe all their past jobs** by reciting the **Official Job Descriptions** (b-o-r-i-n-g) **instead of telling what they accomplished** in those jobs, or how they made themselves valuable to their employers by producing good results.

Now—In More Detail . . .

What is a Good Resume?

A good resume is a **self-marketing tool—a kind of personal advertisement—that shows off your job skills** and their value to a future employer, and the main purpose of a resume is to **help get you a job**

interview. It starts off by **naming your job target** and then **describes your skills, experience, and accomplishments** as they relate to THAT job target.

Writing a good resume is very different from filling out a job application form. **An application form is about JOBS,** and gives just the facts of your employment history. But **a good resume is about YOU,** and how you act and perform in your jobs. *It's very important to see the difference!*

Ten Steps in Creating a Good Resume

(You can do #3 through #10 in any order, but do #1 and #2 FIRST.)

1. **Choose a job target**—also called a job objective.

    For some people this is the most difficult step, but it's also the most important one! *You can't do a great resume without it.* You need to be able to clearly say what job you want so the reader knows how to assess your resume.

    A clear job target says to the prospective employer, **"This resume tells you about ME and how I could perform in THIS job."**

    Actually, the **job target also helps YOU** write a great resume, because it **focuses your attention on your goal** and gives you a reference point for choosing the most important things to say about yourself.

    ▶ A resume without a job target
       is like a book without a title.

2. **Find out what skills, knowledge, and experience are needed to do that kind of work.**

    This step is equally crucial because if you DON'T know what's needed, your lack of understanding will show up on your resume. You won't know what to emphasize and what to leave out, so your resume will not do a good job of selling you to an employer who is looking for people who KNOW the requirements of the job.

    The information about what it takes to do the job can be found in several ways:
    a. In a **classified ad** for the job
    b. In the **company's job description** for the job
    c. In the **D.O.T.** *(Dictionary of Occupational Titles)* at the local employment office
    d. **From someone already working in that field**

    I highly recommend d. above, as one of the BEST ways to find out exactly what skills the job requires. **Find someone who already does that kind of work.** Visit them on the job or at home, and **ask them to tell you all about "what it takes."**

    Career counselors call this wonderful form of research "information interviewing." It's VERY helpful. And don't worry—people DO love to talk about their jobs!

    (The "HOW" of information interviewing is found on page 175.)

3. **Make a list of your two, three, or four strongest skills or abilities** that make you a good candidate for that target job, considering what you now know the job calls for. Here are some *examples*:

✓ Robert Sperling (page 79) felt there were just two main skills involved in the Prep Cook job he was looking for:
   1. Food preparation
   2. Kitchen organization

So he organized nearly everything he had to say under these two skill headings.

✓ Carlene Doonan (page 75) chose three skills areas for a job as Apprentice Baker:
   1. Cooking knowledge
   2. Coordination and teamwork
   3. Speed and accuracy

✓ Sherry Hill (page 170) came up with five categories to show her abilities as an Esthetician:
   1. Sensitive customer service
   2. Clientele development
   3. Creative design
   4. Product expertise
   5. Health knowledge

Having a lot of **specialized knowledge** in your field can be considered the **same as a "key skill"** for this purpose.

4. **For each of these key skills, think of several accomplishments** from your work history to illustrate that skill.

For example, if "Building Construction" was one of the skills you named, like Vic Schwartz on page 40, you might say:

• Directed design of over 20 floor plans, consulting with architects and structural engineers. . .

• Designed and built a specially engineered, 60-foot diameter dome to endure extreme loading conditions. . .

"Work history" in this case means ANY WORK you've done—paid, volunteer, parenting, hobby, *whatever*—that documents the skills and knowledge you need to show for your desired new job.

5. **Describe each accomplishment** in a simple, powerful, **action statement** which emphasizes results that benefited your employer. (This is what I call a **"juicy one-liner."**)

For example, when the skill is Customer Relations:

• Developed a better approach to providing excellent customer service, which won back many of our old customers and expanded our new customer base.

Put the action words near the beginning of the line, and be sure to mention specific, provable, successful results whenever possible.

Don't mention activities you never want to do again!

6. **Make a list of the past jobs you've held, in chronological order.** List your most recent job first, then your earlier jobs. Give the job title, employer, and dates of employment. Include any unpaid work that fills a gap or shows you have the skills for the job.

Here's how it might look:

1993–present	Dispatcher	Billingham's Roofing, Oakland
1990–92	Journeyman Roofer	Billingham's Roofing, Oakland
1985–90	Freelance Roofer	Clients in San Mateo County

OR, like this:

1992–94	Counter Sales	Bellarosa Coffee, Chicago
1990–91	Receptionist	Elementary School, Chicago
1987–90	Homemaker & Student	
1983–87	Asst. Office Manager	Crowley Floors, Chicago

7. **Make a list of your training and education** that's related to the new job you want. This could include correspondence courses, apprenticeships, work-study programs, and relevant workshops. List the name of the school or other place where you have trained, the degree or certificate if any, and the year completed IF it's fairly recent.

You can omit this section if you have no training, no college, and no school courses to list which are related to your new job goal.

"Training" and "Education" can be listed as separate sections on your resume, or (if they are both short) they *could* be combined into one section.

If you can't decide what to include and what to leave out, see pages 181 and 182 in the **"Resume Clinic"** section.

8. **Choose a resume format that fits your situation, either. . .**

- **chronological**, if you're staying in the same field and you have an unbroken employment history; or

- **functional**, if you're making a career change OR you don't have a continuous record of paid employment.

Here's the essential difference between a Functional resume format and a Chronological resume format:

CHRONOLOGICAL	FUNCTIONAL
JOB #1	SKILL #1
something I did in that job	something I did using that skill
something I did in that job	something I did using that skill
	SKILL #2
JOB #2	something I did using that skill
something I did in that job	something I did using that skill
something I did in that job	SKILL #3
	something I did using that skill
JOB #3	something I did using that skill
something I did in that job	
something I did in that job	Job #1
	Job #2
	Job #3

"Chronological" means your jobs are arranged in order by *dates* (usually the most recent first)—this is the traditional way of arranging a resume, and places the emphasis on your JOB TITLES and employment history.

"Functional" means your *work experience* is described by emphasizing the SKILLS involved—putting the descriptive details into skill-group paragraphs that are separate from your bare-bones chronological list of jobs.

This format is especially useful when your RELEVANT skills—the skills required for your NEW job target—are not so obvious when someone looks only at your chronological job history.

For example: If you developed skills through a hobby or volunteer work and you now want to use those skills in a *paid* job, those skills might not even show up in a chronological resume format but they could be made OBVIOUS in a functional format where you're not limited to describing your activities just under job titles.

▶ Still confused? If you can't make up your mind which format is best for you, I'd suggest starting out with a functional format. That will keep you focused on skills relevant to your desired NEW job. Then, if you later change your mind, you can REorganize the same one-liners into a chronological format.

9. **Arrange your action statements** from Step #5 according to the format you chose—either:

    a. Place each action statement **under the appropriate job title** where the action happened (if you chose a **chronological** format)

OR . . .

    b. Place each action statement **under a skill category** if you chose a **functional** format. The skills you listed in Step #3 now can become your skill categories.

When you use a functional format, try to briefly mention, in each action statement, when or where this accomplishment happened, so your experience is more clear and believable.

10. **Summarize your key points at the top of the resume. Make a brief list**—say, five short lines—**of key points** which the new employer will need to know and which will make you look attractive for the new job.

A good summary *could* include:

• Number of years or months of **experience** in that field

• Your **education**, training or certification in that field

• An **accomplishment** or recognition that "says it all," if possible

• Your **key skills** or special knowledge related to this job

• Something about your personal **work style or attitude** toward the job which would look good to an employer

Put that summary at the top of the resume just below your "job target," and set each statement off with a bullet.

When you run into a PROBLEM with any part of your resume, take a look at the resume examples in this book for ideas. If you don't see an answer to your dilemma, then check out the **"Resume Clinic"** section at the back of the book for good solutions. The Clinic starts on page 173.

132 Sample Resumes

1
AUTOMOTIVE and HEAVY EQUIPMENT

2
CONSTRUCTION and MAINTENANCE

3
CUSTOMER SERVICE

4
HOTEL, RESTAURANT, and FOOD SERVICE

5
OFFICE

6
TRADES

7
WAREHOUSE, MANUFACTURING, and ELECTRONICS

8
MIXED BAG

Peter Caparelli
77 Justin Street, Apt. 44
San Francisco CA 94000
(415) 654-3210

Objective: Position as waiter

Summary of Qualifications
★ Over seven years experience as a professional waiter.
★ Demonstrated record of exceptional reliability.
★ Able to think independently and quickly resolve problems.
★ Expertise in anticipating and responding to customer needs.
★ Sophisticated knowledge of wines and liquors.
★ Take pride in providing excellent customer service.

Skills and Experience

Customer Relations

• Developed an effective approach for advising customers on food and wine, e.g.:
-listened for customers' likes/dislikes, to make appropriate suggestions
-using appealing, descriptive phrases to describe dishes
-recommending wines that complement specific entrees
-sensing and responding to the moods and needs of each customer.
• Fostered repeat customers through consistently providing quick, well-timed, and professional service.

Teamwork / Problem Solving

• With 7 years experience, developed a strategy for making quick decisions under high-stress conditions, maintaining composure while prioritizing and orchestrating many job functions.
• Built an exceptional record of reliability—three years without a missed day.
• Earned a reputation as a valuable and cooperative co-worker:
-was fair, honest, and willing to help others when needed
-effectively resolved conflicts at appropriate times
-assisted new managers and other staff to become familiar with restaurant policy

Employment History

1994-present	Lunch/Dinner Waiter	DiMAGGIO'S, San Francisco CA
1990-93	Dinner Waiter	ALVIN SHEPPARD'S RESTAURANT, Berkeley CA
1988-90	Lunch/Dinner Waiter	SHELTER HOUSE RESTAURANT, Portland OR
1985-88	Dinner Waiter	MAISIE'S RESTAURANT, Salem OR

Education

History Major, 1983-85 - Willamette University, Salem OR

Paula R. Fiske
4002 Monte Vista Ave
Oakland, CA 94606
(510) 535-5353

Job Objective

Administrative support position with project management responsibilities

Qualifications

• 10 years providing administrative assistance and project management.
• Experienced in WordPerfect 5.1, Lotus 1-2-3, MultiMate Advantage II.
• Skilled at 10-key by touch and Dictaphone transcription.
• Ability to learn new duties quickly and without supervision.

Experience

1993-1994 Contractual Secretarial Positions
Clients included:
PACIFIC BELL (6 months)
TAX CONSULTANTS INC. (3 months)
UNITED WAY
• Word processed correspondence from handwritten notes and Dictaphone.
• Performed data entry for shipping orders and invoicing.
• Proofread documents, technical specifications, and financial reports.
• Maintained calendars, scheduled meetings, and made travel arrangements.
• Answered phones, screening calls as needed.

1990-1993 Secretary
BASKIN-ROBBINS ICE CREAM, Oakland, CA
• Independently managed projects:
- Monthly manufacturing reports
- Product formula distribution
- Ingredient and flavor tracking system
• Established and maintained highly confidential company files.
• Performed administrative assistance for the Operations Department.

1987-1989 Receptionist
CHILDREN'S HOSPITAL, Berkeley, CA
• Performed reception and typing duties for the Personnel Department.

1984-1986 Clerk-Typist
MERRITT ENGINEERS, Oakland, CA
• Managed all business card orders for company personnel.
• Typed documents and correspondence.
• Reconciled purchase orders and invoices.

Education

Computer Courses: Diablo Valley College, Vista College, College of Alameda

1

AUTOMOTIVE AND HEAVY EQUIPMENT

ANTONIA DRIVER

7123 Johnston Avenue
Pleasant Hill CA 94523
(510) 333-6666

Antonia, a woman in her forties, was sharply focused on what she wanted: a part-time job driving for Federal Express to bring in extra money, as she was supporting her son in college. —Y.P.

Objective: Position as Driver

SUMMARY OF QUALIFICATIONS

- Over 10 years experience driving and delivering in heavy city traffic, with a perfect driving record.
- Thoroughly familiar with East Bay and San Francisco.
- Excellent health and physical strength (aerobics instructor).
- Personable and friendly in dealing with the public.
- High-energy and dependable; proven ability to produce within a demanding work schedule.

RELEVANT SKILLS & EXPERIENCE

DRIVING • DELIVERING • FAMILIARITY WITH BAY AREA
As owner/manager of two small businesses:
- **Purchased and delivered** retail items, furniture, and groceries for business people and homeowners throughout Contra Costa Co. and San Francisco, for over 6 years.
- **Drove a van to pick up merchandise** throughout the East Bay and S.F.
- **Drove a truck or van** for wide range of short-trip errands in urban area.

As volunteer driver:
- **Drove a truck** to transport groups of students, in hundreds of weekly trips to sporting events and field trips throughout the Bay Area.

MAIL HANDLING
- **Batched and sorted a large volume of mail** for Bayside Dental Service, working with sorting/batching/stamping equipment. **Delivered** interoffice mail.
- **Handled important personal/business mail** for individual clients of Take-It-Easy, including cashing social security and disability checks, and paying bills.

CUSTOMER RELATIONS
- Built and maintained a base of **hundreds of satisfied customers**, as entrepreneur, creating and operating two businesses.
  - Developed a reputation among customers as a dependable, reliable, and trustworthy business person.
- Established **cooperative working relations with manufacturer's reps** of dozens of companies supplying merchandise for gift-basket company.

EMPLOYMENT HISTORY

1989-present	Owner	BASKET MAGIC, Gift Baskets
1991	Telemarketing	JOHNSON MANAGEMENT CONSULTANTS, Concord
1984-91	Owner/Operator	TAKE-IT-EASY, Shopping/Delivery Service
1981-83	Receptionist/PBX	UNITED RETAIL CLERKS, Concord
1978-79	Mail Handler	BAYSIDE DENTAL SERVICE, San Francisco

EDUCATION
Diablo Valley College coursework:
•Marketing •Merchandising •Retailing •Psychology

- Resume Writer: Yana Parker -

DALE SIMPSON

P.O. Box 51
Pencil Point, ME 03907
(207) 444-3321

Objective: Position as driver for Britt-ways Corp.

SUMMARY OF QUALIFICATIONS

- Dependable, hard worker who can be counted on to "get the job done."
- Excellent driving record, with over eight years experience behind the wheel.
- Friendly and well liked; good at customer relations.
- Available to relocate.

EXPERIENCE

1992-present Driver/Tour Guide   Trolley Tours, Pencil Pt., ME & Larkspur, AZ
- Drove small tour bus through scenic parts of these two resorts, pointing out sights, providing friendly service, and assisting senior citizens.
- Maintained a perfect driving record, always giving first priority to safety.
- Performed light repair work as needed.
- Recognized as #1 employee within this company of 15.

1991   Sales Representative   Recycled Tractor Parts, Townsend, ME
- Sold used tractor and equipment parts by phone and over the counter.
- Handled inventory, shipping, and nationwide teletype service.

1990   Driver   Oil Recycling, Paris, ME
- Managed pickup and delivery of waste oil (until business was sold).

1989   Sales Representative   Old Fashioned Engine & Parts, York, MA
- Opened and maintained new accounts by contacting targeted prospects.
- Traveled approximately 1,000 miles per week, servicing existing accounts and cold calling.

1986-88   Assistant Manager   CarSearch, Southern, ME
- Performed warehouse duties including processing orders, stocking, shipping, receiving, and locating sources for special orders.
- Promoted to Assistant Manager; handled counter sales and customer service.

1981-86   Driver/Dispatcher   Portland-Bangor Oil, Portland, ME
- Drove oil trucks, providing pickup and delivery service for waste oil recycling.
- Supervised product safety, working with thousands of gallons of oil per week.
- Promoted services as "on-the-road representative" for the company.
- Served as dispatcher in the retail fuel oil division, coordinating deliveries and service calls.

EDUCATION
ABA, Business Administration, University of Maine, Portland

- Resume writer: Susan Ireland -

RAYMOND M. FROHLICH
924 Fulton Street, #306
San Francisco CA 94117
(415) 771-2455

OBJECTIVE: Position as a Driver

SUMMARY OF QUALIFICATIONS

- Over 10 years dependable experience driving cargo and passenger vans while maintaining a perfect safety record.

- Great at training customers, handling all paperwork, and installing company machines.

- Reliable, respectful toward others, and dedicated to getting the job done.

- Able to handle stressful situations responsibly.

- Can perform light repair work as needed.

RELEVANT DRIVING EXPERIENCE

As **Driver/Installer** for PITNEY BOWES, INC., South San Francisco, 1989-93
- Five years driving cargo vans, and installing postage meters, mail machines, and scales.
- Driver-of-the-Month, March 1993. Maintained perfect safety record from 1989-93 while covering San Francisco, East Bay, and Peninsula.
- Trained customers in proper usage of postage meters.
- Handled all paperwork: installation, pickup, meter inspection, cancel order, and log driving reports.

As **Driver** for MORTON DELIVERY SERVICE, Santa Barbara, CA, 1986-88
- Three years pickup and delivery in cargo van, handling official government documents from offices throughout Santa Barbara.
- Delivered special official documents on time to selected drop-off points in Santa Barbara County.

As **Driver** for the U.S. ARMY, Fort Lewis, WA, 1982-85
- Three years operating 2- and 5-ton trucks in the loading and delivery of live ammunition to live firing ranges.
- Prepared pre-maintenance reports for trucks, monthly supply clerk reports, and quarterly inventory ammunition reports.
- Instructed enlisted men in proper ammunition safety.

ADDITIONAL EMPLOYMENT HISTORY

1988-89	Painter/Laborer	St. Anthony's Foundation, San Francisco CA
1986	Building Manager	Evergreen Court Apartments, Lakeside WA

EDUCATION

Truck Driving School — Fort Sill, Lawton OK, 1982
Graduate, De Witt Clinton High School — Bronx NY, 1981

- Resume writer: Kathie Mear of Roving Resume Writers -

CHARLES M. McHENRY

12345 NE Bronze St.
Portland, OR 97230
(503) 305-5030

OBJECTIVE

Truck Driver

HIGHLIGHTS OF QUALIFICATIONS

- 30 years experience in the truck driving industry.
- Hold current C.D.L.
- Skilled in all facets of safe and defensive truck driving.
- Working knowledge of the Portland/Vancouver area.
- Excellent customer problem-solving skills.
- Adept at dispatching, using both telephone and radio.

EQUIPMENT OPERATED

- Gas and diesel semis, doubles, triples, flatbeds, solo, trucks, lift trucks.
- Piggy-back loading and unloading.

RELEVANT EXPERIENCE

- Conducted qualification and road testing to ensure driving competence.
- Handled multi-line phone system to coordinate pickups and deliveries.
- Processed bills of lading and solved any delivery problems.
- Successfully identified and resolved customer problems which led to excellent customer relations.
- Diagnosed mechanical problems called in by drivers, so appropriate action could be taken and schedules met.
- Supervised the loading and unloading of goods, assuring that items were handled with care and placed accurately in warehouse.
- Conducted cold calls to acquire business and promote use of freight service.

WORK HISTORY

Vasquez Transport — TRUCK DRIVER / LOCAL DISPATCHING	1992-present
Dixon Terminals — TRUCK DRIVER, LOCAL	1989-92
Northwest Motor Trucking — TRUCK DRIVER, LOCAL / LINE	1966-89
Robertson Baking Co. — DRIVER / SALESMAN	1963-66

MILITARY

U.S.A.F. Radio Repairman/Truck Driver - Honorable Discharge

EDUCATION

Clackamas Community College - Video Taping
Vancouver High School - Graduate

DRIVING RECORD AND RELATED DOCUMENTS AVAILABLE ON REQUEST

- Resume written by Dislocated Workers Project -

Amy Carter Jones
19000 Sixth Ave. NW
Bremerton, WA 98888
(206) 777-7544

OBJECTIVE

Sales / Customer Service Manager

HIGHLIGHTS

- 14 years experience in the auto parts and service industry.
- Professional attitude toward customer satisfaction, resulting in an excellent reputation with customers.
- Ability to balance books and handle finances in a responsible manner.
- Purchasing experience and expert knowledge of automotive parts.

RELEVANT EXPERIENCE

1990-present **J & D DISTRIBUTORS**, Fremont CA   (import parts wholesaler)
Inside & Outside Sales
Part of a two-person sales team with over a million dollars in sales per year, topping two million the last year.
- Successfully handled busy phones daily, servicing customers while meeting shipping and delivery deadlines.
- Maintained acceptable profit margins without alienating customers, through superior customer service.

1988-89 **BAYSIDE AUTO PARTS**, Piedmont CA   (import parts wholesaler)
Domestic Purchasing and Inside & Outside Sales
Advanced from order-taker to outside salesperson and eventually to domestic purchasing manager.
- Monitored inventory, requested and evaluated price quotes, prepared and placed purchase orders.
- Oversaw receiving procedures and maintained quality control of domestically purchased products.

1982-83 **F & W ENGINES**, Berkeley CA   (VW & Japanese engine rebuilder)
Parts, Service Writing, Bookkeeping, Mechanics
Performed minor mechanical repairs and setups for machine work, as well as managing all phases of daily office operations, including:
- Service writing, estimating, and scheduling of work.
- Bookkeeping, banking, and accounts payable.
- Ordering, receiving, and keeping inventory of parts and supplies.

1981 **IMPORT CAR CENTER**, El Cerrito CA   (retail import auto parts)
Driver, Counter Sales
Worked with retail customers as counterperson.
Received and stocked parts. Made deliveries.

- Resume writer: Yana Parker -

Robert Lawson

39770 Magee Way
Castro Valley CA 94546
(415) 221-6869

> Robert Lawson had been running his own business, but his strength (and interest) was in working with people. This resume helped him go after a job using his technical skills but dealing more directly with people. —Y.P.

Objective: Position as service writer for an auto manufacturer

HIGHLIGHTS OF QUALIFICATIONS

- Outstanding talent for assessing people's needs.
- Proven ability to gain customers' confidence and trust.
- Business acumen in balancing public relations with profitability.
- Work cooperatively with a wide range of personalities.
- 8 years experience in automotive diagnosis and repair.

RELEVANT EXPERIENCE

Needs Assessment/Public Relations
- Generated large volume of repeat business from satisfied customers, maintaining excellent relations through good repair work and sensitivity to clients' overall needs.
- Developed a keen perception for both the spoken and unspoken needs of customers, providing adequate technical information and advice for decision-making, and restoring customers' sense of "being in control."

Technical Knowledge
- Repaired foreign and domestic cars for 8 years, specializing in:
  -electronic fuel injection -SU carburetors   -engine rebuilding.
- 5 years experience in heavy machinery operation and repair.
- Completed two years training in automotive repair at Chabot College.

Business Management
- Started up a successful restaurant business, including leasing/remodeling building, hiring/supervising staff, providing day-to-day management.
- Established and managed auto repair business, handling all aspects.

EMPLOYMENT HISTORY

1993-present	Owner/manager	ROBERT LAWSON FIXES CARS - Davis
1992-93	Mechanic	ALL AROUND AUTO REPAIR - Davis
1989-92	Owner/manager	ROBERT LAWSON FIXES CARS - Davis
1988	Mechanic	WINTERS GARAGE - Winters
1986-87	Mechanic	J & J AUTOMOTIVE - Davis
1980-85	Machine Operator	BOSTROM BERGEN METAL PRODUCTS - Oakland
1978-80	Partner	ALL ONE NATURAL FOODS - Hayward

EDUCATION & TRAINING

Economics, U.C. DAVIS and HAYWARD STATE, 1992-present
Certificate in Auto Mechanics - CHABOT COLLEGE, 1986

Additional Training
Electrical Systems; Tune-up - GENERAL MOTORS TRAINING CENTER
Electronic Ignition; Infrared Diagnosis - SUN PRODUCT TRAINING, San Jose

- Resume writer: Yana Parker -

ZACHARY CURTISS
35 West Harbor Road
Massapequa, New York 11758
(516) 789-8765

OBJECTIVE: SERVICE TECHNICIAN in an Automobile Dealership

HIGHLIGHTS OF QUALIFICATIONS:
- Relate easily with all levels of Co-workers and Customers
- 7 Years Hands-on Experience with Automotive Electronics, Electronic Fuel Delivery Systems and Computers
- Adapt readily to both Domestic and Foreign Car Repair
- Responsible, Capable and Hardworking

EDUCATION:

A.A.S. Degree - AUTOMOTIVE ENGINEERING TECHNOLOGY
SUNY College of Technology   Farmingdale, NY

May 1994   Graduated Cum Laude,   College and National Dean's List

AUTOMOTIVE SERVICE SPECIALIST CERTIFICATIONS:
- Automotive Electricity
- Combustion Engines
- Automotive Transmissions
- Automotive Electronics & Computerized Control

ADDITIONAL RELEVANT COURSE WORK:
Automotive Merchandising and Inspection
Computer Science   Business Management

WORK EXPERIENCE:

AUTOMOTIVE REPAIR BUSINESS   1990 - Present
- Repair, rebuild and maintain over 100 foreign and domestic automobile engines annually
- Manage all aspects of my own business

AUTOMOBILE MECHANIC   1987 - 1989
Rosco Service Station   Northport, NY

- Provided general and preventive maintenance on foreign and domestic automobiles
- Interacted with customers

ASSISTANT MANAGER / NEW CAR DEPARTMENT   1986
Anchor Toyota   Oakdale, NY

- Oversaw Department personnel and operations
- Executed repairs and installation of vehicle options
- Prepared new automobiles for delivery to customers

REFERENCES: Professional References Available Upon Request

- Resume writer: Hinda Bodinger -

James L. Kirk
1285 Colorado Ave.
Berkeley CA 94709
(510) 987-6543

James insisted that there is so much turnover in his field that employers are really looking for evidence of stability. He wanted a "Personal" section that portrayed him as a stable family man an employer could count on. —Y.P.

Objective: Auto Body Repair.

★ Over 20 years experience in quality combination body and paint repairs.

★ Complete set of tools and equipment.

★ Interested in permanent position, good salary, benefits, and possible salary incentive plan.

Experience in:
• Painting (both urethane and lacquer)
• Color matching
• Spot paint
• Complete paint
• Inventory control
• Body repair
• Light frame repair
• Rust repair
• Fabrication
• Welding

Other shop skills:
• Management
• Personnel training
• Equipment maintenance
• Customer relations

RECENT AUTO BODY EMPLOYMENT HISTORY

1991-present KRULLER AUTO BODY, Berkeley CA
Owner/Manager: Marty Ohler • (510) 876-5432

1988-90 T & R CLASSICS, Oakland CA
Mercedes Benz repair
Owner, Clark Kent • (510) 765-4321

1986-87 GEORGE'S AUTO BODY, San Rafael CA

1983-86 MARVEL AUTO BODY, Albany CA
Owner: John Farleigh • (510) 654-3210

1980-83 TOP AUTO BODY (self-employed), Richmond CA

PERSONAL: Age 41, married, 3 children, buying a home in the Berkeley area.

OTHER INTERESTS:
My family, classic cars and boats, fishing, camping, boating.

- Resume written by James Kirk & Yana Parker -

Melvin Bear

600 East 43rd Street, Apt. 2C
New York, N.Y. 10010
(212) 318 - 6000

Skilled auto mechanic, familiar with American and foreign cars, seeking a position to improve service for customers.

Experience

MECHANIC   **Complete Engines, Longwood Avenue, Bronx, N.Y.**   **1993-Present**

Working extensively on building engines for *all* American cars, including installations. Earned award for "*hard work*" in December 1993. Diagnose car problems for customers via telephone and make preliminary suggestions for repairs. Advise customers of basic car maintenance prior to leaving shop. Operate cash register in owner's absence.

MECHANIC/   **Sammy's Auto Work, Bronx, N.Y.**   **1992-1993**
FOREMAN

Worked in garage. Primary accomplishment: Developed in-depth knowledge of air conditioning system, including installations and refilling. Provided tune ups, oil changes. Established excellent rapport with customers by accurately assessing the problem and fixing it. Worked on *Pontiacs, Chryslers, Fords, GMs*, to name a few. Trained new hires.

SUPERVISOR/   **Joe's Motor, Bronx, N.Y.**   **1992**
MECHANIC

Managed all customer service in owner's absence, including routine safety checks at gas station. Learned to repair electrical systems and computerized systems for fuel injection cars: traced the problem via computer, then reassembled. Aimed to please the customer.

ADMINISTRATOR/   **United Nations, Malabo Guinea Equatorial**   **1989-1991**
ASST. MECHANIC

Scheduled 72 cars on a monthly timetable for United Nation officials and "Project" vehicles *(American and Japanese cars)*. Supervised 21 people, including drivers, cleaners, and security personnel. Delegated assignments relating to bodywork, ignition, transmission, tires, and preventive maintenance. Received and delivered cars to officials.

SUPERVISOR   **American Embassy, Malabo Guinea Equatorial**   **1988-1989**

Worked on yacht for the American Embassy, fixing small pickup trucks and small cars *(Oldsmobile, Pontiac, Fords)* in addition to generator plants, and motorcycles for U.S. Government officials. Provided day-to-day care. Affirmed that all cars were performing at maximum level. Handled engine problems, refills, changed brushes, air filters.

MECHANIC/   **Clusa Cooperative League, Malabo Guinea Equatorial**   **1983-1988**
FOREMAN

Worked as U.S. aide. Company contracted by USA to maintain commercial vehicles transporting food from interior in to Malabo. Serviced GMC bed trucks, pickups *(Nissan, Toyota, Mitsubishi, Bedford)*. Promoted to supervisor in 7 months. Assessed inoperable vehicles brought in by commercial truck drivers. Reassembled and replaced broken parts, tuned suspension system. Checked work for accuracy before vehicles left .

Education

National Vocational Training Institute, Accra, Ghana   -   Certificate: Trade Test, Grade Two   1978-1982

Mercedes Benz G.N.T.C. Technical Institute, Accra, Ghana   -   Awarded Diploma   1976-1978

- Resume writer: Margaret Lawson -

ALLAN STARBUCK
121 SE Seaview
Portland, OR 97206
(503) 987-6543

OBJECTIVE

RAILCAR FOREMAN

SKILLS & ACCOMPLISHMENTS

- Skilled in the use of railcar refurbishment equipment.
- Qualified to supervise personnel who are involved with multiple job duties.
- Able to perform maintenance in an efficient and effective manner.
- Increased invoicing at Gordon & Assoc. from $100,000 per year to $800,000.

EXPERIENCE

RAILCAR FOREMAN, Gordon & Assoc., Inc., Portland, OR   1990-1994

- Supervised a 22-person crew in the refurbishment of railcars.
- Directed the rebuilding of over 400 F10VMC freight cylinders, ensuring quality work.
- Maintained, repaired, and used:

Wirefeed welders	Stick welders	Stud welders	Torches
Port-a-Power	Pneumatic tools	Pressure washers	Compressors
			Forklifts

- Correctly installed freight-saver units in over 500 railcars.
- Kept up control logs for incoming and outgoing railcars, and properly completed bills of lading and other associated paperwork for over 2,000 railcars.

MAINTENANCE TECHNICIAN, Opticorp, Portland, OR   1986-1990

- Set up and maintained planned maintenance for the production facility, reducing equipment down-time by 50%.
- Designed pneumatic systems to improve airflow for lens cutting machines.
- Performed general plumbing for the entire production facility.
- Rebuilt motors to extend life of cylinder machines such as edgers and blockers.
- Maintained and repaired conveyor belt systems, ballast light systems, and some parts of HVAC system.

EDUCATION

Mt. Hood Community College, 1994 — Portland OR

REFERENCES AVAILABLE UPON REQUEST

- Resume written by Dislocated Workers Project -

JOHN JOBSEEKER

2855 West Cactus Road #28   Phoenix, Arizona 85329   (602) 789-1200

OBJECTIVE: To obtain a Supervisory position in a Vehicle Maintenance, or Warehouse Facility.

HIGHLIGHTS OF QUALIFICATIONS

- ▶ Quality, detail and cost oriented, with proven ability to identify, analyze and solve problems.
- ▶ Proven competence in working with others to focus activity on continuous improvement and cost effective value added work.
- ▶ Perform effectively despite sudden deadlines and changing priorities.
- ▶ Highly reliable self starter; can be counted on to complete assignments.
- ▶ Strong leadership, and planning skills; keeps a sharp eye on the bottom-line.
- ▶ Ability to determine the cause and justify the resulting cost overruns of completed projects.
- ▶ Possess excellent communication and inter-personal skills; speak Spanish on a conversational level.
- ▶ Demonstrated ability to motivate, increase morale, train and increase productivity while reducing costs through team building and leading by example.

SUMMARY OF EXPERIENCE

Performed work in the following capacities: Garage Foreman, Equipment Operator Trainer, Equipment Pool Foreman, Supervisor in Trucking/Crane Department, Supervisor in Warehouse, and Journeyman Mechanic.

REPRESENTATIVE ACHIEVEMENTS

- Conducted a study to analyze loads and hauling vehicles resulting in downsizing and reduced costs by $80,000 annually, and received a $5,000 company excellence award.
- Developed a crane operator certification program to satisfy requirements of A.N.S.I. B.30.5 1990; program adopted company wide.
- Reduced warehouse payroll costs by re-designing work processes to eliminate the need for 3 positions resulting in an approximate savings of $180,000 annually.
- Implemented program to repair and recycle used warehouse pallets saving $12,000 annually.
- Achieved a 15% increase in employee productivity in first 6 months as Warehouse Supervisor.
- Achieved a 100% customer satisfaction level in hauling services.
- Designed and implemented computerized work requests for hauling services reducing customer response time.
- Received Excellence Award for participation in C.D.L. program as 3rd party examiner.
- Implemented an employee managed safety program in Hauling Services providing for 1,500,000 Department safe driving miles.
- Streamlined work processes in Hauling Services to provide for 40% reduction in staff and equipment.
- Negotiated leases with purchase options in Equipment Pool on 5 pieces of equipment saving. approximately $40,000 when compared to rented contracts and new purchases.

continued - page two

JOHN JOBSEEKER - page two

EMPLOYMENT HISTORY

ARIZONA PUBLIC SERVICE - Phoenix, AZ   **5/71 to present**
Positions: **Supervisor, Central Stores & Hauling Services**   3/93 to present
- Manage daily activity of 44 people, administer budget ($5 million) for Warehousing & Hauling & Crane Operation.

Hauling Services Supervisor   1/88 to 3/93
- Managed budget & 16 people involved in Crane & Hauling activity including oversize/overweight loads & general freight in a Flatbed Operation.

Equipment Pool Foreman   4/86 to 3/88
- Managed approximately 12 people & 200 pieces of equipment including backhoes, trucks & cars. Administered rental contracts for construction equipment.

Garage Foreman   10/85 to 4/86
- Supervised 8 mechanics, 2 mechanic helpers & 2 apprentices performing maintenance & preventive maintenance on approximately 100 pieces of equipment and vehicles.

Journey Equipment Mechanic   5/77 to 10/85
- Performed maintenance and repairs on construction & utility equipment.

Apprentice Equipment Mechanic   5/73 to 5/77
- Participated in O.J.T. apprentice training & classroom in algebra & automotive theory classes.

Mechanic's Helper   5/71 to 5/73
- Worked in Parts Room, changed & repaired tires, performed light vehicle maintenance.

EDUCATION AND TRAINING

Bachelor of Science Degree in Human Resources - Ottawa University, Phoenix, AZ (expected completion 3/94)
A.A. Degree in General Studies - Glendale Community College - 1985
A.A. Degree in Automotive Technology - Maricopa Technical College - 1977
Journeyman Equipment Mechanic Apprenticeship completed at A.P.S. - 1976
Completed 60 hour seminar in Organizational Change & Continuous Improvement at A.P.S.
Attended 16 hours training in Administering a Labor Agreement
Attended 16 hours training by Arizona Attorney General's Office in Alternate Dispute Resolution
Current qualified as a C.D.L. Examiner (3rd Party)

ASSOCIATIONS

Member of Executive Board - Arizona Motor Transport Association

COMMUNITY ACTIVITIES

Volunteer Activity for March of Dimes
Active in several A.P.S. Volunteer Community Activities
Volunteer Mediator for State Attorney General's Office

REFERENCES AND EVALUATIONS FURNISHED UPON REQUEST

- Resume writer: Bernie Stopfer -

Arnold Filbertson
3333 Woodacre Road
Redwood City, CA 95555
415-777-8888

OBJECTIVE

Peninsula Region Fleet Management Team Member for PG&E.

SUMMARY OF QUALIFICATIONS

- Over ten years experience in Peninsula Region fleet management.
- Nine years service in innovative leadership at PG&E.
- Successful supervisor for achievement of company goals.
- Committed to building a world-class fleet organization.

SUCCESS FACTOR ACCOMPLISHMENTS

QUALITY & EFFICIENCY

- In upgrading corporate identity, saved PG&E $81,000 by painting 80 vehicles in-house instead of contracting work out.
- Developed specifications and floor plan of new garage facility in Daly City, incorporating innovative strategies to maximize operational efficiency and minimize costs of necessary relocation.
- Responded to a department need by designing a crane truck to pick up 5,000 lbs. at 55 feet, adding an important and heavily-used piece of equipment to the division fleet.
- Initiated in-house smog program at the Daly City Garage to cut costs, and designed vapor-recovery system for mobile fuel tankers to meet EPA and CARB certification requirements.
- To support company promotion of natural gas, replaced inoperative, badly-designed pumping station by constructing a highly reliable mobile station at one-tenth the cost.

MANAGING FOR RESULTS

- As member of the Fleet Management Improvement Project, identified $850,000 in potential savings to PG&E budget and procurement procedures.
- Successfully encouraged employees to increase technical skills. For example, three Peninsula Division mechanics have completed smog certification training, saving money and providing services for other PG&E units.
- Provided counseling, lab results, training, and technical assistance to support division departments in reducing hazardous waste risks.
- As Project Manager, constructed new vehicle washing facilities to bring division fleet into environmental code compliance.

SAFETY

- Supervised Peninsula Division fleet services personnel for eight years with no lost time or automotive accidents.

-Continued-

Arnold Filbertson
Page Two

PG&E LEADERSHIP

1993-present	Coordinator	PENINSULA DIVISION SATELLITE DOWN-LINK
	Member	FLEET MANAGERS ADVISORY COUNCIL
	Project Manager	DALY CITY OFFICE RELOCATION
1988-present	Advisor	PENINSULA DIV. COMMUNICATION COMMITTEE
1986-present	Coordinator	PENINSULA DIVISION HAZARDOUS WASTE
1985-present	Coordinator	PENINSULA DIVISION SECURITY
1989-90	Peninsula Region Delegate	FLEET MANAGEMENT IMPROVEMENT PROJECT
1988-89	Chairman	PENINSULA DIVISION SAFETY
1985	Vice Chairman	PENINSULA REGION UNITED WAY

PG&E EMPLOYMENT HISTORY

1986-present	Fleet Services Supervisor & Building Supervisor (1989-present) & Hazardous Waste Coordinator (1987-present)	PENINSULA DIVISION
1985-86	Acting Superintendent	PENINSULA REGIONAL GENERAL SERVICES
1984-85	Fleet Services Supervisor	PENINSULA DISTRICT (DALY CITY)
1983-84	Assistant to Superintendent	PENINSULA REGIONAL GENERAL SERVICES
Previously:	Relief Garage Foreman (8 yrs) Garage Apprentice Instructor (2 yrs) Journeyman Mechanic (8 yrs)	CENTRAL DIVISION

PROFESSIONAL DEVELOPMENT

Courses in management and supervision from:
  -PG&E (Situational Leadership)   -University of Michigan
  -PSEA   -Zenger Miller   -Diablo Valley College

- Resume writer: Jenny Mish -

RONLYN R. HENEGAR

75 Brown Road
Montrose, Colorado 81401
(303) 654-3210

OBJECTIVE: **A position as a heavy equipment operator**

QUALIFICATIONS

- Over 9 years experience as an operator on heavy equipment.
- Operated a D9 dozer on the McPhee Dam Project.
- Consider the overall project as important as my direct responsibilities; creative and proud of my work.
- Learn quickly, willing to work hard; known for physical and mental strength.
- Work as a Dozer Instructor at Rancho Murieta Training Center, which has the reputation of being the best in the world.

EXPERIENCE

Dozer Operator

- Operated D9; D8H; D7; D6D; D6C; D5; and Kamatsus.
- Pioneering, building roads, logging, and finishing in very steep, rocky, dangerous terrain. Successful as a finish hand with clay fill on D9 - McPhee Dam Project.
- Offshore work; mixing mud from a dredger. Able to keep up with larger dozers while operating a D7.
- Successful at finish work with large dozers, saving blade time and money.

Blade Operator

- 12 and 14 Cats; rough blade haul roads, ditching.
- 18 Cat; haul road maintenance.

Backhoe Operator

- Trenches; remove silt from ponds; lay pipe.

Excavator Operator

- Bantam and Cat 245; steep pioneer road pulling up huge granite rock from slope; finishing fill slopes.

Loader Operator

- 988; 980; 950; loaded trucks with shot rock.
- 966; grade check.

Linkbelt Operator

- 18 ton crane; tearing down mining operation.

Oiler

- 140 and 60 ton cranes; moving, rigging, putting together 140 ton trucks.

Scraper
- Cut and fill.

Grade Checker
- 8-mile project.

- CONTINUED -

RONLYN R. HENEGAR

Page two

EXPERIENCE - continued

Compactor

- Roller.
- 825 compactor.

Dozer Instructor

- D9; D8H; D6D; D6C; D5.
- Wrote and followed curriculum. After being on the job only one month, was trusted to write my own curriculum.
- Directed safety meetings.
- Trained over 150 people, majority being men; 148 students passed the course.
- Taught apprentices and journeymen: leach ditching, sloping, pioneering, finishing, pushing scrapers, following grade stakes.
- Oversaw C-Testing for non-union members to become union journeymen.
- Developed handout on techniques of moving dirt.
- Served as member of review board, determining disciplinary action.
- Successfully solved everyday personnel and logistical problems by making good decisions and using sound judgment.

WORK HISTORY

1989-present	**Dozer Instructor**
	RANCHO MURIETA TRAINING CENTER, Rancho Murieta, CA
1987-1989	Family Leave
1985-1987	**Heavy Equipment Operator**
	SIERRA CONSTRUCTORS, San Francisco, CA
1985	**Dozer Operator**
	GUY F. ATKINSON (NKA Sierra Constructors), Terminal Island, CA
1980-1984	**Dozer and Blade Operator, Oiler**
	GUY F. ATKINSON, McPhee Dam Project, Dolores, CO
1979	**Grade Checker**
	SCHMIDT & TIAGO Grand Lake-West Vail, Denver, CO

EDUCATION

Operating Engineers (Local 9) Apprenticeship Program, 1979

PERSONAL PROFILE

Over the past 11 years, I have made a place for myself in what is typically known as a man's world by working hard and being accountable for my own responsibilities. I have earned the reputation of being a fast and accurate operator. Whenever necessary I have effectively handled any personnel problems related to being a woman in this occupation, without costing management time, headaches, or money. 1 strongly feel that my experience and enthusiasm would be a good addition to any company. I am available for interviews at your convenience. References available on request.

- Resume writer: Vicki Law-Miller -

GEORGE PIKE
336 Cartwright Avenue
Winnipeg, Manitoba R2H OJ5

1-555-9898

Objective: A position as Heavy Duty Mechanic / Equipment Operator

SUMMARY OF QUALIFICATIONS

- Journeyman Heavy Duty Equipment Mechanic (Interprovincial) with thirteen years experience.
- Recognized by Esso for providing an effective preventive truck maintenance program that allowed the company fleet to earn a 5,000,000-Kilometer Safe Driving Award.
- Willing to travel. Honest, hard-working, dependable, punctual.
- Confident in my experience, knowledge, and ability to make things run efficiently.

MECHANICAL EXPERIENCE & SKILLS

As a contract mechanic for Esso, maintained the entire Winnipeg Fleet of nineteen units in excellent working order, handled all aspects of truck maintenance and repair:

- Developed and implemented a scheduled maintenance program which reduced breakdowns and increased equipment longevity.
- Made hundreds of repairs, replacing worn parts and ensuring correct vehicle operation and safety.
- Purchased quality parts and tires at competitive prices, and assisted in selecting additions to the fleet.
- Trained apprentices in mechanical repairs and maintenance.
- Installed on-board computer systems to upgrade existing equipment.
- Certified equipment condition and capacity.

WORK HISTORY

1989-1994	Driver	Northern Petro
1985 -1988	Mechanic	Esso Petroleum
1983 -1985	Salesman	Electrolux
1981 -1983	Driver	Fouillard Bros.

EDUCATION

Graduate of Red River Community College as a
Journeyman Heavy Duty Equipment Mechanic (Interprovincial), 1980

PROFESSIONAL SEMINARS
- Defensive Driving Course -Driver Certification (Petro Canada)
-Extinguishing Small Oil Fires; and Spill Cleanups (Esso)

References Available On Request

- Resume writer: Ron Bartlette -

ARMANDO DeJesus

7222 S.E. Susan St.
Portland, OR 97206

Home Phone (503) 765-4321

OBJECTIVE : To obtain a position as an **Aircraft Maintenance Technician**

HIGHLIGHTS OF QUALIFICATIONS
- Eight years professional experience in aircraft maintenance.
- Proficient in analyzing system malfunctions.
- Ability to perform comprehensive bench repair, adjustment, overhaul, modification, inspection and testing of aircraft components using hand tools and testers.
- Knowledgeable in complex system modifications.
- Resourceful, hardworking, and a fast learner.
- Work well with others.

WORK EXPERIENCE
- Tested avionics equipment under simulated or actual operating conditions to determine performance and air-worthiness.
- Accompanied flight crew to determine and record system performance during test flights.
- Set up and operated ground test equipment to perform functional tests.
- Calibrated, installed, and repaired equipment to prescribed specifications.
- Measured physical dimensions of parts to ensure proper tolerance, and checked adjustments before releasing repaired or overhauled components.
- Modified systems, using blue prints, wiring diagrams, service bulletins, and engineering orders.
- Inspected avionics equipment for defects, such as loose connections and frayed wire, and for accuracy of assembly and installation.

EMPLOYMENT HISTORY
Aircraft Maintenance Technician—Boeing, Portland, OR (1994)

Avionics Technician—Desert Air Center, Tucson, AZ (1991-93)

Avionics Technician—Mideast Aircraft Maintenance Company, Abu Dhabi, U.A.E. (1988-90)

Avionics Line/Hangar Mechanic—Philippine Airlines, Manila, Philippines (1984-88)

EDUCATION AND TRAINING
BS, Electrical Engineering, Technological Institute of the Philippines, Manila, Philippines

Basic Aircraft Training, Digital Circuits and Microprocessors Course, and
B-747 Ground Electrical Engineers' Course, Philippine Airlines, Manila, Philippines

B-747 Ground Handling Course, Desert International Airlines, Jakarta, Indonesia

B-747 Avionics Course and B-747 Environmental Systems Course, Desert Air Center, Marana, AZ

B-737 Systems Maintenance Familiarization, Boeing, Portland, OR

LICENSE: FAA A&P # 563699336

- Resume written by Dislocated Workers Project -

akiko

2
CONSTRUCTION AND MAINTENANCE

Willard Silva

9976 East 12th Street
Oakland, CA 94601
(510) 900-7567

Construction/General Labor

Summary

- Get along well with employers and coworkers
- Worked both as a crew member and independently
- Experience handling tools, pesticides, fertilizers in a safe manner

Construction Labor

- Operated jackhammers, compressors and power tools
- Built and placed forms, plywood and wall systems
- Installed doors and windows prefab or framed
- Prepared walls for painting
- Constructed deck beams and columns

Concrete Placement

- Constructed concrete forms
- Poured concrete by pump, bucket, barrow and shovel
- Dug, spread and leveled dirt and gravel using pick and shovel

Landscaping

- Planted and pruned trees and shrubs
- Mowed, watered and maintained lawns
- Installed sprinkler systems
- Operated hand and power tools

Painting

- Painted interiors and exteriors using brushes and rollers
- Performed prep work including masking, sanding and filling holes
- Removed old paint using paint remover and wire brush

Related Experience

Construction/General Laborer Self-employed, 1989-93, Oakland, CA
Warehouse, Berkeley Outlet, 1984-89, Oakland, CA

Education

Diploma, Oakland High School, Oakland, CA

- Resume written by Roving Resume Writers -

CARTER CUMBERLAND
545 Whitney Court
Reno, NV 76767
404-676-8686

JOB OBJECTIVE

A position as supervisor or working foreman for residential construction.

SUMMARY OF QUALIFICATIONS

- Owned and operated residential construction business.
- Supervised various successful building projects.
- Experienced in customer relations.
- Scheduled and directed subcontractors and employees.
- Able to interpret blueprints, estimate costs, and bid jobs.

RELEVANT ACCOMPLISHMENTS

- Quickly resolved problems that might have hindered progress or created disputes, communicating clearly between subcontractors and employees.
- Accumulated extensive knowledge of building products and practice from ground to roof, with hands-on experience in:

Excavation	Foundations	Framing
Siding	Roofing	Finish
Detail	Troubleshooting	Repairs

- Participated in the development and construction of 35 custom homes.
- Supervised crews of up to 9 employees:

  Scheduled work and assigned tasks.
  Trained workers on-the-job.
  Watched for safety hazards.
  Made sure the work got done on time.

EMPLOYMENT HISTORY

1990-present	*Owner*	Pinewood Construction, Reno, Nevada
1987-90	*Framing Foreman*	Roger Kroll Construction, Pyramid Lake, Nevada
1985-87	*Carpenter*	William Darning Victorian Remodeling, Leeds, England
1984-85	*Mason*	John Schofts Construction, Bridgeport, New Hampshire
1980-84	*Plate maker*	Good Ads Print Shop, Coastline, New Hampshire

- Resume written by Carter Cumberland -

STEPHEN P. PARKER
1038 Shattuck Avenue
Berkeley CA 94707
(510) 566-3421

Objective: Handyman/Office Assistant for the Nature Company headquarters

SUMMARY OF QUALIFICATIONS

• Self-motivated; able to learn anything on my own initiative.

• Excellent record of dependability and reliability.

• Lifetime interest in nature and nature studies.

• Wide range of manual skills.

WORK HISTORY

1980-present **Nature Photographer**   Freelance, part time, NY and West Coast.
• Published photos in national and regional magazines; agency represented.

1984-86 **Maintenance Worker**   SOUTHSIDE MALL, Oneonta NY
• Repaired and maintained plumbing, door hardware, and groundskeeping equipment.
• Light carpentry as needed.
• General cleaning, building security, opening and lock-up.

1984 season **Bicycle Mechanic**   ALL-AMERICAN SPORT SHOP, Oneonta NY
• Repaired and maintained all types of bicycles.
• Fabricated parts as needed.

1979-83 **Auto Mechanic**   VAN'S AUTO SERVICE, Oneonta NY
• Repaired and maintained all makes of automobiles and light trucks.
• Developed expertise in brakes, suspension, exhaust, tuneups, tire repair, mounting and balancing.

1975-79 **Dept. Mgr./Stock Clerk**   GREAT AMERICAN FOOD STORES, Cooperstown NY
• Ordered and rotated stock; generally supervised dairy department.

- Resume writer: Yana Parker -

Gerard Villaseñor

2020 Thomas Drive • Sunnyvale, CA • 94086

(408) 734-9365

Objective: Position as Roofing Superintendent.

Highlights of Qualifications

- Energetic, enthusiastic, dedicated professional.
- Self-motivated; knows what it takes to get the job done.
- Inspire and support others to work at their highest level.
- Good decision-maker; resourceful and responsible.
- Talent for picking the right people for the job.
- Ability to prioritize, delegate, and motivate.

Roofing Construction Experience

New Construction

- Worked extensively in new construction for commercial and industrial projects, including $750,000 Hydro-tech waterproofing project for Codorniu Winery in Napa; Bentonite waterproofing and single-ply PVC membrane for New Children's Hospital at Stanford; and single-ply EPDM and two-piece tile for Monterey Sports Center.
- Incorporated variety of roofing and waterproofing techniques, most notably for Syntex Evergreen in San Jose, which used BUR, Polyken, Mameco Vulkem, Xypex, and a complete paver system on pedestals.
- Reviewed plans and developed schedules with architects, contractors and subcontractors, assuring proper coordination, efficiency and profitability.
- Supervised crews for all types of roofing and waterproofing:
  - BUR: hot, cold and modified;
  - single-plies: EPDM, PVC, PIB, Hypalon;
  - fluid applied: roof membranes, traffic topping;
  - steep roofing: composition shingles, tile, shakes;
  - waterproofing: sheet membranes, blacklines, Bentonite.
- Dispatched tractor-trailers, 3X dump trucks, debris bins, asphalt tankers and truck-mounted crane.

Reroofing

- Achieved consistent high quality control in compliance with building codes and inspection standards.
- Assured strict adherence to projected scheduling and costs.
- Interacted with variety of roof consultants, building inspectors, and owners or their representatives for effective scheduling and maximum quality control.
- Completed wide range of projects involving Tremco materials, working closely with their sales and technical reps.
- Coordinated sheet metal, mechanical, electrical, plumbing and core drilling subcontractors as the prime contractor for various reroofing projects.
- Handled wide range of public works, including NASA, Cupertino School District schools and City of San Jose.

Repairs and Maintenance

- Dispatched personnel promptly for leak calls and other needed repairs.
- Scheduled and satisfactorily completed minor roof maintenance work in a timely manner.

Work History

1987-present	Field Production Superintendent (1990-present)	Billingham's Roofing Co., San Jose
	Dispatcher/Assistant Superintendent (1988-90)	"
	Journeyman Roofer (1987-88)	"
1984-87	Freelance Roofer	Clients in Santa Clara, San Mateo counties
1971-84	Foreman (1976-84)	Andy's Roofing Company, Mountain View
	Journeyman Roofer (1973-76)	"
	Apprentice (1971-73)	"

Education

Roofing Apprenticeship Program, Local Union 95 • San Jose City College, 1971-73

Ethnic Studies, Foothill College, 1972-73

- Resume writer: Sallie Young -

Vic Schwartz

2020 Dwight Way, Apt. C
Berkeley CA 94704
(510) 540-7873

OBJECTIVE

A position as Lead-Based Paint Inspector and Consultant.

HIGHLIGHTS

- Over 17 years experience in building construction.
- Recent training in toxic lead inspection, management, and abatement.
- Willing to work long hours, crawl through dirt, work alone or with a gnarly team to complete projects and do them *well*.
- Committed to positive change for the environment.
- Willing to travel.

RELEVANT ACCOMPLISHMENTS

LEAD-BASED PAINT

- Completed 2 weeks of training and earned certification in the inspection, management, and abatement of lead-based paints:
  - Developed special interest in risk assessment to inform the public about the health and environmental dangers of leaded paints.
  - Studied the history, use, health effects, and management of lead-based paints.
  - Learned inspection techniques such as X-ray fluorescent spectrum analysis and atomic absorption testing, to determine lead content of paint.
  - Became acquainted with techniques and procedures for handling hazardous materials and disposing of hazardous wastes.
- Conducted independent library research to discover current laws and regulations, health research, and environmental impacts of lead contaminated soil and water.
- Attended recent lecture to learn about lead contamination in single-family residences at monthly meeting of the Home Inspectors Association in Sacramento.

BUILDING CONSTRUCTION

- Awarded U.S. Patents for heavy-duty geodesic dome construction hardware:
  - Designed connectors to join wooden struts into pentagonal and hexagonal panels.
  - Engineered complex ledger hangers to support angled second-floor joist connections,
  - Maximized safety and durability with unusually strong materials, consistently exceeding Uniform Building Code standards.
- Directed design of over 20 floor plans, consulting with architects and structural engineers to develop foundations, interior walls, stairways, lofts, cupolas, dormers, skylights, escape windows, garages, decks, fireplaces, and heating and ventilation systems.
- Designed and built a specially-engineered 60' diameter dome to endure the extreme loading conditions in Eagle River, Alaska, pleasing a church congregation with an attractive and sturdy sanctuary.

- Continued -

Vic Schwartz

CONSULTATION

- Established and maintained industry-wide reputation for high quality customer service by providing technical support to owner-builders, contractors, and architects. For example:

  - Explained geodesic dome construction to building inspectors in municipalities nationwide to assist them in applying local codes to unfamiliar structures.

  - Assisted customers with blueprint interpretation and building permit regulations.

- Wrote user-friendly assembly manual, precise technical correspondence, and descriptive promotional materials detailing geodesic dome construction.

- Taught 2-day seminars in the history and construction of geodesic domes, assisting students in choosing among dome designs and housing options.

WORK HISTORY

1990-present	**Full-time Student**	
1978-90	**Owner/Operator**	Timberline Geodesics, Berkeley CA
1973-78	**Carpenter**	Timberline Construction, Berkeley CA

CERTIFICATION, EDUCATION, & AFFILIATIONS

Certificates in Inspection, Management, & Abatement of Lead-Based Paint, June 1993
University of California at Berkeley Extension, Berkeley CA

B.A., with emphasis in Environmental Research and Writing, expected August 1993
New College of California, San Francisco CA

National Association of Home Builders, former member

- Resume writer: Jenny Mish -

1200 Cambridge Avenue
Pasadena, CA 44444

222-999-8888

JOB OBJECTIVE: A position in Construction Management.

SUMMARY OF QUALIFICATIONS

- Over ten years experience in construction management.
- Over six years experience in municipal building inspection.
- Recognized expert in providing design assistance to architects and contractors.
- Strong track record in managing complex projects on deadline while maintaining high quality standards.

RELEVANT ACCOMPLISHMENTS

1984-present TRIANGLE STUCCO, Pasadena
General Manager

Managed all personnel, materials, and equipment for up to 30 jobs daily for a high-volume, high-quality stucco company.

- Supervised and scheduled up to 30 skilled workers at any given time, continually upgrading employee skills and maintaining unusually low turnover for the industry.
- Submitted over 500 bids annually, and successfully managed a weekly budget of $20,000.
- Inspected all work to maintain a company reputation for high quality, and to ensure compliance with California codes.
- Served as liaison between owners, contractors, and architects, and performed excellent stucco work on the homes of several highly-pleased architects.
- Provided crucial troubleshooting and coordination between specialty contractors to minimize leaks and other problems.
- Checked plans daily and made recommendations to architects for design changes to reduce leaks and to ensure use of high-quality materials and methods.

1976-84 CITY OF PASADENA
Building Inspector (1978-84)

Checked construction plans and inspected over 20 buildings daily (over 30,000 total) to maintain compliance with codes and ordinances.

- Established an outstanding reputation for fairness while inspecting large commercial projects for compliance with UBC and Title 24, and residential projects for compliance with building, plumbing, mechanical, and electrical codes and the zoning ordinance.
- Checked plans for thousands of new and existing construction projects for compliance with the California Administrative Code, Uniform Building Code, and the City of Pasadena Zoning Ordinance.
- Made recommendations and assisted architects and contractors in developing alternate methods or materials, to adjust plans for safety, structural soundness, and compliance with codes.

-Continued-

CITY OF PASADENA (continued)

Housing Inspector (1977)
Implemented a new Federally-funded program designed to ensure Title 24 compliance for existing rental units, resulting in the upgrade of many units in Pasadena.

Residential Security Project Supervisor (1976)
Designed and developed a self-sustaining project which reduced the residential burglary rate in Pasadena by 45%, supervising 9 employees to meet first year goals in three months.

Previously: *Carpenter (2 years)*
Painter (1 year)
Machine Operator (2 1/2 years)

LICENSES AND SPECIALIZED TRAINING

ICBO Certificates in Building and Combination
California Contractor's License
Parex Applicator's Certificate
Dryvit Applicator's Certificate
City of Pasadena Plan Checking Workshop
ICBO Title 24 Energy Standards Workshops
Intensive Business Management Training with HTH Consulting
Classes in Codes, Bookkeeping, and Welding at local community colleges

Note how Richard's previous 5-6 year experience is referred to on page two without need for detail. (Richard is deaf, but he decided to wait for the interview to reveal his disability.) —J.M.

- Resume Writer: Jenny Mish -

BRIAN BRIARSSON
7676 West Highway 421
Silver City, NM 98765

(123) 456-7890

SUMMARY

Experienced in pipeline and **oil field construction work**.
Since 1986, **specialist in asbestos abatement**, including job management and crew supervision.

WORK HISTORY

1989-present

GENERAL SUPERINTENDENT, SPRAY SYSTEMS ENVIRONMENTAL, PHOENIX, AZ
Superintendent for asbestos abatement contractor at Chino Mines of Hurley, NM. Supervise 30-person crew, set up jobs, oversee safety, order materials, assure that job is done on time.

• Current job involves setting up freestanding asbestos containments around 70-foot-high boilers in a working copper smelter. This has been accomplished with no disruption to plant operations or personnel.

1986-89

SUPERINTENDENT, BCP CONSTRUCTION, PHOENIX, AZ
Asbestos abatement for schools, hospitals, and office buildings from Kentucky to California. Ran crews of one to four workers.

• Supervised complete asbestos abatement project for three floors of a highrise building (Mera Bank) in Phoenix, AZ.

1980-86

APPRENTICE WELDER, WAYNE HOUSTON WELDING, MEDICINE HAT, ALBERTA, CANADA
General welding duties, pipe cutting, and job set-up.

1975-80

ASSISTANT DRILLER, ROUGHNECK; VARIOUS OIL COMPANIES, ALBERTA, CANADA
Worked on large oil rigs.

EDUCATION & TRAINING

1989   Advanced Supervision of Abatement, Georgia Inst. of Technology.

1988   Certificate, abatement work in schools under
        Asbestos Hazard Emergency Response Act, Hager Labs.

1987   Abatement Supervisor Training, Georgia Inst. of Technology.

1985   Certificate, Welder First Class, Southern Alberta Inst. of Technology.

- Resume writer: Jan Hurley -

BRUCE W. JOHNSON

256 East 2nd North
Apartment C
Green River, Wyoming 82935
(307) 875-6053

Bruce's resume problem was that he has worked as a construction electrician for a great number of different contractors, working through the union halls. His solution was to group the most significant work projects into one or two time periods in his work history. (Note: This resume was current in 1992.) —Ed.

Objective: Position for underground or surface mine maintenance.

HIGHLIGHTS OF QUALIFICATIONS

* 13 years experience in the electrical industry.
* Successfully completed 4 years in the Wyoming Electrical Apprenticeship.
* Licensed Journeyman Electrician in Wyoming and Washington.
* Certified arc welder.
* Versatile and multi-skilled person.
* Talented in finding more efficient and effective working procedures.
* Wyoming CDL licensed with hazardous and cargo endorsements.
* Competent and reliable professional, committed to top quality work.

RELEVANT SKILLS AND EXPERIENCE

* Installed surface and underground, motor control, logic control, instrumentation and fiber optics for new processes in mines.
* Installed and maintained industrial, commercial, residential electrical wiring and equipment.
* Read schematic diagrams and blueprints for installation of new process controls.
* Diagnosed, estimated costs and implemented repairs of electrical problems.
* Qualified in tig welding and the operations of oxy/act for metal fabrication.
* Skilled in the operation, safe handling and care of hand and power tools.
* Experienced in the operation of heavy equipment and rigging.

EMPLOYMENT HISTORY

1992	**Electrician**	BAYVIEW ELECTRIC, FMC Corp., Green River, WY
1991-92	**Equipment Operator**	WYOMING HIGHWAY DEPARTMENT, South Pass Camp, WY
1985-91	**Electrician**	working primarily for the following companies:

        NORBY ELECTRIC, Chevron Plant, Rock Springs, WY

        BAY VIEW ELECTRIC, FMC Corp., Green River, WY

        AUTOMATION ELECTRIC, Bair Oil, WY

        DEVOGE ELECTRIC, Rhone Poulenc, Green River, WY

        WRIGHT, SCHUGART & HARBOR, Longview, WA

1984-85	**Maintenance Electrician**	EIELSON AIR FORCE BASE, Fairbanks, AK
1983-84	**Electrician**	

        M and J ELECTRIC, FMC Corp., Green River, WY

        WESTLAND ELECTRIC, Evanston, WY

1979-83	**Apprentice Electrician**	with the Wyoming Joint Electrical Apprenticeship, Casper, WY

EDUCATION AND TRAINING

Graduate, WYOMING JOINT ELECTRICAL APPRENTICESHIP
Completed an Arc Welding Course at WESTERN WYOMING COLLEGE
Presently taking an Instrumentation Class at WESTERN WYOMING COLLEGE

References Available Upon Request

- Resume written by Bruce Johnson -

JOHN SCHIZLINSKY

234 Cromwell Circle
Campbell River, British Columbia
(123) 456-7890

Objective: Position in construction and maintenance

SUMMARY OF QUALIFICATIONS

- Hands-on knowledge of virtually all phases of construction.
- Resourceful in solving problems and maximizing resources.
- Special ability to learn by "doing it" thoroughly.
- Enjoy a challenge; work hard to do the best job possible.

RELEVANT EXPERIENCE

Repair and Maintenance Skills

- Repaired and maintained old farm house; replaced complete north wall; installed windows, door trims, baseboards and moldings.
- Built large shed from start to finish.
- Renovated kitchens.
- Performed all phases of carpentry work.
- Used and maintained all types of tools.
- Repaired lawn mowers, jet pumps, piston pumps, and ski-doos.

Construction; Installation

- Performed all phases of construction from start to finish: ...carpentry ... brick work ... concrete finishing ... electrical work ... plumbing ... drywall and lathing ... painting ... all types of roofing ... sheet metal work.
- Installed air-tight furnace, including chimney, duct work, and electrical work.

Client Relations; Supervision

As Manager and Assistant Manager, supervised the Parts Department:
- Developed thorough knowledge of all parts and kept informed on any new products; found items for customers without delay.
- Assessed customers' needs and advised on parts required; explained cost and benefits of products to customers in relation to their needs.
- Checked that parts were installed promptly and work done to the customer's satisfaction.
- Always available to help customers solve problems and willing to put in extra hours.

WORK HISTORY

1990-present	*Service Attendant*	Automotive Dept., Hugh Lakeland, Campbell River, B.C.
1981-89	*Muffler Installer*	Carline Muffler, Campbell River, part-time
1982-84	*Muffler Installer*	Steve Marshall Ford, Campbell River
1981	*Construction*	Frank Gagne Excavating, Campbell River, B.C.
1974-81	*Roofer/Foreman*	Bayfield Roofing & Sheet Metal, Toronto
1975	*Manager*	National Muffler Halifax, N.S.

- Resume writer: Katannya van Tyler -

BOB MATTISON

4321 N. 42nd Drive
Phoenix, AZ 85019

(602) 555-2159

My goal was to paint a lively and interesting picture of Bob using his skills, experiences where he went above and beyond the call of duty. His resume immediately generated interviews and job offers. —S.Y.

Objective: Position in maintenance and repair.

HIGHLIGHTS OF QUALIFICATIONS

- Enthusiastic, dependable, self-motivated; assumes responsibility necessary to get the job done.
- Work cooperatively with a wide range of personalities.
- Equally effective working alone or as a member of a team.
- Skilled in handling the public with professionalism and diplomacy.
- Strong skills in organizing work flow, ideas, materials, people.
- Hired, trained and supervsied work crews.
- Takes pride in achieving the best possible results.

WORK HISTORY

1992-Present **Engineer,** SCOTTSDALE PLAZA RESORT, Scottsdale, AZ

9/91-11/91 **Engineer,** OMNI HOTEL (formerly PHOENIX SHERATON), Phoenix, Arizona

8/90-6/91 **Engineer,** CROWN STERLING SUITES HOTEL (formerly EMBASSY SUITES BILTMORE), Phoenix, Arizona

8/88-8/90 **Chief Engineer,** WOOLLEY'S PETITE SUITES HOTEL, Tempe, Arizona

5/87-8/88 **Owner,** MAINTENANCE AND REPAIR, Phoenix, Arizona

6/85-5/87 **Maintenance Worker,** J.P.H. ENTERPRISES, Indio, California

MAINTENANCE SKILLS

Appliances, Carpentry, Electrical, Fencing, Flooring, Locks, Painting, Plumbing, Pools & Spas, Roofing Irrigation and Sprinklers
Air Conditioning, Refrigeration and Heating

EDUCATION

Air Conditioning & Refrigeration
College of the Desert, Palm Desert, California

Electronics
DeVry Institute of Technology, Phoenix, Arizona

PROFESSIONAL EXPERIENCE

Building Repair
- During a monsoon storm in Phoenix, climbed hotel roof to check drains; upon discovering six inches of water and drains patched over with roofing cement, immediately cut through patches and cleared the drains.
- Within three hours, completely rebuilt apartment complex stairs that collapsed after two heavy tenants moved in; added joist hangers and extra supports underneath to meet legal specs and ensure future stability.
- When a four-inch copper pipe burst and flooded a ground-floor room, removed all furniture, pulled up carpet and dug four feet deep to repair the pipe; after drying, filled in hole, poured concrete, installed carpet and put back furniture.
- Replaced broken windows, made screens, hung doors and jambs, hung and patched drywall, textured and painted walls, installed electrical switches and outlets, moved phone jacks, rewired disconnect and breaker panels, installed and repaired lighting.

Mechanical Repair
- During breakfast rush hour, quickly removed stuck soda dispenser solenoid, which caused Dr. Pepper to flood the entire waitress station; temporarily adjusted unit until Coca-Cola repairman arrived.
- Repaired chillers, boilers, water softeners, ice machines, washers, dryers, motors, pumps and other equipment for various establishments; also troubleshoot elevators and escalators.
- Fixed hotel restaurant equipment, including grills, ovens, refrigerators, dishwashers, etc.

Customer Service
- Regularly earned commendations for diplomacy and courtesy toward hotel guests and apartment tenants during work-related encounters.
- Developed cooperative working relationships with management, staff and contracted help; was left in charge of operations of Woolley's Petite Suites for a week when managers and staff went to Florida to participate in a hostile takeover of three hotels.
- Resolved wide range of customer problems, including patiently and diligently working to pry a broken key from a hotel room lock, earning a letter of commendation from the guest who "appreciated his control in a trying situation."

Construction & Maintenance

MATTISON

- Resume writer: Sallie Young -

Robert had been owner/operator of a bar for 12 years, and wanted to get out of the business, since the general image of alcohol has deteriorated. We made two versions of his resume, this one including his supervisory and management experience, and the following version without. —J.M.

Robert Clinton

3337 Kansas Street
Fremont, CA 96565
(510) 656-6565

OBJECTIVE

A position as a Maintenance Supervisor.

HIGHLIGHTS

- Over twelve years experience in management and maintenance.
- Strong ability to build staff teamwork.
- Knowledgeable in carpentry, plumbing, and electrical repairs.
- Haven't missed work due to illness in over ten years.

RELEVANT EXPERIENCE

1982-present **Operations and Maintenance Manager, Super Stop Lounge, Fremont**
Performed all maintenance and repairs for 2000 sq. ft. building, and managed staff and daily financial operations of small business grossing $200,000 annually.
MANAGEMENT
- Hired, supervised, and scheduled 4 customer service employees, maintaining good teamwork and very low turnover.
- Balanced daily cash reports, made deposits, and kept accurate financial records.
- Ordered and tracked over $2000 monthly in supplies.
- Arranged promotional activities such as softball teams, tournaments, barbecues, and picnics for Big C customers and potential customers.
MAINTENANCE
- Performed routine electrical system maintenance and troubleshooting. For example:
  -Replaced ventilation and refrigeration fans, lighting fixtures, and circuit breakers.
  -Installed an additional electrical circuit to upgrade refrigeration equipment.
- Replaced plumbing fixtures, drain lines, and portions of main sewer line to keep the system in good working order.
- Maintained attractive building appearance, for example:
  -Repaired plaster and painted exterior walls.
  -Planted stone planters and cared for plants.
  -Recovered vinyl upholstery on chairs, stools, and bar rails.
  -Kept exterior neon sign in proper working order.
  -Replaced rain gutters, down spouts, and roof flashing, preventing water damage.

1989-94 **House Restoration, Independent, Oakland**
Prudently invested $40,000 in supplies and renovated a house to increase property value.
- Rewired 75% of electrical system and upgraded service from 30 to 100 amps.
- Updated entire plumbing system, adding a sink and bringing all pipes to code.
- Totally redesigned kitchen floor plan, producing a more functional workspace.
- Removed exterior stucco to replace termite-damaged wood, and subcontracted with a plasterer to re-apply stucco.
- Upgraded wood windows by replacing them with insulated aluminum frame windows.
- Designed and built a patio and Japanese-style rock garden.

EDUCATION

Business Administration coursework, 3 years
California State University at Hayward and Merritt College

- Resume writer: Jenny Mish -

Robert Clinton

3337 Kansas Street
Fremont, CA 96565
(510) 656-6565

OBJECTIVE

Building Specialist for Pacific Bell.

HIGHLIGHTS

- Over twelve years experience in building maintenance.
- Knowledgeable in carpentry, plumbing, and electrical repairs.
- Able to complete work on deadline.
- Haven't missed work due to illness in over ten years.

RELEVANT EXPERIENCE

1982-present **Maintenance Manager, Super Stop Lounge, Fremont**

Assessed and performed all maintenance and repairs for 2000 sq. ft. building.

- Performed routine electrical system maintenance and troubleshooting. For example:
  - Replaced ventilation and refrigeration fans, lighting fixtures, and circuit breakers as needed.
  - Installed an additional electrical circuit to upgrade refrigeration equipment.
- Replaced plumbing fixtures, drain lines, and portions of main sewer line to keep the system in good working order.
- Maintained attractive building appearance, for example:
  - Repaired plaster and painted exterior walls.
  - Planted stone planters and cared for plants.
  - Recovered vinyl upholstery on chairs, stools, and bar rails.
  - Kept exterior neon sign in proper working order.
  - Replaced rain gutters, down spouts, and roof flashing, preventing water damage.
- Installed security door and changed and maintained lock sets to ensure building security.

1989-94 **House Restoration, Independent, Oakland**

Renovated 60 year-old two-bedroom house, and re-landscaped grounds.

- Rewired 75% of electrical system and updated service from 30 to 100 amps.
- Updated entire plumbing system, adding a sink and bringing all pipes to code.
- Totally redesigned kitchen floor plan, producing a more functional workspace.
- Removed exterior stucco to replace termite-damaged wood, and subcontracted with a plasterer to re-apply stucco.
- Upgraded wood windows by replacing them with insulated aluminum frame windows.
- Designed and built a patio and Japanese-style rock garden with a bridge, rock paths, and bonsai plants.

Previously: **Upholstery Assistant (1 year), Carlo Vinoletti Upholstery, Fremont**

EDUCATION

Business Administration coursework, 3 years
California State University at Hayward and Merritt College

- Resume writer: Jenny Mish -

Robert Verdi

5678 Seymour Ave.
Richmond CA 94805
(510) 236-1999

Objective: Position as Park Supervisor with regional park district.

PROFILE

★ Over 25 years professional experience in horticulture,
developing excellent knowledge of landscaping and plants.
★ Lifelong interest and background in gardening.
★ Excellent working relations with the public, and with
co-workers and employees of all ethnic groups.
★ Proven record of reliability and responsibility.
★ Skill in planning, coordinating and supervising projects.

RELEVANT EXPERIENCE

SUPERVISION, TRAINING, SAFETY

* As Landscape Maintenance Supervisor at Teklon:
-**supervised and scheduled** 35 permanent gardeners and 6 foremen
-**trained and evaluated** the above employees, teaching:
...safe use of power tools ...principles of horticulture ...chemical pest control.

* **Supervised** 20-40 CETA gardeners, hundreds of seasonal gardening helpers,
and students at UC Berkeley working at Botanical Gardens:
-presented **safety guidelines** at mandatory weekly safety meetings
-followed-up and **monitored attendance** and **productivity**
-**taught** proper use of equipment and tools
-**taught** pruning techniques, weed control, turf management
-organized and planned field trips to botanical sites.

* **Trained and supervised** hundreds of seasonal gardening helpers, students at
UC Berkeley working at Botanical Gardens.

PARK TECHNICAL EXPERIENCE

* Operated all **equipment and power tools**:
...walk mowers ...riding mowers ...gas and electric trimmers ...lawn edgers
...lawn vacuums ...generators ...rotary reel and gang mowers ...tractors
...turf equipment and attachments ...chain saws ...weed eaters ...brush cutters.

* **Maintained grounds and greenhouses** at UCB Botanical gardens, involving:
...small engine repair ...concrete construction ...paving
...repair of patios/driveways/foundations ...greenhouse construction ...excavating
...grading (residential, commercial) ...industrial lot cleaning ...tree removal
...slide repair ...erosion control ..plumbing ...drain cleaning
...sprinkler system installation ...maintenance of athletic fields
...fertilization ...chemical applications (weed control) ...rototilling ...sod lawns
...pest control ...irrigating ...planting ...mowing ...pruning ...special soil mixing.

* Maintained school district truck; excellent driving record.
* Maintained indoor plants at Teklon offices and school administration offices.

- Continued on page two -

RELEVANT EXPERIENCE
(continued)

ADMINISTRATION

- Submitted daily **reports** to Teklon, following inspection of work sites, reporting damage, equipment and materials needed, and tasks remaining to be done.
- **Interviewed** and **hired** gardeners for Teklon.
- **Verified** and submitted weekly employee **time-sheets** for both CETA and Teklon.
- **Coordinated** field trip arrangements for CETA workers: selected botanical sites to visit, and rearranged work schedules to accommodate special trips.
- Developed estimates for Teklon landscape **contracts**.
- **Organized** retirement dinners for School District gardeners.

LIAISON, COMMUNITY RELATIONS

- **Led tours** of Botanical gardens for student groups and garden clubs.
- Served as **liaison** between CETA gardeners, District teachers, and administrators.
- **Mediated** minor grievances and approved landscaping requests of Homeowners Association, as landscape maintenance supervisor for Teklon contractors.

EMPLOYMENT HISTORY

1990-present	*Landscape Gardener*	VENTURI GARDENING, self employed
1989-90	*Facility Caretaker*	ROSSMOOR COMMUNITY, Walnut Creek
1987-89	*Landscape Gardener*	VENTURI GARDENING, self employed
1974-87	*Gardener/Assistant Foreman*	OAKLAND UNIFIED SCHOOL DIST.
	Gardener Caretaker, live-in	OAKLAND UNIFIED SCHOOL DIST. Chabot Science Center
1972-74	*Landscape Maintenance Supv.*	TEKLON, Landscaping Division, Concord (building contractors)

EDUCATION & TRAINING

Horticulture course work, MERRITT COLLEGE
- •Horticulture •Greenhouse Management •Plant Diseases •Herbicidious Plants

Horticulture Workshops, UCB BOTANICAL GARDENS:
- •Plant Identification •Plant Maintenance •Propagating •Spraying

Supervisory Training, OAKLAND SCHOOL DISTRICT

- Resume writer: Yana Parker -

George C. Clark

545 Pacific Avenue
Alameda, CA 94501

(510) 524-5442

OBJECTIVE: Chief Engineer in Real Estate Services for California State Automobile Assoc.

SUMMARY OF QUALIFICATIONS

- 30 years experience as Stationary/Marine Engineer.
- Hold Merchant Marine License and California State Contractors' Licenses.
- "Organized, dependable, safety conscious, and prompt in the discharge of required tasks," according to supervisor's evaluation.
- "Demonstrated self-reliance to a remarkable degree," according to supervisor's evaluation.
- "Known to be resourceful in solving unique problems and frequently demonstrated willingness and ability to assume greater responsibilities."
- Excellent relationships with co-workers.

ENGINEERING EXPERIENCE

1980-present   *Stationary Engineer*
CALIFORNIA STATE AUTOMOBILE ASSOCIATION, San Francisco, CA
Maintained, repaired, and installed HVAC equipment.

- Recommended energy conserving 02 trim systems for thermal pak boilers in Building 4, with average savings of $5,000/year in fuel costs.
- Modified domestic hot water heating system in Building 3, resulting in 24-hour availability of hot water for after-hours working departments.
- Set up long-lasting domestic hot water heating to replace old system that required complete renewal every 5 years, in Building 1 and 2.

1973-80   *Plumbing Contractor*
ISLAND PLUMBING & HEATING, Alameda, CA
Specialized in repair, remodel, and new construction to residential, commercial, and light industrial customers.

- Installed fixtures and plumbing to meet handicapped code in Building 4 men's and women's restrooms at CSAA, at less cost than hiring a contractor.

1971-73   *QMED Engineer*
MILITARY SEA TRANSPORTATION SERVICE (MERCHANT MARINE), Oakland, CA
Served as Fireman, Oiler, Junior Engineer, and Refrigeration Engineer.

1964-71   *Stationary Engineer*
COUNTY OF ALAMEDA, Oakland, CA
Maintained 40 County buildings HVAC.

- continued -

1963-64   *Stationary Engineer*
CITY OF RICHMOND, Richmond, CA
Watchstander in Civic Center Central Plant.

EDUCATION & TRAINING

Liberal Arts
Laney College, Alameda

Correspondence Coursework in the Military equivalent to AA degree:
Completed all courses related to Boilerman from 3rd class to Chief
U.S. Coast Guard Marine Engineering (preparation course for officers candidate school)
Association of Energy Engineers Boiler Optimization Seminar
Association of Energy Engineers "Fundamentals of Energy Management"

CERTIFICATES & LICENSES

Merchant Marine License #550-50-8211: Authorized to sail on any steamship of
   unlimited horsepower as Fireman, Oiler, Junior Engineer, Watertender, Electrician,
   or Refrigeration Engineer.
   - Upgraded to "QMED" rating in 1990: Qualified for any position in the Engine
   Department.

California State Contractors' Licenses #340785 for:
   - B-1 General Contractor
   - C-36 Plumbing Contractor

- Resume writer: Alina Ever -

Jerry P. Hall

1126 Eighteenth Avenue • Redwood City, CA 94063 • (415) 362-4092

JOB OBJECTIVE: Foreperson in outside maintenance at See's Candies

SUMMARY OF QUALIFICATIONS

- Highly skilled in service and repair of mechanical and electrical components.
- Over five years experience in outside maintenance and service.
- Take pride in quality workmanship and complete customer satisfaction.
- Excellent supervisor; professional and courteous with employees and customers.

RELEVANT EXPERIENCE

ELECTRICAL/MECHANICAL SKILLS

- Brought Robinson residence up to electrical codes by installing 50% new electrical wiring and hardware, using standard home wiring materials and procedures.
- Set up electrical conduit lines from main power source to various points of use, including switches, receptacles, light fixtures, pumps, and timers at Robinson residence.
- Diagnosed electrical and mechanical problems, such as tripped breakers, burnt fuses, frayed wires, faulty electrical motors, and broken appliances; and made necessary repairs.
- As mechanic at Arvak (incorporated into Western Overhead), repaired garage doors, garage door openers, and industrial washers, dryers, and folders.

CARPENTRY SKILLS

- Removed and replaced kitchen and bathroom floors, stud walls, and cabinets, as well as built deck and doorway eaves at Robinson residence.
- Installed window and pedestrian door frames as self-employed handyman.

MANAGEMENT SKILLS

- Managed own business, involving customer service, accounts, and purchasing.
- Supervised and trained four installers at Western Overhead Door.
- Thoroughly explained in lay terms the functions of garage doors and openers to customers at Western Overhead Door.

PLUMBING SKILLS

- Removed and replaced steam boiler, hot water heaters, water lines (copper, brass, and galvanized pipe) at Robinson residence, Homebase, and as self-employed handyman.
- Removed and reset drain and sewer lines (plastic, ceramic, and cast iron).
- Set and repaired PVC water lines above and below ground at Robinson residence.

RECENT WORK HISTORY

1993-present	Garage Door Installer	EDCO Electronics, Hayward
1993	Self-employed Handyman	Robinson residence, Lafayette
1992-93	Customer Service Technician	Western Overhead Door, Honolulu
1990-92	Owner/Foreperson	Wise Garage Doors, Corvallis (accounts included Homebase, Albany Paper Mill)
1989-90	Garage Door Installer	Garage Doors Unlimited, Clayton

- Resume writer: Alina Ever -

Stacy & Alan Fees
310-555-8517

5555 W. 24th Street #2
San Pedro, CA 90731

OBJECTIVE
Apartment Management

HIGHLIGHTS

♦ In-depth knowledge of <u>all</u> aspects of apartment management.

♦ Experienced in bookkeeping, labor, and public relations.

♦ Efficiently and independently run 19-unit building in addition to simultaneous assistance with 5- & 4-unit buildings.

♦ Computer literate for ease and efficiency of administrative work.

♦ Seven years experience.

EXPERIENCE

Wide range of Plumbing skills including:
- Installation of toilets, and garbage disposals (including rewiring);
- Installation and repair of bathroom and kitchen fixtures including valves and nipples in walls;
- Roto rootering with small and large snakes;
- Trouble-shooting problems that don't have obvious solutions;
- Some knowledge of copper pipe repair;

Interior and Exterior work consisting of:
- Painting and spackling, refinishing, staining and varnishing;
- Magnacite repair and paint;
- *Proper* installation of racks and rods (with inserts);
- Carpet cleaning;
- Laying linoleum tile; re-grouting and caulking ceramic tile
- Gardening and landscaping;
- Repairing rain gutters;
- Deadbolt and entry lock installation *from scratch*;
- Shower door installation;
- Pool maintenance;
- Door hanging and re-screening;
- Total refurbishing of apartments;
- Signage for buildings;
- Minor electrical: wall switches, outlets;
- Order and pick-up of all materials needed;
- Knowledge of installation of large appliances;
- Knowledge of installation of both louvered and regular windows;

Administrative Work
- Diplomatic tenant relations and investigation;
- Bookkeeping, rent collection, deposits;
- Maintain tenant communications through newsletters and notices,

Other work includes:
Making and installing custom-made draperies as **Supervising Assistant Manager** for *Dienos Draperies, Santa Maria* 1980-1983.

References available upon request

- Resume writer: Lauri Callen -

R. Wayne Terry

One Cabrillo Street, #108
San Francisco, CA 94118
Phone (415) 750-1466
Pager (415) 245-0769

Objective: **Apartment manager for 12-24 unit building**

Summary of Experience

- 15 + years real estate/facilities management experience.
- Excellent people skills with ability to defuse conflicts and solve disputes.
- General mechanical, plumbing, and electrical repair knowledge.
- Thorough and well organized record keeping abilities.
- Extensive experience with budgets, controlling costs and managing income.
- Able to handle eviction proceedings, lease/tenancy negotiations and follow landlord/tenant laws.
- Responsible and mechanically inclined individual able to screen and select suitable tenants and protect the owner's interest.

Work History

Supervisor, Building Management, Office of Support Services   1989 to present
State Bar of California

- Managed housekeeping, janitorial, and maintenance of all mechanical systems for approximately 100,000 square feet of building space.
- Selected, coordinated and supervised vendors (landscapers, janitors, security guards, electricians, plumbers, painters, etc.)
- Monitored buildings on a regular basis to ensure that buildings met City code requirements.
- Implemented safety policies and procedures.
- Managed construction and remodeling projects.
- Solicited and negotiated contracts.

Owner / Project Manager, Spacetech   1986 to 1989

- Planned and coordinated business and office relocations from start to finish:
  ...space needs assessment ...property search ...lease negotiations
  ...office space planning and design ...tenant improvement and construction management ...move planning and coordination
  ...equipment and furnishings research and acquisitions.
- Dealt with architects, inspectors, and a host of contractors and city officials to implement efficient relocation.

Buildings Operations Manager, Werner Erhard and Associates   1976 to 1986

- Oversaw 500,000 square feet of office space and public assembly space.
- Managed large staff and departments for shipping & receiving, office supplies, telecommunications, reception, secretarial staff, and garage operation.
- Successfully provided a stable foundation of services to an organization that was in a constant state of growth and reorganization.

References available upon request

- Resume written by Maurine Killough -

3

CUSTOMER SERVICE

MELANIE DOBSON
441 Tiburon Drive #441
Alameda, CA 94501
(510) 454-4545

JOB OBJECTIVE: Cruise Line Excursion Staff, Hostess, Front Desk or Reservations Clerk.

SUMMARY OF QUALIFICATIONS

- Nine years related experience in customer service.
- Tour director trained by the International Tour Management Institute.
- Extensive travel experience.
- Service-oriented, loyal, and adaptable employee.
- Warm and enthusiastic personality.

RELEVANT ACCOMPLISHMENTS

CUSTOMER SERVICE

- As Assistant Manager of Cozy Cove Bar and Grill:
  - Dramatically increased wine sales by educating customers about wine choices.
  - Insured high level of customer satisfaction by responding quickly to changing customer needs and by prioritizing quality service.
  - Sensed customer moods and preferences, and thoughtfully assisted customers in making selections which brought them satisfaction.
  - Handled irate customers and complaints in friendly manner.
- Served as communications liaison for annual fundraising campaign, enjoyably answering questions and solving problems between Texaco USA and United Way.
- Provided full range of customer service needs on busy switchboard for Allied Steamship.

DIRECTING ACTIVITIES

- As a tour guide, designed and conducted customized small group tours of San Francisco.
- Arranged all aspects of field trips, and designed and led games, arts & crafts, and team sports at MSU Day Care Center.

ORGANIZATIONAL SKILLS

- As Assistant Manager for Cozy Cove Bar and Grill:
  - Planned and directed advertising, menus, entertainment, decorations, and staffing of special events.
  - Hired, trained, scheduled, and supervised 12 employees.
- Coordinated all materials, registrations, guest speakers, and room reservations for management training sessions as United Way liaison at Texaco USA.
- Assessed needs and preferences of traveling Texaco employees, and made appropriate travel arrangements.

-Continued-

WORK HISTORY

1993-present	Receptionist/Secretary, ALLIED STEAMSHIP CO., San Francisco, CA
1985-93	Assistant Manager, COZY COVE BAR AND GRILL, Vallejo, CA
1992	Tour Guide, VOLUNTEER CENTER, City of San Francisco, CA
1983-85	Administrative Assistant, TEXACO USA, San Francisco, CA
1982-83	Activity Coordinator, MSU DAY CARE CENTER, Bozeman, MT

EDUCATION

INTERNATIONAL TOUR MANAGEMENT INSTITUTE, San Francisco, CA
Courses included:
Local, Domestic, and International Tour Directing
Tour Management Ethics and Principles
Extensive Field Training.

CPR AND FIRST AID CERTIFICATION, American Red Cross, Alameda, CA

P.A.D.I. CERTIFIED SCUBA DIVER, Great Reef Diving, San Francisco, CA

MONTANA STATE UNIVERSITY

HEALD BUSINESS COLLEGE

TRAVEL

CARIBBEAN:
Antigua, Barbados, Grand Cayman, Jamaica, Martinique, Puerto Rico, St. Maarten, St. Thomas.

EUROPE:
Austria, England, France, Germany, Italy, Switzerland, Yugoslavia.

NORTH AMERICA:

Canada: British Colombia (Vancouver and Victoria).

Mexico: Acapulco, Cozumel, Cuernavaca, Playa Del Carmen, Mexico City, Taxco.

U.S.: Arizona, California, Colorado, Florida, Hawaiian Islands, Nebraska, Nevada, New York, Virginia, Washington, Washington D.C., Wyoming.

- Resume writer: Jenny Mish -

Customer Service

Colleen Davis
3434 Raleigh Lane
Raleigh, NC 34343
343-343-3434

OBJECTIVE

A position as North Carolina Edison Customer Services Assistant (Scheduler).

SUMMARY OF QUALIFICATIONS

- Thirteen years NCE experience.
- Outstanding customer service skills.
- Consistently evaluated as an excellent employee.
- Able to build strong working relationships with co-workers, and employees.
- Won three Ideas In Action Awards for cost-cutting proposals.

RELEVANT ACCOMPLISHMENTS

SCHEDULING

- As Sales Assistant & Purchasing Agent for an interior design firm, coordinated logistics for multi-million-dollar installation contracts.
  - Investigated pricing, availability, and delivery schedules to wisely select thousands of fixtures and furnishings.
  - Prepared complex bids including installation timelines and detailed pricing.
  - Ordered, purchased, and tracked delivery of all materials, ensuring that damaged goods were replaced quickly to meet installation deadlines.
  - Double-checked millions of critical details on invoices for accuracy.
  - Maintained frequent contact with hundreds of vendors to quickly identify and solve delivery problems, ensuring that installation dates were met.

CUSTOMER SERVICE

- Conveyed dignity and respect to hundreds of thousands of NCE customers, taking the extra step to provide more than one-stop service.
  - Offered alternative payment plans and cost reduction suggestions to customers with credit problems.
  - Handled emotional customers with delicacy, listening empathetically while maintaining company policy.
  - Offered referrals to elderly customers who might need Gatekeeper's services.

STAFF SUPERVISION

- Supervised three employees at Weier & Hoffman and four employees at Temco, delegating projects and monitoring daily tasks.
  - Built teamwork by eliciting problem-solving from each member.
  - Evaluated employee performance formally and informally, providing positive feedback and suggestions for skill development.
  - Interviewed and hired office support staff of four at Resort World, and trained employees at both positions.

WORK HISTORY

1984-present	**Customer Service Representative** **Utility Clerk**	NCE, Raleigh
1982-84	**Sales Assistant & Purchasing Agent**	WEIER & HOFFMAN, Raleigh
1981-82	**Office Manager**	TEMCO PROPERTIES, Raleigh
1977-80	**Utility Clerk**	NCE, Raleigh

EDUCATION

Business coursework, Raleigh Community College

- Resume writer: Jenny Mish -

Name Colleen Davis   JOBS No. CSA 419

SECTION III - Qualifications for This Position

Fill in below the 3-5 requirements listed as "critical" on the job bulletin. Then outline qualifications, including experience, accomplishments and results, for those critical job requirements. Limit comments to space provided. Additional information should be included in your resume.

Critical Requirement #1   CUSTOMER FOCUS

I have made customer service my first priority for thirteen years at NCE. I have developed a high level of skill in responding effectively to customers, communicating respect for them while solving the problem at hand. Every customer feedback form I have received has been excellent, and each day there are many examples of my commitment to placing the customer first.

Critical Requirement #2   BUSINESS UNDERSTANDING

I have been able to keep the big picture in mind in hundreds of customer service contacts weekly, providing gentle pressure when necessary to meet NCE goals without sacrificing customer relations. In addition, I have coordinated the research, ordering, and tracking of materials for multi-million-dollar interior design projects for another employer, requiring a complex daily understanding of costs, deadlines, and logistical management.

Critical Requirement #3   MANAGING FOR RESULTS

I have successfully supervised employees in two positions, delegating and monitoring their work, and providing frequent informal positive feedback and support in meeting goals. At NCE, as a Quality Improvement Team member, I provided significant direction and leadership in improving morale at the Raleigh office.

Critical Requirement #4   TEAMWORK

As supervisor of two office support teams, I used the same skills which make me an outstanding customer service representative to create strong group cohesion. In every capacity, I have built consistently good working relationships with supervisors, co-workers, employees, and customers. I have passed this team building on to others as a Quality Improvement Morale Team member, and as a United Way campaign team leader.

Critical Requirement #5   QUALITY AND EFFICIENCY

I have received three Ideas In Action Awards for my suggestions to improve NCE office efficiency. In a previous position for an interior design firm, I researched and planned the delivery of thousands of supplies for multi-million-dollar design projects, ensuring that detailed invoices were extremely accurate, and supervising delivery to ensure that cost-saving deadlines were met.

I declare that all the information submitted is complete and true to the best of my knowledge.

_____   _____
                Employee Signature   Date

JOSEPHINE TILLER
2222 Hawthorne Street #15
Boulder, CO 87878
(787) 787-7878

Objective: Position as Supermarket Checker or Head Clerk.

SUMMARY OF QUALIFICATIONS
- 16 years experience in the grocery industry, as checker, head clerk, and cashier.
- Excellent reputation with customers as a competent, knowledgeable and helpful professional.
- Enjoy my work, and consistently greet customers with a smile.
- Honest, reliable, and productive.

RELEVANT SKILLS & EXPERIENCE

CUSTOMER SERVICE
- Developed a reputation for **excellent customer service** by:
  -acknowledging the customer's presence and making eye contact.
  -greeting customers in a friendly manner, and giving them full attention.
  -taking time to answer a question or find someone else who can.

- Served as **product expert** on sophisticated items, directing customers to:
  ...exotic spices and ingredients   ...ethnic foods ...unusual gourmet items.

- **Increased sales** in the higher profit Natural Foods Department (and increased customer satisfaction) by **advising customers** on bulk alternatives to name-brand items.

SUPERVISION
- As Head Clerk, **managed "front end"** of the store:
  -**prepared daily schedules** for staff of up to 18 clerks, to assure maximum checkstand coverage at all times.
  -**assigned staff** to cover peak hours and continuous stocking.

- **Trained** new clerks in procedures, policies, and customer service.

ADMINISTRATIVE
- **Balanced** checker's **cash drawer** with consistently high level of accuracy.

- As **Office Cashier** for one year:
  -accurately balanced books and balanced deposits
  -answered phones   -prepared daily sales report   -made deposits
  -processed returned checks   -prepared monthly sales report for HQ.

EMPLOYMENT HISTORY

1978-present	**Retail Clerk, journey level**	WHOLESOME SUPERMARKET, Boulder and GOODWIN'S MARKET, Boulder (bought by Wholesome in 1982)
1978	**Buyer's Assistant**	J.C. PENNEY'S, Boulder
1973-78	**Manager's Assistant**	RUTHANN'S Clothing Store, Spokane WA

EDUCATION
Business Classes, 1977 - SPOKANE COMMUNITY COLLEGE

- Resume writer: Yana Parker -

Francine Walker

510-565-5656

5656 Tolleson Drive
El Sobrante, CA 95656

JOB OBJECTIVE: A position as an Airline Ticketing Agent.

SUMMARY OF QUALIFICATIONS

- Sixteen years experience in customer satisfaction.
- Extremely reliable and conscientious.
- Fast, accurate, and thorough worker.
- Confident, professional manner and appearance.

RELEVANT ACCOMPLISHMENTS

CUSTOMER SERVICE
- As organizer of over 50 retreats for Alcoholics Anonymous:
  - Took reservations for 75 participants per retreat.
  - Assigned rooms according to personal preferences and special needs.
  - Tactfully explained limitations in preference availability, and listened with empathy when preferred choices were not available.
  - Personally welcomed participants at check-in desk, matching reservations with records, orienting guests to facilities, and resolving unforeseen complications.
- Successfully responded to personal concerns of young people as Counselor's Troubleshooter at El Sobrante High School and assisted elderly people to alleviate anxieties about burial arrangements on behalf of Beth El.
- As a receptionist, directed thousands of phone calls and welcomed in-person guests with courtesy, screening and taking accurate messages when appropriate.

ORGANIZING AND PROBLEM-SOLVING ABILITY
- As organizer of over 50 retreats for Alcoholics Anonymous:
  - Contacted and retained well-known personalities to lead retreats, and made VIP arrangements for their transportation, lodging, and other needs.
  - Sent personalized confirmations several weeks before the retreat including maps, menus, room and roommate assignments, and arranged transportation for all who requested such help.
  - Assisted members of four other Alcoholics Anonymous regions to set up retreats parallel to ours.
- As a collector, contacted debtors and tactfully but firmly requested payment, arranged for payment options, and litigated small claims when necessary.

WORK HISTORY

1978-present	RETREAT ORGANIZER, Alcoholics Anonymous, Vallejo, CA
1993-present	SECRETARY, Beth El Burial Association, Pinole, CA
1990-92	COUNSELOR'S TROUBLESHOOTER, El Sobrante High School, El Sobrante. CA
1988-93	COLLECTOR, Business Systems, Oakland, CA; & Building Concepts, Berkeley, CA
1980-87	RECEPTIONIST, McMartin's Clothing, Orinda, CA; Singer Mortgage & Inv. Co., Oakland, CA

EDUCATION

Lotus 1-2-3 and WordPerfect 5.1, Martinez and Richmond Adult Schools, CA

- Resume writer: Jenny Mish-

Customer Service

Margaret Ann Peterson

3400 Atlas Road, #2308
Richmond, California 94806
(510) 758-1755

OBJECTIVE

A Ground Support position with an emphasis on Reservations or Customer Service

SUMMARY

- Over 10 years experience in Customer Service/Sales.
- A true professional; able to remain poised and level-headed under pressure.
- Recognized for being an excellent problem solver regarding customer relations and business transactions.
- Very personable, outgoing, and able to relate to people from diverse cultures.

RELEVANT SKILLS AND EXPERIENCE

CUSTOMER SERVICE

- Handled customer relations for Keegan Management Co.:
  - Trained sales representatives in:
    - Quality service
    - Professional company representation
    - Effective interpersonal relations
    - Add-on sales techniques
  - Resolved customer complaints in person and over the phone.
- Represented Alfred W. Ferrise, M.D. Weight Loss Centers to the public:
  - Introduced new customers to the program, giving full explanations and answering questions.
  - Counseled clients who had difficulty following the program, offering them encouragement, support, and friendly advice.

ORGANIZATIONAL SKILLS

- Oversaw operations in 11 of Keegan Management's offices in Cincinnati, OH:
  - Maintained accurate financial record using IBM and Tandy PCs.
  - Scheduled up to 60 client appointments per day.
  - Trained staff regarding office procedures and policies.
- Directed the administration of 30 Weight Loss Centers throughout Northern California, involving daily operations, personnel, and business development.

WORK HISTORY

1993-present	Independent Travel	Throughout the U.S. including Alaska and Hawaii
1986-93	Regional Manager	Keegan Management Co., dba: Nutri System,
	Troubleshooter	San Francisco Area and Cincinnati, Ohio
	Trainer	
	Office Manager	
1978-85	Head of Operations	Alfred W. Ferrise, M.D. Weight Loss Centers,
	Office Manager	Sacramento, CA.
	Receptionist	

TRAINING

Numerous seminars on Sales, Public Relations, and Customer Service

- Resume writer: Susan Ireland -

Joan Serina

545 Bridgeview Drive, #54
San Francisco, California 94123
(415) 123-4567

Joan's ancient history with another airline was highlighted at the top of this resume, which she successfully used to return to the job market after a few years working full-time at home. —S.I.

OBJECTIVE

A position in Ground Support with United Airlines.

HIGHLIGHTS

- Former Flight Attendant for Braniff Airlines.
- Over 7 years in customer service; committed to delivering top-quality service.
- Ability to represent the company with professionalism, poise, and integrity.
- Adept at solving immediate and long-term problems.
- Teamworker who sees the whole picture while focusing on primary responsibilities.

RELEVANT SKILLS & EXPERIENCE

CUSTOMER SERVICE
- Served tourists and business professionals of diverse cultures at the Mark Hopkins Hotel and Gulliver's Restaurant, accommodating their travel and time pressures.
  - Consistently provided top-quality service, receiving commendations from customers and management.
  - Put customers at ease by acknowledging their need for explanations and information.
  - Frequently volunteered tourist information to travelers.
- As Supervisor of Gulliver's Restaurant:
  - Maintained a high standard of employee appearance and work performance.
  - Collaborated with chef to ensure highest quality food preparation.
  - Oversaw customer reservations and seating.
- As Salesperson at Shreve & Co. (fine jewelry and crystal):
  - Worked in an organized sales team to offer comprehensive expertise on all products.
  - Assisted customers in locating products and making purchasing decisions.
  - Received excellent reviews on covert shopping evaluations.

PROBLEM SOLVING
- As Supervisor at The Top of the Mark and at Gulliver's, effectively resolved customer complaints regarding food, service, and payments.
  - Stepped in at last minute to cover employee shortages, without any attention being drawn to the problem.
  - Managed large crowds during rush hours, providing extra customized service.
  - Re-prioritized duties during peak times to keep front-line operations running smoothly.

WORK HISTORY

1990-present	**Full-time Parent**	
1988-90	**Restaurant Supervisor Cocktail Server**	Gulliver's Restaurant, Burlingame
1986-88	**Hostess/Cocktail Server**	Top of the Mark, Mark Hopkins Hotel, San Francisco
1984-86	**Retail Salesperson**	Shreve & Co., San Francisco, CA
Previously	**Flight Attendant**	Braniff Airlines, Love Field, Dallas, TX

EDUCATION AND TRAINING

Braniff International Hostess Training Program, Dallas, TX
Performing Arts, Northwest Missouri State University, Springfield, MO

- Resume writer: Susan Ireland -

Customer Service

JoAnn Brook

500 Madill Ave.
Antioch, CA 94509
510-635-7777

OBJECTIVE: A position in **Customer Service**

SUMMARY

- Extensive background in customer service.
- Demonstrated ability to handle several tasks at once.
- Won recognition from all previous employers, for outstanding service.
- Successful in dealing with difficult customers.

RELEVANT EXPERIENCE

1991 to present   WAL-MART, Pittsburg, CA
Retail Sales Representative, Assistant Department Manager
- Received two awards for outstanding customer service in the shoe department.
- Frequently requested by repeat customers for assistance in selecting shoes.
- Promoted from sales to assistant department manager.

1986-90   MORE TO LOVE, Walnut Creek, CA
Sales Clerk, Buyer
- Received bonuses for increasing store profits over 100%.
- Selected and priced items; set-up displays; created promotional materials.

1981-85   AMERICAN RIVER COLLEGE BOOKSTORE, Sacramento, CA
Cashier
- Perfectly balanced cash drawer for duration of employment.

1979-81   COLONY KITCHEN, Carmichael, CA
Waitress

EDUCATION

1979   EASTERN ADULT EDUCATION CENTER Sacramento, CA
Office Procedures, Certificate of Completion; and completed GED

- Resume writer: Rhonda Findling -

Deborah A. Eggers

_(415) 876-5432_

881 Marin Ave.
Hayward, CA 94541

JOB OBJECTIVE: A position in Customer Service

HIGHLIGHTS OF QUALIFICATIONS

- Strong customer service skills; diplomatic and patient.
- Organized; good at following through.
- Flexible; able and willing to learn new things.
- Professional in appearance and work attitude.
- Clerical skills include: typing, ten key, data entry, and phone systems.

RELEVANT ACCOMPLISHMENTS

CUSTOMER SERVICE

- As **Customer Service Representative** for TAYLOR MADE, INC.:
  - Increased number of accounts at Taylor Made, Oakland Business Center by 70%.
    - ..Created an efficient customer account file for invoicing which encouraged frequent use by customers.
    - ..Participated in telemarketing campaigns to existing accounts regarding new services and promotions.
    - ..Personally presented all available services to customers in the store.
  - Maintained public relations with top Bay Area accounts including: Golden State Warriors, Equitec, Sir Speedy, and Copy Mat.
  - Responded to customer inquiry calls using my ability to identify with the consumers' needs and problems.
  - Performed on-line troubleshooting: identified problems, gave technical advice, filed service requests and followed up on scheduling.

- As **Customer Service Representative** for PLATT MUSIC CORPORATION:
  - Answered as many as 60 calls a day from angry customers regarding missed shipment; guaranteed them delivery as soon as possible.
  - Researched lost orders and traced shipments.
  - Checked stock availability to fill scheduled deliveries.

CLERICAL

- In entry-level positions at TAYLOR MADE and PLATT MUSIC CORP.:
  - Performed data entry using ten key and alpha to update inventory records and enter customer service call information. Functioned as backup for receptionist.
  - Balanced receipts with daily register tapes; reported weekly and monthly sales totals to management, using a spreadsheet format.

- As **Clerical Assistant** at BROKERS SERVICE OFFICE:
  - Maintained numeric filing system.
  - Typed detailed insurance forms with a high rate of accuracy.

WORK HISTORY

Presently	**Clerical**	RYALS & ASSOCIATES, Oakland
1991-1994	**Customer Service**, Bus. Center	TAYLOR MADE OFFICE SYSTEMS, Oakland
1990-1991	**Clerical Assistant**	BROKERS SERVICE OFFICE, Castro Valley
1987-1990	**Customer Service**, Deliveries	PLATT MUSIC CORP., Hayward
1985-1987	**Clerical**	KELLY SERVICES, Hayward

EDUCATION
Liberal Arts, Chabot Jr. College, Hayward

- Resume writer: Susan Ireland -

Customer Service

BOB FOGEL
3003 S.E. Baseline
Portland, OR 97266
(503) 777-5252

Objective: Position as Customer Service Supervisor

PROFESSIONAL EXPERIENCE

Supervision

- Supervised up to 80 people which included hiring, firing, and training.
- Successfully met production requirements for several different departments.
- Developed a time study for each job on production line, which resulted in job standards being established for each position.
- Maintained safety standards by developing and enforcing policies as a safety coordinator.
- Inspected products to ensure quality standards were met.

Customer Service

- Demonstrated ability to listen effectively to customers, and resolve their problems, which resulted in both cost savings and excellent customer relations.
- Successfully defused angry customers by using patience and excellent listening skills.
- Entered data for accessory orders, using Foxpro on a Wyss computer.
- Quoted estimates for purchase of equipment.
- Troubleshot problems with equipment, which included instruction on proper use, location of nearest repair center, or return of equipment to factory.
- Provided technical information to other repair centers using schematics to solve complex problems.

Training

- Taught basic electronics at Lowery Air Force Base for three years.
- Trained testers and assemblers in proper methods of testing, cleaning, & boxing equipment.
- Trained staff in the inspection of cassette tapes.

Achievements

- Developed and implemented a procedure for screening incoming units which resulted in a cost savings of approximately $50,000 per month
- Selected "Technician of the Year."

WORK HISTORY

MESSAGE PHONE INC., Clackamas, OR	1980-1994
Customer Support	1993
Lead - Foreman - Senior Technician	1992
Supervisor	1990
Customer Service Technician	1981
Line Technician	1980

Military - Retired U.S. Air Force - Electronics

EDUCATION

Marketing and Management classes, Clackamas Community College
Technical, Electronic, and Supervisory Training

- Resume written by Dislocated Workers Project -

ANTHONY ROBINSON
609 Seventh Street
San Francisco, CA 94111
(415) 333-3344

OBJECTIVE

A customer service/telemarketing position:
•Cold Calls   •Fundraising   •Surveys   •Sales   •Management

HIGHLIGHTS OF QUALIFICATIONS

- Five years telemarketing experience.
- High level of energy and enthusiasm, from the first call of the day to the last.
- Exceptional telephone personality.   • Able to dial by touch.

RELEVANT SKILLS AND EXPERIENCE

Survey Interviewing
- Quickly established rapport with interviewees, maintaining an average of 110-120% of quota for survey completion.
- "No matter how bad the market, Tony has the tenacity of a pit bull, yet is always warm and friendly." (From manager's evaluation.)

Fundraising
- Solicited the highest donation received in a major campaign, and requested an additional $200 for a total of $1,400 from a single donor.
- Consistently awarded bonuses for increasing donation revenue.

Management/Sales
- Developed effective telemarketing scripts for theatre/seminar ticket sales and fundraising campaigns as an Assistant Marketing Director.
- Trained and managed part-time staff of four: Coached telemarketers in delivery, timing, and closing.

EMPLOYMENT HISTORY

1993-94 **Telemarketing Interviewer,**
   Market Research Strategies, Boston, MA
1991-93 **Assistant Marketing and Public Relations Director,**
   Performance Multimedia, Boston, MA
1989-91 **Telemarketing Interviewer,**
   The New Chicago Group, Boston, MA
1984-89 **Manager,**
   Bucci for Men, Boston, MA

- Resume written by Roving Resume Writers -

Customer Service

Frank Hampton

(415) 775-6500

620 Sutter St.
San Francisco, CA 94102

JOB OBJECTIVE: Customer Service Representative /Receptionist

HIGHLIGHTS OF QUALIFICATIONS

- Over 5 years in the customer service field.
- Effective communicator; attentive listener, patient, and diplomatic.
- Represent employer intelligently and professionally.
- Sincerely enjoy working with people, in person and over the phone.
- Good sense of humor.

RELEVANT EXPERIENCE

CUSTOMER SERVICE

- **As Telemarketing Representative for Lillian Jones Associates:**
  - Made over 1000 calls per week to promote products, resulting in a high rate of returns.
  - Developed an effective phone selling technique involving:
    1. Listening carefully for key concerns of the customer.
    2. Finding a way to interest potential buyer in the product.
    3. Representing the company in a positive light.

- **As Information Guide at The Museum of Natural Science:**
  - Answered questions and disseminated information to the public regarding exhibits, schedules, and locations.
  - Sold books and gift items, making suggestions when appropriate.

ORGANIZATIONAL

- **As Executive Secretary for The Alumnae Association,** a foundation that gave grants to worthy causes:
  - Managed all secretarial functions for the Executive Associate.
  - Assisted in the preparation of the Annual Report and the Board Reports.
  - Responded to written and telephone requests for detailed information about Fund programs.

- **As Telemarketing Representative at Lillian Jones Associates:**
  - Utilized an ITC mainframe to make calls and register responses.
  - Categorized lead cards according to customer response for future use by the company.

WORK HISTORY

1990-1994	Telemarketing Representative	LILLIAN JONES ASSOCIATES, New York City
1989	Secretary/Receptionist	THE WRIGHT FOUNDATION, New York City
1986-1988	Information Guide	THE MUSEUM OF NATURAL SCIENCE, New York City
1984-1986	Child Activity Supervisor	COMMUNITY HOMELESS SERVICES, New York City

EARLIER RELEVANT EXPERIENCE

6 years	Executive Secretary	THE ALUMNAE ASSOCIATION, New York City

EDUCATION

Writing, Anderson Community College, Philadelphia, PA
Liberal Arts, Boston University, Boston, MA

- Resume writer: Susan Ireland -

Carol Pilson
434 Victoria Street
San Francisco, CA 94132
(415) 767-7676

OBJECTIVE

A Sales/Customer Service position

SUMMARY OF QUALIFICATIONS

- Genuinely enjoy helping people through consultative sales.
- 10 successful years in sales; winner of several awards.
- Motivated, hard worker.

PROFESSIONAL ACCOMPLISHMENTS

SALES

- Consistently exceeded personal monthly quotas by as much as 50%
- Won "Salesperson of the Quarter" for opening most new accounts.
- Earned reputation as key player in branch sales team that always won quarterly company sales awards.
- Built a loyal customer base by using a consultative sales approach.

CUSTOMER SERVICE

- Provided friendly advice to a wide range of people, promoting Wells Fargo's customer-oriented image.
- Helped customers and merchants identify services/products that best suited their needs.
- Educated customers on how to fill out forms and how to use various banking services.

ADMINISTRATIVE

- Authorized to open and close the vault.
- Balanced up to $40,000 in personal daily transactions.
- Routinely operated office equipment including computers, faxes, and adding machines.

WORK HISTORY

1993-present	Family Management		
1972-1993	Wells Fargo Bank, San Francisco	**Customer Service Rep**	(20 yrs.)
		Receptionist	(1 yr.)

EDUCATION

A.A., Psychology, Diablo Valley College, Pleasant Hill, CA

Psychology, University of California, Davis

- Resume writer: Susan Ireland -

Customer Service

Arnie Lawlor

(415) 646-6464

1432 16th Avenue
San Francisco, CA 94122

JOB OBJECTIVE: A position in Customer Service within the hospitality industry

SUMMARY OF QUALIFICATIONS

- Five years experience working in the hospitality/entertainment mecca of Las Vegas.
- Competent at managing responsibilities in a high-volume atmosphere.
- Personable and flexible; work extremely well with co-workers.
- Skilled at interacting with patrons of all socioeconomic backgrounds.

RELEVANT EXPERIENCE

CUSTOMER RELATIONS

**As Cashier Auditor/Supervisor at Harrah's Hotel & Casino and
Casino Cashier at Harvey's Hotel & Casino:**

- Served up to 2000 customers per night, including celebrities, convention attendees, and tourists from all walks of life.
- Provided prompt, courteous service, often selling over $15,000 in coins during a shift.
- Assisted patrons with directions and information regarding entertainment, restaurants, etc.

As Attendant at Nevada State University Fitness Center:

- Functioned as receptionist, handling inquiries, reservations, and equipment sign-outs.
- Refereed NCAA team sports (1AA division); monitored weight room activities.

SERVICE MANAGEMENT

As Cashier Auditor/Supervisor at Harrah's Hotel & Casino:

- Conducted on-site audits at each cashier booth on the casino floor, directing cash amounts totaling $800,000.
- Selected to perform maximum security tasks including main bank operations.
- Oversaw the coin delivery team, ensuring each booth's quotas were maintained.
- Supervised 12 cashiers; counted out coin booths at the end of the shift; reconciled and reported balances to management.
- Directed staff positioning during the shift to ensure full customer service at all times.
- Helped organize slot tournaments, designed to increase the number of high-rated players.

WORK HISTORY

1992-1994	Cashier Auditor/Supervisor	HARRAH'S HOTEL & CASINO, Las Vegas, NV
1989-1991	Casino Cashier	HARVEY'S HOTEL & CASINO, Las Vegas, NV
1988-1989	Attendant	NEVADA STATE UNIVERSITY FITNESS CENTER, Las Vegas, NV

- Resume writer: Susan Ireland -

4

HOTEL, RESTAURANT, AND FOOD SERVICE

Maureen McGivern
2376 Shawn Drive
San Pablo, CA 94806
(415) 724-1866

OBJECTIVE

Master Cake Decorator

HIGHLIGHTS

- Over seventeen years decorating cakes for large and small events, both formal and informal.
- Trained by California State Champion Cake Decorator.
- Artistic, with an eye for color and innovative design.
- Adept at working with clients to customize orders.

PROFESSIONAL EXPERIENCE

1981-present **Manager**
Maureen's Originals (Wedding & Party Service), Pinole

- Commissioned to create a cake for the Prince of Nigeria.
- Selected by *Wedding Wish Book* for page 1 photo, displaying bridge wedding cake for 500 which I decorated.
- Contracted by hotels, caterers, and corporations such as Classic Caterers, Chevron Corporation, and Days Hotel for cake orders.

- Decorated party and wedding cakes, offering the ability to duplicate complex designs from photos.
- Specialized in creative designs, incorporating colors of party and decor.
- Met with clients to discuss their event and customize services to meet their needs and budgets.
- Hired, trained, and supervised staff.

1977-81 **Head Baker/Decorator**
Party Time Catering, San Pablo

- Managed full-time baking operations for this busy service which catered to events of up to 5,000 people.
- Decorated over 2,000 cakes for either informal and formal events.
- Increased profitability by performing cost analysis on cake baking/decorating.

TRAINING

Trained by Chuck Aldridge, former California State Champion Cake Decorator

- Resume writer: Susan Ireland -

CARLENE DOONAN

2731 Southgate Dr.
Berkeley CA 94702
(415) 525-9934

Carlene's resume is designed to show an employer that she can make a successful transition from retail management to the world of food. She does this by focusing on her recent training, and showing how her retailing skills can be applied to the new position. To top it off, she lets them know she has passion and commitment to add to her skills. —Y.P.

Objective: Position as apprentice baker, with opportunity for quality training and increasing levels of responsibility.

HIGHLIGHTS OF QUALIFICATIONS

- Work hard, learn fast, willing and able to assume responsibility.
- Passion for food; commitment to producing highest quality products.
- Experience with successful retail design and display.
- Good team player; work well with all kinds of people.

RELEVANT EXPERIENCE

Cooking Knowledge
- Studied with master chef, Ken Wolfe, learning:
  - principles and techniques of food preparation
  - importance of quality and freshness of ingredients
  - chemistry and effects of combining ingredients
  - coordinated timing of food preparation
  - innovative approaches to traditional cooking principles
  - balancing flavors within a dish and within a meal.

Coordination/Teamwork
- Maintained and supervised a balanced flow of inventory for Rialto theatre food concession and for Miasma retail gift store:
  - monitored sales including seasonal fluctuations
  - researched to determine best prices, by phone and at trade shows
  - assured correct stocking and display.
- Coordinated timing and priority of tasks, as store manager.
- Worked in a finely tuned sales team to expedite customer services.

Speed/Accuracy
- Handled large volume of customers in minimum time, selling theatre tickets and selling retail merchandise.
- Accurately counted, recorded and deposited cash receipts for retail store.
- Prepared puff-pastry dough in cooking class, consistently completing in record time.

EMPLOYMENT or WORK HISTORY

1990-present	*Store Manager*	MIASMA gift/novelty store, Berkeley
1987-90	*Assistant Manager*	MIASMA gift/novelty store, Berkeley
1986-87	*Theatre Manager*	RIALTO THEATRE GROUP, Berkeley
1985-86	*Clerk/Counter Sales*	RIALTO THEATRE GROUP, Berkeley

EDUCATION & TRAINING

Liberal Arts - Laney College 1972-75
Classes in Cooking Principles, with Ken Wolfe, Master Chef

- Resume writer: Yana Parker -

Robert Finkler

555 Valley Street, Apt. 65
San Francisco, CA 84111
(415) 888-8808 or 888-0188

EMPLOYMENT OBJECTIVE: Assistant Pastry Chef

HIGHLIGHTS OF QUALIFICATIONS

- Two years restaurant and hospitality experience.
- Work well under pressure as part of the team.
- Good organizational skills.
- Neat and "clean-as-you-go" work habits.
- Well-groomed appearance.
- Polite, respectful, and courteous manners.

EXPERIENCE AND SPECIALIZED SKILLS

PASTRY:
- Learned techniques and principles of bakery trade at the well-known La Baguette Bakery.
- Studied under Pierre Brousseau, French Pastry Chef.
- Baked cakes of all kinds, including wedding cakes, cupcakes, cheesecakes, angel food cakes, and fruitcakes.
- Prepared tarts, cookies, croissants, and assorted French pastries.
- Decorated hundreds of desserts for elegant presentations using colored icings, fruit, flowers, etc.

BANQUET:
- Catered large banquets at Columbus Country Club.
- Prepared attractive salads, sandwiches, and entrees for over one hundred people.
- Made cakes and other desserts on head baker's day off.

FOOD PREP:
- Assisted chef by cleaning vegetables and meats.
- Cut, chopped, and grated assorted food elements.
- Assembled and accurately measured ingredients.

HOSPITALITY EMPLOYMENT HISTORY

Food Prep	Vista Bar & Grill, Norman, KS	1994
Bakery Asst; Pantry	Columbus Country Club, Columbus, OH	1993
Asst. Pastry Chef	La Baguette Bakery, Norman, KS	1990
Dishwasher	Le Chateau, Binghamton, PA	1988
Dishwasher	Pinnochios, Norman, KS	1986-87

EDUCATION

Rose College, Oklahoma	Business Management & Computers	1986/90
Vocational Rehabilitation, Oklahoma	Food Service Etiquette	1984

- Resume writer: Sasha George, Roving Resume Writers -

ALICE Q. HAU

102 Fifth Street
Lobster Point, CA 94000
(514) 134-6666 (Message)

Objective: **A position as a cook.**

HIGHLIGHTS OF QUALIFICATIONS

- Over 30 years cooking experience.
- Skilled in American-style cooking;
  some knowledge of French and Italian cuisine.
- Catered for large and small parties.
- Completed cooking training program.
- Responsible, efficient and flexible.

RELEVANT EXPERIENCE

1990-1994   **Cook and Housekeeper,** Mr. and Mrs. Gerome Friday
Created menus based on family food preferences.
Shopped regularly to buy fresh produce and meats.
Prepared all family meals, including breakfasts, lunches,
    dinners, snacks, and special treats.
Cooked meats, entrees, soups, made salads, and baked desserts.
Planned, prepared, and served food and drinks for guests and
    parties of up to 16 people.
Performed general housekeeping.

1986-1989   **Cook and Housekeeper,** Mr. and Mrs. Frederick Jones
Planned, cooked and served family meals, including
    parties (same as above).
Managed general housekeeping and child care.

1983-1985   **Child Care,** Mr. and Mrs. Coopers
Prepared light meals and provided primary care for three children.

1979-1982   **Cook and Housekeeper,** Mrs. Jeannine Crisp
Performed all daily cooking and housekeeping.

EDUCATION
Completed cooking training program at Paul Peter's Cooking School, Lota, CA

- Resume written by Roving Resume Writers -

Candice Cakebread
704 Foothill Drive
San Rafael, CA 95407
(415) 266-1759

This woman was relocating to a new area and going through major changes in her life. She was a creative and experienced woman with no resume to reflect her talents or personality.—M.K.

"I live on good soup, not fine words." - Moliére

Objective: Food prep, baking or counter person; part-time.

Summary of Qualifications

◆ Gourmet vegetarian cooking and baking are my specialty.

◆ Able to work in a fast-paced, intense environment smoothly.

◆ Experienced with international and theme meals.

◆ I am a fast learner and am willing to be on call.

Experience

1991-present   • *Catering* - **Taste Catering**
On-call food prep pantry in kitchens and on-site service for up to 1,600, including Art Museum parties.

1991   • *Catering* - **Bank of America**
Catered staff luncheons for up to 15. Introduced vegetarian additions to menu.

1991   • *Food Prep/Kitchen Staff* - **Renaissance Faire/Mullah's Turkish Coffee House**
Prepared food for two meals twice daily, for 200 meat and vegetarian entreés including salads, vegetables, grains, and desserts.
Counter work, made coffees and chai, served foods, and cashiered.

1991   • *Deli Person* - **Other Avenues Collective Food Store**
Purchased spices, worked in deli, and assisted in joint decision making.

1989 - 1990   • *Kitchen Manager & Cook* - **Isis Oasis Retreat Center**
Oversaw kitchen production, planned vegetarian, macrobiotic, chicken and fish menus. Ordered and bought local produce. Participated in nutritional workshops, catered weddings and parties up to 150.

1989   • *Head Cook/Meat Chef Assistant* - **Cirque de Soleil**
Planned varied menus, shopped wisely and prepared two delicious meals twice daily including soups, salads, entreés, vegetables and grains for 150.

1986 - 1989   • *Baker* - **Taste of Honey**
Wholesale and retail baking including pies, bars, cookies, cakes, rugelach, tarts, pastries, etc. Worked with alternatives to white flour, sugar, wheat, dairy and egg products. Made soups, lasagna, sandwiches. Counter work, made coffees, espressos, smoothies. Served baked goods and lunch food, cashiered, maintained inventory. Weekend supervisor.

- Resume written by Maurine Killough -

Robert P. Sperling

2233 La Honda Avenue
Oakland, CA 94999
(415) 441-4141

Robert's experience at a five-star restaurant is the key in this resume, which minimizes his degree and former career in forestry. —S.I.

OBJECTIVE

A position as a prep cook

HIGHLIGHTS

- Over three years experience at a 5-star restaurant, two years as prep cook.
- Meticulous worker; attentive to quality and detail.
- Quick learner; eager to further my cooking knowledge and skills.
- Able and willing to assist in any aspect of restaurant work when necessary.

RELEVANT SKILLS & EXPERIENCE

at Chez Jean-Paul:
PREPARATION

- Butchered a wide variety of meats and seafood, developing good knife and portioning skills.
- Made lamb and pork sausage for pizza, grilling, and pastas.
- Cooked soups that reflected seasonal menu changes.
- Gained familiarity with braising, breading, fat frying, and grilling.
- Prepared a wide range of vegetables used for salads, appetizers, and entrees.
- Cooked all house stocks for cafe and restaurant.
- Made fillings and toppings for pizzas and calzones.

KITCHEN ORGANIZATION

- Ordered kitchen supplies including dry goods, dairy, oils, spices, meats, and produce; ensured inventory could accommodate a constantly changing menu.
- Organized and maintained three walk-ins, tracking items carefully for efficient and timely use.
- Reported daily to chef regarding walk-in inventory.
- Prioritized prepping duties to meet deadlines in a crowded kitchen.

WORK HISTORY

1991-present	*Prep Cook* *Garde Manger* *Farm Liaison*	Chez Jean-Paul Restaurant & Cafe, Berkeley
1987 & 1989	*Procurer of Goods* *Bus Boy/Waiter*	Chez Jean-Paul Restaurant & Cafe, Berkeley
1987-1991	*Forester*	US Forest Service, Sierraville/Truckee University of California, Berkeley Brewster Pines Company, Modoc

EDUCATION

B.S., Forestry, University of California, Berkeley, 1986

- Resume writer: Susan Ireland -

WALTER A. LOWELL III

7130 New Forest Court #2 • Clinton, Maryland 20603 • (301) 292-4967

CAREER OBJECTIVE: Position as CHEF in a restaurant.

SKILLS SUMMARY

* Over 15 years of successful experience in food service, preparing various types of gourmet food, and specializing in southern-style foods.
* Certified in Food Technology and trained as a steward.
* Skilled in all kitchen equipment and various cooking techniques.
* Training and skills as a butcher.
* Committed to providing total quality service in culinary arts.

EDUCATION

Certificate of Completion, 1986 - **Chief Steward**
Harry Lundeburg School of Seamanship; Piney Point, Maryland

Food Service Institute, 1982 - 1984; New Orleans, Louisiana

PROFESSIONAL EXPERIENCE

Chief Cook, <u>Southern Diner</u>; Waldorf, Maryland   **1992 - Present**
* Prepare meats institutional-style by roasting, stewing, and baking to ensure the restaurant provides tasty southern cuisine to its customers.
* Prepare fresh vegetable dishes which balance flavors with that of the coordinating meat dishes.
* Blend spices and herbs to complement the meat and vegetable dishes.
* Received several cash awards for providing Total Quality Management within the restaurant.

Chief Steward, <u>Seafarers International Union</u>; Camp Springs, Maryland   **1980 - 1992**
* As a member of the steward department in the Merchant Marines, I was assigned to various ships on sea duty.
* Advanced from Messman to Chief Steward over the span of 12 years, taking on responsibilities as Third Cook, Baker, Chief Cook and finally as Chief Steward.
* Maintained officer's quarters and dining area.
* Prepared assigned foods and maintained designated kitchen area.
* Took inventory, ordered and stocked galley, making sure sufficient supplies of food and utensils were available.
* Planned menus for five meals per day, ensuring that meals were nutritious and well balanced.
* Scheduled kitchen staff to provide sufficient service to the passengers and crew.

- Resume writer: Wanda Jenkins -

LEE CRAIG
254-39 Peachtree Lane
Bayside, New York 11364
(718) 229-0123

OBJECTIVE: Executive Chef in charge of Corporate Dining Facilities and Events

HIGHLIGHTS OF QUALIFICATIONS
Graduated with honors from the Culinary Institute of America
Over 10 years successful experience in restaurants and catering
Effective manager with proven ability to train, motivate and direct staff
Consistent performance of highest quality and creativity levels within budget
Full range of experience in developing and presenting menus of diverse ethnic and cultural styles

RELEVANT SKILLS & EXPERIENCE

MANAGEMENT:
- Managed kitchen and support staff of 10 - 20, preparing menus for off-premise events
- Supervised and coordinated presentation of events ranging from elegant seated dinners, to corporate cocktail and large theme parties - Clients included:
  Tiffany, Philip Morris, Citibank, The NYC Ballet, Boys Harbor, Ann Taylor, Julliard
- Maintained and often surpassed a targeted 25% food cost
- Developed and implemented policies and standards of quality for private catering business
- Directed a cafeteria-style lunch operation serving 50 - 90 members daily
- Supervised and produced menu preparations for lunch, dinner, brunch, catered events and daily specials at a 125-seat "healthy foods" restaurant
- Purchased all food for 300-seat restaurant and banquet facilities
- Trained staff in basic skills; taught seasoned employees enhanced preparation and presentation skills
- Directed layout and design of two full-service kitchens

TECHNICAL & CREATIVE EXPERTISE:
- Instituted a plan for menu and recipe development for own catering company, significantly increasing menu repertoire
- Created standardized recipe and accurate costing systems
- Conceived and priced menu for 160-seat restaurant serving lunch, dinner and brunch
- On-site chef for events ranging from seated dinners for over 100 to cocktail parties for over 1000
- Designed, developed and executed menus including the following:
  Regional American, French and Italian; Middle Eastern, English Teas and Spa Cuisines

EMPLOYMENT HISTORY

1989-1994	PARTNER/EXECUTIVE CHEF	Lee Craig Catering	NYC / The Hamptons
1984-1989	HEAD CHEF	S.K. Williams Catering	NYC / The Hamptons
1983-1984	CONSULTANT	The West End Cafe	New York City
1982-1983	DAY PRODUCTION CHEF	Natalie's	New York City
1980-1982	RECEIVING STEWARD/LINE COOK	Windows on the World	New York City

EDUCATION

THE CULINARY INSTITUTE OF AMERICA   Hyde Park, NY

Associates in Occupational Science - 1980   Graduated with Honors, Perfect Attendance

- Resume writer: Hinda Bodinger -

Hotel, Restaurant, & Food Service

Thomas Mackey

333 Lenore Court • Oakland, CA 94609 • **(510) 444-3333**

JOB OBJECTIVE

Position as Professional Bartender

> Here is a good example of how you can use the "Summary" to emphasize just about everything important to the next employer.—Ed.

SUMMARY OF QUALIFICATIONS

- Proven reputation as a bartender with over 10 years experience.
- Built a large and loyal customer base through offering friendly attitude and professional service.
- Able to efficiently handle all situations.
- Expert knowledge of food and wine.
- Top priority to maintain cleanliness and neatness in bar area.

EMPLOYMENT EXPERIENCE

1988-94 *Bartender*
MCGEE'S BAR & GRILL, Alameda, CA
As Head Bartender, worked a variety of shifts from morning to closing for very successful and popular business serving wide range of customers – businesspeople, families, and sports enthusiasts.

- Managed all facets of opening and closing.
- Consistently worked all busy shifts, including St. Patrick's Day, New Year's Eve, Super Bowl Sunday, and World Series.
- Served all types of customers in a friendly and efficient manner.
- On daily basis, set up bar to handle any size crowd.
- Ensured customers enjoyed a relaxed and comfortable atmosphere by controlling potentially disruptive situations.

1985-88 *Night Loader*
HORIZON BEVERAGE, Oakland, CA
Organized daily loading instructions and used fork lift to load route trucks.

1981-85 *Manager*
CHEF ROMANO PIZZA, Alameda, CA
Managed a very busy take-out and delivery pizza business.

1977-81 *Bartender*
ALAMEDA GOLF COURSE RESTAURANT & BAR, Alameda, CA
Tended large volume bar for business that included two golf courses serving up to 200,000 golfers a year.

- Coordinated food and beverage for many golf tournaments.
- Worked all busy shifts, including dozens of special functions.

TRAINING

First Aid and CPR Training, 1992
Red Cross, Alameda, CA

- Resume writer: Alina Ever -

Darlene Best

1289 Third Avenue Apt. A • San Francisco, CA 94122 • **(415) 123-4567**

JOB OBJECTIVE: Professional Waiter at Greens Restaurant.

OVERVIEW

- Over 15 years experience as professional in food and beverage industry.
- Attained substantial return business by maintaining consistently friendly attitude and professional service.
- Committed to full-service dining experience.
- Particularly adept at responding to customer needs, including special dietary requests and questions about wine.
- Adapts well to changing kitchen climates.
- Maintains clean and organized work area.
- Basic knowledge of domestic and international wines.

FOOD & BEVERAGE EXPERIENCE

1988-present *Waiter*, **LITTLE CITY ANTIPASTI**, San Francisco, CA
- Achieved one-third of personal sales through repeat customers.
- Consistently turned tables quickly and profitably.

1986-88 *Waiter*, **GIFT CENTER**, San Francisco, CA
Worked private parties, conventions and regular cocktail shifts.
- Dealt skillfully with many people of different nationalities and was often requested for repeat functions.

1984-86 *Waiter*, **CHARLEY BROWN'S**, Burlingame, CA
Promoted from luncheon shift to cocktail service.
- Won Charley Brown Award for top monthly sales.
- Single-handedly and calmly responded to injury accident of kitchen worker by using First Aid skills.

1986-87 *Reservations*, **ERNIE'S**, San Francisco, CA
Handled reservations, coat check and hostessing.
- Ensured privacy for famous customers by diverting phone calls and reporters.
- Recognized and greeted customers by name.

1977-85 *Waiter*, **SCOMA'S DON NUNCIO**, San Francisco, CA
Performed cocktail service, reservations, banquets and hostessing.
- Hired as original staff.
- One of few who received cash bonuses and favorable comments from owner.

EDUCATION

A.A., Liberal Arts
City College, San Francisco

- Resume writer: Alina Ever -

PETER CAPPARELLI
77 Justin Street, Apt. 44
San Francisco CA 94000
(415) 654-3210

Objective: Position as waiter in a top-quality restaurant.

SUMMARY OF QUALIFICATIONS

★ Over seven years experience as a professional waiter.
★ Demonstrated record of exceptional reliability.
★ Able to think independently and quickly resolve problems.
★ Expertise in anticipating and responding to customer needs.
★ Sophisticated knowledge of wines and liquors.
★ Take pride in providing excellent customer service.

RELEVANT SKILLS & EXPERIENCE

CUSTOMER RELATIONS
- Developed an effective approach for advising customers on food and wine, e.g.:
  -listened for customers' likes/dislikes, to make appropriate suggestions
  -using appealing, descriptive phrases to describe dishes
  -recommending wines that complement specific entrees
  -sensing and responding to the moods and needs of each customer.
- Fostered repeat customers through consistently providing quick, well-timed, and professional service.

TEAMWORK/PROBLEM SOLVING
- With 7 years experience, developed a strategy for making quick decisions under high-stress conditions, maintaining composure while prioritizing and orchestrating many job functions.
- Built an exceptional record of reliability—three years without a missed day.
- Earned a reputation as a valuable and cooperative co-worker:
  -was fair, honest, and willing to help others when needed
  -effectively resolved conflicts at appropriate times
  -assisted new managers and other staff to become familiar with restaurant policy and operations.

EMPLOYMENT HISTORY

1994-present	Lunch/Dinner Waiter	DiMAGGIO'S, San Francisco CA
1990-93	Dinner Waiter	ALVIN SHEPPARD'S RESTAURANT, Berkeley CA
		THE PINK PEPPER*, San Leandro CA
1988-90	Lunch/Dinner Waiter	SHELTER HOUSE RESTAURANT, Portland OR
1985-88	Dinner Waiter	MAISIE'S RESTAURANT, Salem OR
		(*Same owner)

EDUCATION

History Major, 1983-85 - Willamette University, Salem OR

- Resume writer: Yana Parker -

JOHN SHENN
401 Eighth Street
San Francisco, California 94103
(415) 446-4646

Objective: Hotel or restaurant •Food Server •Dining Room Staff •Porter

HIGHLIGHTS
- Eight years experience meeting customers' needs.
- Knowledgeable in hotel restaurant operations and procedures.
- Fast learner: I ask questions and follow detailed instructions.

ATTITUDE & APPEARANCE
- Hardworking and efficient, with a "can-do" attitude.
- Neat, professional appearance.
- Respectful; enjoy working with people from diverse cultures.
- Bilingual in English and Armenian.

SPECIALIZED SKILLS

Customer Service
- Often requested by repeat customers.
- Welcomed customers with a smile, seated them and made them feel at home.
- Remained aware of customer needs and provided guests with:
  - clean silverware   -pressed linens   -fresh flowers
  - -ice water   -ashtrays   -condiments   -special requests.
- Took detailed orders for shipping and glasswork, and resolved problems in person and over the telephone.

Food Service
- Catered banquets of up to 50 people in hotel dining room:
  - set up room   -set up buffet   -served food and drinks
  - -took drink orders   -bussed and cleaned up.
- Prepared and served breakfast buffets including egg dishes, breakfast meat platters, fresh fruit plates, rolls and pastries.

Cash Handling
- Correctly prepared bills, calculated tax, and tracked tips.
- Accurately made change and completed credit card transactions.
- Operated electronic cash register and processed end of evening accounts.

WORK EXPERIENCE

1994-present	Waiter/Banquet Server	Hotel Eastmont Cafe	San Francisco, CA
1994	Merchandise Handler	Diversified Freight	Hayward, CA
1986-93	Residential Contractor	Armandine Glass Co.	Glendale, CA

- Resume written by Roving Resume Writers -

JAMES A. PETER
146 Parker Street
San Francisco, CA 94122
(415) 454-4545

OBJECTIVE: Restaurant • Management Trainee • Cook • Food Prep
(Long term goal: to own and manage a restaurant and bar)

HIGHLIGHTS OF QUALIFICATIONS

- Over seven years experience in varied restaurant positions.
- Responsible and hardworking team player.
- Enjoy working weekends, holidays, and long hours.
- Quick learner with a "can-do" attitude.

RELEVANT SKILLS AND EXPERIENCE

1994- present   *Restaurant Worker*   Taco Bell Restaurant , San Francisco, CA
- Prepped food items safely, neatly, and efficiently.
- Received deliveries, stored stock items, and rotated fresh foods.
- Operated cash register and made accurate change in a fast-paced setting.

1993   *Deli Man*   Shop Rite Supermarket, North Bergen, NJ
- Assumed all counter responsibilities in a busy full-service deli:
  -prepared and cooked hot foods -provided complete customer service
  -operated electric slicers and cheese graters -maintained cleanliness of work area.
- Safely handled and stored fresh seafood according to special training.

1988-93   *Night Manager*   Roy Rogers Restaurant, Union City, NJ
- Trained and prepared weekly work schedules for up to 40 employees, ensuring that restaurant was appropriately staffed at all times.
- Accurately performed end of business day inventory, and made weekly supply orders to ensure adequate stock.
- Prepared weekly payroll and complied with government regulations.
- Followed and promoted corporate guidelines in all operations.

1987-88   *Grill Cook*   Roy Rogers Restaurant, Union City, NJ
- Grilled and prepared meats, sandwiches, and other entrees.
- Checked that food was cooked properly and served in proper sized portions.
- Controlled food wastes during slow period times.

1987   *Dishwasher*   Roy Rogers Restaurant, Union City, NJ
- Maintained health and safety standards in the restaurant.
- Checked and cleaned bathrooms in accordance with local health regulations.

EDUCATION

Saddle Associates Franchise Management Training Seminars, Union City, NJ
Memorial High School, West New York, NJ

- Resume written by Roving Resume Writers -

JIM CHRISTEN

6789 Webster Street, Apt. 7
Oakland CA 94609
Home: (415) 123-4567 • Work (415) 789-1234

Jim has had quite a struggle keeping his life on track, but his personal turmoil doesn't have to show up in his resume. —Y.P.

Objective: Position with a hotel or restaurant,
•Management Trainee •Banquet Service •Waiter or •Front Desk

SUMMARY OF QUALIFICATIONS

- Practical experience in every phase of restaurant work.
- Reputation as a supervisor able to keep employees both productive and satisfied with their jobs.
- Willing to go out of my way to make guests comfortable and their dining experience pleasurable.
- Learn quickly, and able to work under pressure.

RELEVANT EXPERIENCE

SUPERVISION

- As Assistant Manager, supervised restaurant staffs of up to 45, overseeing all day-to-day operations, including:
  - setup/opening - breakdown/closing of restaurant - scheduling
  - stocking - preping - setup of cash drawers.

FOOD SERVICE

- As **waiter** at K&L's, worked shifts handling up to 20 tables.
- Set up and closed down for **banquets** at the Park Blvd Hotel.

CUSTOMER SERVICE

- Effectively handled difficult restaurant customers, using an approach of:
  - listening carefully to complaints and doing whatever I can to resolve the problem;
  - maintaining a positive attitude even with customers who are hard to please.

EMPLOYMENT HISTORY

July '87-present	**Assistant Manager**	K&L ICE CREAM, Oakland
1987 fall	**Banquet Set-up** (part-time)	PARK BLVD HOTEL, Oakland
1984-87	**Groundsman/Pruner**	BARTON TREE SERVICE, Alameda
1977-84	**Cashier/Delivery**	STATE ST. PHARMACY, San Francisco
1976-77	**Busperson/Salad Prep**	LA PETIT CAFE, San Francisco

- Resume writer: Yana Parker -

Henry Lee

This resume aims to show that Henry has stuck with it in the fast-food field, accumulating the management expertise needed to supervise food service at a large amusement park. —Ed.

(408) 343-3434

3232 Angeles St., #2323
Santa Clara, CA 95051

JOB OBJECTIVE: Area Supervisor for restaurants at Great America

HIGHLIGHTS OF QUALIFICATIONS

- 12 years experience in fast food restaurant management.
- Proven record in retaining employees for long period of time.
- Maintain excellent cost controls while increasing profitability.
- Have genuine enthusiasm for Great America.

PROFESSIONAL EXPERIENCE

General Manager   MCDONALD'S, INC., **San Jose**, C A   **1994-present**
- Increased annual sales by 15% in 1989 through efficient management practices.
- Coordinated plans created by McDonald's International with subordinate managers, instituting new product offerings and local promotions.
- Supervised the Co-Manager, Assistant Manager, and Shift Managers, handling three shifts a day, seven days a week.
- Reviewed operations daily to ensure fresh food, clean environment.

Area Supervisor   MCDONALD'S OF SANTA CLARA, **Santa Clara**, CA   **1991-1994**
- Supervised overall operations of three McDonald's Restaurants, holding weekly meetings for managers to resolve problems and give updates on new procedures.
- Conducted training seminars for managers of seven McDonald's Restaurants.
- Advised management concerning:

  - Product cost control
  - Inventory ordering
  - Labor guidelines
  - Sales reporting
  - Promotions
  - Customer service

Restaurant Manager   JACK-IN-THE-BOX RESTAURANT, **San Jose**, C A   **1989-1991**
- Directed a crew of 18 young employees on the night shift, requiring close supervision.
- Closed the restaurant each night; balanced daily cash receipts, inspected premises for cleanliness and security, and locked up.

Manager   ARCADIA, **San Jose**, C A   **1989-1991**
- Managed two video arcades, providing a fun-filled atmosphere for a youth-oriented clientele.
- Oversaw a staff of five. Administered bookkeeping, banking, and promotions.

Restaurant Manager   DENNY'S RESTAURANT, **Santa Clara**, CA   **1986-1989**
- Served as first manager for two Denny's which opened up new, thriving territories.
- Implemented company policies and procedures that maintained their national reputation.
- Hired and trained 25 personnel to cover the full range of operations.
- Worked closely with middle management to resolve problems.

Restaurant Manager   TACO BELL, **Tucson, AZ**   **1981-1986**
- Opened two new restaurants in Tucson, one of which achieved the highest volume sales among Arizona Taco Bells, in spite of its remote location.
- Named "Manager of the Month" for high sales, low food and labor costs, and high inspection rating.

- Resume writer: Susan Ireland -

Wendi Kennedy

4128 Pacific Street
San Francisco, CA 95200

(415) 332-4413

OBJECTIVE

A position as a Coordinator in a Catering or Special Events Department.

HIGHLIGHTS

- 15 years in events coordination, specializing in catering.
- Strong interpersonal skills; effective in both independent and collaborative settings.
- Well versed in social etiquette, having served diplomats, celebrities, and corporate leaders.
- Organized, with the ability to delegate to get the job done.
- Talent for prospecting and acquiring quality, cost-effective resources.

PROFESSIONAL EXPERIENCE

MANAGEMENT

As Chef of the Executive Dining Room, Royal Bank of India, New York:
- Organized all culinary aspects from menu planning to presentation of luncheons and parties, serving up to 150 guests.
- Supervised permanent and temporary staff, preparing extensive hors d'oeuvres for monthly parties and occasional private events.
- Set up a new cafeteria which provided efficient service for company staff.
- Purchased all food and supplies, maintaining a high quality inventory while staying within the budget.

As Private Chef for the First Family at The White House for four years:
- Prepared and presented breakfasts and lunches in the Private Quarters, serving the family and occasional guests.
- Adhered to precise schedules, sometimes needing to present meals within minutes.

CATERING

As Caterer for Bank of Integrity, Famous People Magazine, and private residences:
- Planned and executed over 100 events, both formal and informal.
- Created menus and designed table settings to express a variety of themes.
- Hired and supervised kitchen and serving staff.
- Devised work schedules to ensure successful event coordination.

PUBLIC RELATIONS

- Established an extensive resource network, by consistently developing contacts among celebrities, business associates, and friends.
- Promoted products and companies at events such as The Food and Wine Society Demonstration and Tuborg Beer promotion parties.

WORK HISTORY

1982–present	*Caterer*	Bank of Integrity, New York, N.Y. Famous People Magazine, New York, N.Y. Private Residences, New York and San Francisco
1991–92	*Chef*	Mr. & Mrs. Charles Celebrity, San Francisco
1983–88	*Chef, Executive Dining Room*	Royal Bank of India, New York, N.Y.
1978–82	*Private Chef for First Family*	The White House, Washington, D.C.

EDUCATION

AA, Occupational Studies in the Culinary Arts, Culinary Institute, Hyde Park, N.Y.

- Resume writer: Susan Ireland -

Hotel, Restaurant, & Food Service

Roseanne Dearly

777 99th Ave., #3334
San Francisco CA 94444
415-888-1234

OBJECTIVE

A position as Banquet Manager at a large luxury hotel.

SUMMARY OF QUALIFICATIONS

- Over twelve years progressively responsible experience managing banquets.
- Experienced in union relations and training quality-focused staff.
- Special expertise in off-premise catering.
- Highly productive but relaxed under pressure.

PROFESSIONAL EXPERIENCE

1982-present WESTIN ST. FRANCIS HOTEL, San Francisco CA

Assistant Banquet Manager (1987-present)

Oversaw all logistical and staffing arrangements for thousands of functions and meetings for a premier San Francisco hotel with 35,000 sq. ft. of function space and catering sales of $10 million annually.

EVENT PRODUCTION

- Collaborated closely with catering and convention service sales staff to design personalized floor plans, decor, logistics, and staffing for small and large events.
- Coordinated logistics between departments involved in presenting functions (including kitchen, beverage, and service staff).
- Received feedback from satisfied clients for consistent and thorough attention to detail and delivery of complex functions.
- Organized over 25 off-premise caterings for functions at corporate sites and public venues including: -City Hall   -Davies Hall   -Nordstrom's
    -De Young Museum   -Fort Mason   -Aircraft carriers for Fleet Week

ADMINISTRATION

- Consistently met labor cost goals through proper scheduling.
- Prepared capital improvement budget and researched $5-25,000 in cost-effective purchases annually to maintain high-quality equipment and props.
- Designed, purchased, and maintained linens, props, and accessories for dozens of decorative theme parties such as safari, fiesta, garden, underwater, and San Francisco scenes.

PERSONNEL MANAGEMENT

- Adapted and implemented guest-focused programs to elicit useful policy input from line staff, resulting in improved performance and productivity.
- Hired, evaluated, disciplined, and supervised over 100 employees in accordance with labor laws and three union contracts.
- Arranged and supervised mentoring relationships to train two dozen captains.

Senior Captain (1984-87)

Captain (1981-84)

Junior Captain (1980-81)

- Resume writer: Jenny Mish -

Randall Santili

430 Arguello St., #34, San Francisco, CA 94132   **(415) 333-3633**

OBJECTIVE: Hotel Management Trainee or a position in Food and Beverage Management.

SUMMARY OF QUALIFICATIONS

- Three years experience in highly regarded hospitality environments with emphasis on management.
- Degree in Hotel and Restaurant Management anticipated Fall 1996.
- Diploma in Hotel Administration and Food Technology.
- Multilingual: Hindi, Basic French, Basic Spanish.

HOSPITALITY EXPERIENCE

Assistant Food & Beverage Manager, Carnival Cruise Lines

- Assisted in the management of:
  - **16 beverage outlets** - Scheduled and supervised 40 bartenders and bar waiters, managed weekly inventories, ordered stock, and balanced daily accounts.
  - **Two guest dining rooms** (each with 650 seating capacity) - Supervised 140 dining room personnel for table and buffet service.
  - **Five employee dining rooms** - Oversaw general operations for serving three meals a day to 900 employees.
  - **Room service for 2800 guests** - Ensured prompt and courteous service for 1200 guest rooms.
  - **One main kitchen** - Scheduled utility assignments for 70 employees, oversaw equipment repairs, and maintained hygiene standards according to U.S. Public Health regulations.
- Improved Customer Service by co-creating "Carnival College," a fleetwide training program for all service personnel.
  - Designed curriculum and instructed four-week sessions.
  - Instituted standards requiring graduation with score of at least 80%.
- Prior to being promoted to Assistant F&B Manager, trained in all positions of the department.
- Received certificates in: U.S. Public Health, Responsible Alcohol Service, Back Safety Awareness, and Training with Video.

Vacation Trainee

- Gained hands-on experience in five-star hotels. Areas of training included restaurant, bar, front office, kitchen, housekeeping, and room service.

WORK HISTORY

1994-present **Full-time Student**, Hotel/Restaurant Management Program, San Francisco City College
1991-94   **Assistant F&B Manager**, Carnival Cruise Lines, Miami, FL
Concurrent with Education:
Summer '90 **Vacation Trainee**, Taj Mahal Group of Hotels, Bombay, India
Winter '89   **Vacation Trainee**, Oberoi Sheraton Hotels, Bombay, India

EDUCATION

A.A., Hotel and Restaurant Management, San Francisco City College, Fall 1996
Diploma in Hotel Administration and Food Technology, 1991
Sophia Shree B. K. Somani Polytechnic, Bombay, India
Recipient of award for outstanding service

- Resume writer: Susan Ireland -

Denise Wallport

23 Westerly Court
San Francisco, CA 94111
(415) 430-9878

OBJECTIVE

Front Desk or Front Office Clerk in a San Francisco luxury hotel.

KEY QUALIFICATIONS

- Five years experience producing satisfied customers.
- Dependable employee, willing & able to fill in for others when necessary.
- Track record in creating and keeping repeat clientele.
- Team player who works well under pressure.

RELEVANT SKILLS & EXPERIENCE

CUSTOMER SERVICE
- As Front Desk Clerk at the San Francisco Airport Hilton:
  - Received bouquet of exotic flowers in appreciation of excellent customer service.
  - Praised frequently on customer comment cards.
- As Jewelry Manager at Whole Earth Access:
  - Received many letters of thanks from satisfied customers.
  - Developed loyal clientele of regular customers.
  - Effectively responded to customer needs and concerns by placing special orders, arranging for repairs, and graciously accepting returns.

ORGANIZATIONAL
- As Jewelry Manager at Whole Earth Access:
  - Conducted daily and monthly inventories of watch and jewelry department grossing $15,000 monthly.
  - Produced daily, weekly, and monthly bookkeeping records and sales reports.
  - Maintained product information files on over 30 lines of jewelry.
  - Handled paperwork for special orders, repairs, and returns.
- As Front Desk Clerk at the San Francisco Airport Hilton, streamlined service to customers by learning about and coordinating efforts with related departments.

OFFICE
- At the San Francisco Airport Hilton:
  - Providing substitute and relief staffing as needed:
    Booking up to 20 customers daily as Reservations Agent.
    Answering up to eight lines as PBX operator.
  - Printed, verified, and highlighted reports on customer arrival, departure, VIP's, groups, and investors using NSI computer system on IBM PCs.
- Type 35 wpm.

EMPLOYMENT HISTORY

1994-present	Front Desk Clerk	SAN FRANCISCO AIRPORT HILTON, South SF
1991-94	Jewelry Manager & Sales Associate	WHOLE EARTH ACCESS, San Francisco
1989-90	Retail Sales Associate	HEADLINES, San Francisco
1989-90	Office Clerk	MCCUTCHINS & ASSOCIATES, San Francisco

EDUCATION

Currently attending Skyline Community College, San Bruno
Will be attending San Francisco State University, Fall 1993

- Resume writer: Jenny Mish -

Al Murfield
330 S. Becker, #222, Santa Monica, CA 95959
434-3434

OBJECTIVE

A position as Front Office Manager for a luxury resort.

HIGHLIGHTS

- Three years luxury hotel front office experience; over eight years in customer service.
- Highly knowledgeable of interdepartmental luxury hotel operations.
- Talented trainer and supervisor capable of building strong working teams.
- Skilled at interpreting Hotel Information System reports.

RELEVANT EXPERIENCE

1991 & 1993 GLACIER PARK INC., Glacier National Park, Montana

Night Auditor & Front Office Manager, East Glacier Park Lodge, 1993 Summer Season

Performed all daily accounting, and filled in for front office manager's unexpected long-term absence at 155-room resort hotel, including front office, gift shop, dining room, lounge, snack bar, golf shop, and gas station.

- Reconciled daily receipts and posted data to spreadsheets, tracing discrepancies and ensuring accuracy in every detail.
- Trained and supervised front office crew of 14 in customer service and front office procedures, receiving frequent praise for skill in managing people.

Front Office Manager, Many Glacier Hotel & Swiftcurrent Lodge, 1991 Summer Season

Managed seasonal opening of two resort lodges, totaling 296 rooms. Oversaw all front office functions and substituted for general managers on days off and when needed.

- Supervised 24 employees (front office, night auditors, security staff), creating weekly schedules, providing performance feedback, and building strong cooperative teams.
  - Trained employees in all front office operations, including cash handling, customer service, switchboard, record keeping, park policies and regulations.
  - Provided leadership for young workers who moved into management.
- Coordinated interdepartmental practices to ensure quality customer service.
- Ensured compliance with detailed National Park Service regulations and inspections.

1991-1993 LOEWS SANTA MONICA BEACH HOTEL, Santa Monica, California

Front Office & Reservations Supervisor, October 1991-May 1993

Supervised staff in front office and reservations functions for 354-room luxury hotel.

- Trained and supervised employees in customer service, cashiering, reconciling receipts, marketing, phone procedures, and computer data entry.
- Improved customer service and streamlined reservations procedures.
- Routinely used HIS and deciphered complex computer reports.
  - Researched archival tapes to verify commissions and determine negotiated rates.
  - Created and updated computer files, set up special billings; posted commissions for travel agents, groups, conventions, and various corporate accounts.
- Served as safety coordinator, ensuring compliance, staff training, and hazard reduction.

Previously: **Hotel Front Office Clerk,** *South Lake Tahoe, California,* Summer Season
Food Service Management, *Tempe, Arizona,* 2-1/2 years
Retail Sales, *Mesa and Phoenix, Arizona,* 2-1/2 years

- Resume writer: Jenny Mish -

Hotel, Restaurant, & Food Service

Paul J. Littleson

995 Marlboro Street, Suite 915
San Felipe, CA 94000
(306) 479-5614
(leave message with Marjorie Peabody)

Objective: A position as a housekeeping supervisor

Highlights of Qualifications

- Over 18 years of professional housekeeping service.
- Motivated, independent, self-starter.
- Well organized, efficient and highly productive.
- Special talent for working with all types of people.

Experience and Specialized Skills

Special Projects Supervisor
- Coordinated the refurbishing of rooms in a five-star hotel.
- Supervised maintenance of various flooring surfaces, each requiring special attention.
- Planned, designed, and installed a full service hotel laundry at the Hi-Star Hotel.

Troubleshooter
- Successfully solved special maintenance problems in a five-star hotel.
- Initiated an in-house carpet cleaning program adapted for various types of special carpet. This program eliminated the need for the costly services of an outside contractor.
- Supervised the replacement and repair of damaged surfaces, furniture, etc.

Assisted Executive Housekeeper
- Supervised a housekeeping staff of 40 in an upscale hotel.
- Maintained a high level of quality control by paying special attention to detail.
- Designed and implemented a plan that greatly improved the productivity of a large housekeeping staff.

Education and Specialized Training

Madera Peninsula College	Courses studied: hotel department management in conjunction with Triple Treat Inn training program	1980-1981

Employment History

Lead Shelter Volunteer	Secular Community Services	San Felipe, CA	1994
Housekeeping Supervisor, Special Projects	Hi-Star Hotel	Castro, CA	1991-1992
Acrylic Cleaner	Madera Atrium	Madera, CA	1989-1991
Room Inspector	Sanford Hotel	San Felipe, CA	1987-1988
Lead Housekeeping Supervisor	Red Linx Inn	Omega, NE	1985-1987
Housekeeping Advisor	Brighton Hightop Inn	Princeton, AZ	1983-1985
Housekeeping Supervisor	Triple Treat Inn	Houston, TX	1981-1983

- Resume written by Roving Resume Writers -

5

OFFICE

Jane Howland

98765 Geary Blvd.
San Francisco, CA 94121
(415) 123-4567 (message telephone)

Objective: A Clerical Office Position

Highlights of Qualification

- Over two years office experience.
- Strongly self-motivated, punctual, and follow directions accurately.
- Responsible, reliable, and friendly.
- Professional appearance and manner.

Relevant Skills and Experience

- Paid close attention to accuracy, especially with numbers, in clerical tasks such as sorting, filing, and looking up information at Wells Fargo Bank and Cal Trans.

- Updated state transportation department records, making sure that each entry was clear and complete.

- Used PC to update records at Wells Fargo, using word processing and accounting programs.

- Copied and filed documents so that daily work done at Wells Fargo and Cal Trans was correctly documented and all files were complete.

- As a clerk in the dead-letter department of the U.S. Postal Service:
    - Searched for senders using files and computer records.
    - Coded and filed mail for successful final delivery.
    - Filled out necessary forms to track addresses and postage.
    - Worked with minimum supervision, and maintained confidentiality at every step.

- As security guard of a bank, received and directed customers, paying attention to details, and providing assistance when needed.

- Worked as team player, cooperating well with other employees in every job.

Work History

Full-time Parent - Managed household finances, 1989-94 & 1984-86
Security Guard - American Protective Services, San Francisco, CA, 1989
Mail Clerk - U.S. Postal Service, San Francisco, CA, 1988
Office Assistant - Wells Fargo Bank, San Francisco, CA, 1987
Office Assistant - Cal Trans, San Francisco, CA, 1983

Business Training

School of Business and Commerce, San Francisco, CA, 1989
Academy of Stenography, San Francisco, CA, 1986-1987

- Resume written by Roving Resume Writers -

Carl F. Rosarita
201 Seventh Street
San Francisco, CA 94103
(415) 898-8989

OBJECTIVE: A general office work position:
• Clerical   • Typing   • Bookkeeping

SUMMARY

- Over 12 years experience working in a variety of office settings.
- Accurately type 70 WPM.
- Quick learner who can easily adapt to new responsibilities.
- Cooperative and dependable; get the job done efficiently.

OFFICE SUPPORT SKILLS

General Office

- Developed skill and competence in many clerical procedures, including:

-Typing	-Answering phones	-Payroll Accounting
-Filing	-Distributing mail	-Shipping and Receiving
-Issuing Receipts	-Inventory Controls	-Keeping Records

Bookkeeping

- As Billing-Rate Clerk, balanced over 100 accounts and sent statements at the end of month.
    - Assisted credit manager in account collection by phone and mail, decreasing unpaid by 20%.

- Maintained bondable status continuously through to the present.
    - Reliably handled and tallied large sums of cash for Highway Express and Omega Line.

Communications and Interpersonal

- Established and maintained good rapport with co-workers and clients in every position.

    - Courteously provided information and customer assistance at Cruise Ship Services and at Pat O'Brien's.
    - Served as liaison to improve communication between various departments at Cruise Ship Services, Pat O'Briens, Highway Express, and Omega Line.
    - Answered and directed telephone calls as a temporary office worker.

WORK EXPERIENCE

Typist	The Reporter, San Francisco, CA	1994
Temporary Office Worker	Kelly Services, New Orleans, LA	1993
Driver	Cruise Ship Services, New Orleans, LA	1991-1992
Doorman	Pat O'Briens, New Orleans, LA	1985-1990
Billing-Rate Clerk	Highway Express, New Orleans, LA	1981-1985
Payroll Operator	Omega Line Steamship, New Orleans, LA	1977-1981

EDUCATION

Soule Business School, New Orleans, LA
Completed courses in **Accounting & Typing**. Courses planned in computers & word processing.

- Resume written by Roving Resume Writers -

Paula R. Fiske

4002 Monte Vista Avenue • Oakland, CA 94606 • (510) 535-5353

JOB OBJECTIVE

Administrative support position with project management responsibilities

QUALIFICATIONS

- 10 years providing administrative assistance and project management.
- Experienced in WordPerfect 5.1, Lotus 1-2-3, MultiMate Advantage II.
- Skilled at 10-key by touch and Dictaphone transcription.
- Ability to learn new duties quickly and without supervision.

PROFESSIONAL EXPERIENCE

1993-1994 **Contractual Secretarial Positions**
Clients included:
PACIFIC BELL (6 months)
TAX CONSULTANTS INC. (3 months)
UNITED WAY

- Word processed correspondence from handwritten notes and Dictaphone.
- Performed data entry for shipping orders and invoicing.
- Proofread documents, technical specifications, and financial reports.
- Maintained calendars, scheduled meetings, and made travel arrangements.
- Answered phones, screening calls as needed.

1990-1993 **Secretary**
 BASKIN-ROBBINS ICE CREAM, Oakland, CA

- Independently managed projects:
    - Monthly manufacturing reports
    - Product formula distribution
    - Ingredient and flavor tracking system
- Established and maintained highly confidential company files.
- Performed administrative assistance for the Operations Department.
- Acted as information source to outside contractors, realtors, and company
  employees at all levels regarding status of ongoing facility projects.

1987-1989 **Receptionist**
 CHILDREN'S HOSPITAL, Berkeley, CA

- Performed reception and typing duties for the Personnel Department.

1984-1986 **Clerk-Typist**
MERRITT ENGINEERS, Oakland, CA

- Managed all business card orders for company personnel.
- Typed documents and correspondence.
- Reconciled purchase orders and invoices.

EDUCATION

Computer Courses: Diablo Valley College, Vista College, College of Alameda

- Resume writer: Susan Ireland -

LINDA GIANNI
343 Alegria Avenue #404
Oakland, CA 94644
(510) 343-3434

OBJECTIVE

Office support staff to an accountant or controller.

HIGHLIGHTS

- Recent graduate of Heald Business College Accounting Program.
- Prior experience as accountant's assistant.
- Proficient at Lotus 1-2-3 and dBase III Plus.
- Efficient, detail-oriented, and skilled at time management.

RELEVANT SKILLS & EXPERIENCE

COMPUTER AND TEN-KEY SKILLS

- Developed skills and knowledge through extensive hands-on computer instruction at Heald Business College:
  -120 hours **Lotus 1-2-3** ; 120 hours **dBase III Plus**; 120 hours Bedford Accounting software.
- Increased **ten-key speed** to **150 strokes per minute** and typing speed to 50 words per minute as student at Heald Business College.

BOOKKEEPING SKILLS

- As Assistant to Controller for Bellarosa Coffee Company:
  -Updated and **maintained clear A/P and A/R account records using Accpac** Accounting and Wizard Mail Order software.
  -Regularly **audited product inventory** calculations.
  -Double-checked all monthly store inventory statements for accuracy.

OFFICE MANAGEMENT

- Represented Computer Resources for Computer Learning to dozens of customers daily, providing a professional first impression.
- **Answered and directed query calls on 15 incoming lines** in an efficient and friendly manner at Resources for Computer Learning.
- Researched, compiled, and distributed daily current availability listings for three offices of LBL Locations, an apartment rental service.
- **Ordered, stocked, and distributed office supplies** for Resources for Computer Learning and LBL Locations.

WORK HISTORY

1992-1993	**Assistant to Accountant** **Counter Sales**	BELLAROSA COFFEE COMPANY, San Francisco, CA
1990-1991	**Administrative Assistant** **Receptionist**	RESOURCES FOR COMPUTER LEARNING, San Francisco, CA
1985-1989	**Homemaker and Student**	
1983-1984	**General Office Manager**	LBL LOCATIONS, San Francisco, CA

EDUCATION

Accounting Certificate Program Diploma, April 1994
GPA 4.0, Heald Business College, Oakland, CA
Courses included: Accounting Principles   Spreadsheets
     Computerized Accounting   Business Math
City College of San Francisco, San Francisco, CA

- Resume writer: Jenny Mish -

CRYSTAL MITCHUM

1922 Fourth Street
Concord, California 94722
(510) 656-5454

OBJECTIVE

An accounting or office manager position in a medical setting

HIGHLIGHTS

- 7 years in medical hospital accounting; 5 years in medical management.
- 13 years at Kaiser; thoroughly familiar with hospital accounting procedures.
- Knowledgeable about insurance contracts and regulations.
- Reduced over 90-day accounts receivable down to an 8% average.

PROFESSIONAL EXPERIENCE

1992-present F. RALPH KNUDSON, M.D. (Internal Medicine and Gastroenterology), Concord
Office Manager

- Managed all accounts receivable, accounts payable, and medical billing problems.
- Delegated computer, billing, and diagnostic procedures to office staff.
- Reconciled bank accounts for the doctor's two small companies.
- Produced and analyzed monthly financial statements to confirm a balanced accounts receivable system.
- Maintained an 8% monthly average for over 90-day accounts receivable.

1978-1992 KAISER HOSPITAL, Walnut Creek
Office Manager (1989-1992)

- Managed the Endocrine Department, a private, three-physician office.
- Hired, trained, and supervised staff of five.
- Generated an accurate accounts receivable and accounts payable system.
- Served as liaison to hospital personnel regarding overhead statements and payroll.
- Reviewed insurance contracts, recommending profitable ones to the group.

Staff Accountant (1987-1989)

- Consistently received excellent reviews throughout a major regional merger.
- Prepared monthly physician settlements, calculating billing costs, Medicare and Medi-Cal payments.
- Analyzed information from several departments including Budget and Outpatient.
- Prepared payroll entries for over 1000 employees.
- Worked with both hospitals' general ledgers throughout the merger.

Accounting Clerk (1984-1987)

- Maintained records on all restricted funds, home health insurance, pension plans, tax shelters, and other payroll deductions.
- Reconciled cash receipts and rental income.
- Prepared journal entries for several income and expense accounts.

(Continued)

KAISER HOSPITAL (Continued)

Bookkeeper (1982-1984)
- Served as floating bookkeeper in the Accounting Department.
- Assisted in preparation of bi-weekly payroll.

Medi-Cal Authorization Control Coordinator (1978-1982)
- Served as liaison among Medi-Cal personnel, hospital staff, and physicians.

1973-1978   EAST MOUNTAIN HOSPITAL, Klaggett, OR
(a small community hospital)
Utilization Review Coordinator

1970-1971   ST. JOSEPH'S HOSPITAL, Portland, OR
Laboratory Aide

EDUCATION

Accounting, Diablo Valley Community College

Continuing education in:
        Medical office management
        Insurance reimbursement
        Collections
        Medicare

COMPUTER SKILLS

LOTUS 123
Quattro, Mega West (medical A/R system)
Quicken
WordPerfect

PROFESSIONAL AFFILIATION

The Contra Costa Medical Office Managers' Group
Treasurer (1993-94), Member (1990-present)

- Resume writer: Susan Ireland -

Diane Plesantte
201 Eighth Street
San Francisco, CA 94103
(415) 123-4567 (message)

Objective: A reception or medical assistant position.

Highlights of Qualification

- Experienced medical assistant and receptionist.
- Certificate in medical assisting from BOCES vocational school.
- Sensitive, caring and professional attitude toward staff, patients, and their families.
- Friendly and outgoing, with a pleasant manner and phone voice.

Relevant Skills and Experience

Technical Expertise
- Developed medical skills and efficiency on the job and at BOCES:
    - -taking patients' temperature
    - -recording pulse & respiration level
    - -monitoring blood sugar
    - -assisting to distribute medications
    - -setting up intravenous poles
    - -urinalysis testing
- Prepared patients for X-rays and physical examinations.

Administration
- Recorded daily vital signs in patients' medical records.
- Operated busy switchboard and fielded calls of all sorts.
- Routinely used office equipment including:
    - -PC-DOS programs including WordPerfect
    - -ten-key calculator by touch
    - -typing 68 WPM accurately
- Processed receivables and serviced accounts for marketing firm.

Patient & Family Services
- Communicated with families about patients' daily condition.
- Assisted elderly clients in a wide variety of tasks in home settings.
- Advocated for patients' rights and needs; referred clients to local agencies.
- Assisted clients in scheduling medical appointments.

Work History
Marketing Assistant	Carousel Marketing, San Francisco, CA - 1994
Receptionist	YWCA, Portland, OR - 1990-93
Health Assistant	Fireside Homes-Tara Corp., Portland, OR - 1990-92
Nurses Aid	River Mead Manor, Portland, OR - 1989

Education and Training
Certificate training for Alzheimer's Disease, MLK High School, Portland, OR
Nurses' Aide and Health Assistant Certificate, BOCES Vocational School, NY
Graduate, John F. Kennedy High School, NY

- Resume written by Roving Resume Writers -

Harriet would like to move toward retirement by taking a job with less responsibility than the one she currently holds. She chose a functional format so that she could highlight her second-to-last job as an Administrative Assistant. —S.I.

Harriet Smith

(415) 584-8733

P.O. Box 8831
San Francisco, CA 94159-2103

JOB OBJECTIVE: Administrative Assistant

HIGHLIGHTS OF QUALIFICATIONS

- 8 years experience in office management as an Administrative Assistant.
- Strong organizational skills; able to supervise support staff effectively.
- Excellent verbal and written communicator; adept at drafting correspondence.
- Collaborate easily with co-workers and work well independently.

PROFESSIONAL ACCOMPLISHMENTS

ADMINISTRATIVE SUPPORT

As Administrative Assistant for Total Success Community Developers:

- Managed communications with financial institutions investing in Total Success' multi-million-dollar projects.
  - Conducted nation-wide research to determine which financiers should be approached.
  - Initiated contact with CEO's of potential investors.
  - Worked closely with President and Board Chairman to create formal investment proposals.
  - Coordinated meetings and legal procedures to fulfill contractual requirements.
- Handled extensive travel reservations including air and ground transportation and hotels.

As Manager of Patient Accounts for Arthur Brown, M.D.:

- Drafted correspondence and transcribed reports/narratives for this four-doctor surgical office.
- Acted as liaison between doctors, patients, and hospitals to coordinate appointments.

OFFICE MANAGEMENT/SUPERVISION

As Administrative Assistant for Total Success Community Developers:

- Oversaw complete remodeling of seven executive offices and the reception area; worked closely with interior decorator to create a professional, prestigious environment.
- Supervised a support staff of four, responsible for bookkeeping, typing, phones, filing, supply inventory, and general office procedures.
- Planned regular interdepartmental meetings to synchronize company efforts and trouble-shoot organizational problems.

As Manager of Patient Accounts for Arthur Brown, M.D.:

- Supervised a support staff of two who compiled in-depth insurance records, processed mail, maintained patient records, answered phones, etc.
- Managed AR and insurance billings; determined individual credit and collections policies.

SKILLS

- Word Processing, 80 wpm: Word Perfect, Pfs Write, and Wordstar. • Dictaphone

WORK HISTORY

1986-present	**Manager, Patient Accounts**	Arthur Brown, MD, F.A.C.S., San Francisco
1982-1985	**Administrative Assistant**	Total Success Community Developers, Stockton
1979-1982	**Clinical Secretary**	Pacific Hospital, San Francisco
1977-1979	**Billing Secretary**	Harrison Medical Center, Redding

EDUCATION

Business, Laney College, Hayward

- Resume writer: Susan Ireland -

Elaine M. Daniel

2233 Walrafen Court, #43
Atlanta GA 50606

703-434-4343

JOB OBJECTIVE: Administrative Assistant.

HIGHLIGHTS

- Nineteen years administrative experience solving office problems.
- Consistently received exemplary performance evaluations.
- Skilled liaison in building teamwork and implementing management strategies.

PROFESSIONAL ACCOMPLISHMENTS

1990-94   *Office Manager*
UNITED CLEANING SUPPLY CO., Atlanta, GA
Managed office operations and assisted Vice President of United's regional distribution center.

- Dramatically increased efficiency and reduced errors by cross-training office staff so that each order was handled by one person instead of four.
- Increased professionalism and developed cohesive esprit de corps within office environment by respecting staff and expecting employees to meet goals.
- Oversaw processing and delivery of all supply orders taken at five branches throughout Georgia.
    - Trained fifteen staff members to ensure consistency and coordination throughout system.
    - Created and implemented computer coding which improved customer service by prioritizing orders based on delivery schedules.
- Maintained operations with no loss of continuity after computer was seriously damaged by a lightning strike.
    - Found clever ways to send and receive orders using fax machines, telephones, and branch computers.
    - Made hardware repairs with telephone coaching from manufacturers.
    - Installed new computer system and did troubleshooting to work out the bugs.
- Earned unusual confidence and trust of VP, who described me as the most professional person he had ever met.

1988-90   *Administrative Assistant*
CASPER SYSTEMS, INC., Atlanta, GA
Provided logistical and office support for Director of Marketing of the country's first library software firm.

- Tracked proposals and contracts for over a hundred library computer systems.
- Prepared and delivered documentation packages to accompany software, including up to 50 pounds of manuals for installation and use.
- Made logistical arrangements to deliver equipment and documentation to trade shows in the U.S. and Canada.
    - Complied with detailed Canadian regulations restricting electronics imports.

- Continued -

Elaine M. Daniel
Page Two

1985-88   *Administrative Assistant*
WESTERN AUTO SUPPLY, INC., Sacramento, CA
Served as personal assistant to Vice President, and liaison between VP and 20
salespeople for an automotive parts manufacturer and distributor.

- Served as eyes and ears of Vice President in gathering key information from
  sales force, passing on pertinent details to be used in decisionmaking.
- Maintained frequent contact with sales reps to troubleshoot problems and pass on
  price lists, promotional materials, and logistical information about trade shows.
- Created and implemented strategies to solve problems, such as computer
  systems which:
    - Created monthly financial and sales reports, and computed sales commissions.
    - Distributed catalogs and tracked activities of customer base of 4600.

1975-85   *Office Manager*
BRIGHT SHADES, INC., Sacramento & Oakland, CA
Started two California branch offices for Portland-based window covering company.

- Created office systems for new Oakland branch, gradually increasing office
  support services from one to nine customer service representatives.
- Revived flailing Sacramento branch office, retaining accounts by hiring and
  training new customer service staff and establishing effective office operations.
- Streamlined computerization by training office staff in computer system use.
- Retrained nine customer service representatives to support new product line
  after merger with Houston Davis venetian blinds.

> Elaine is a classic "pink-collar" worker: highly skilled
> in office work, but with no formal education and little
> leverage to get the compensation she deserves. She's a
> modest person, so she needed a resume showing the
> depth of her very substantial accomplishments. —J.M.

- Resume writer: Jenny Mish -

DOREEN S. MULDOON

1224 Seymour Avenue
Berkeley, CA 94444
(510) 434-4343

OBJECTIVE

Executive Assistant in a progressive Bay Area company.

SUMMARY OF QUALIFICATIONS

- Eleven years experience as an Executive Assistant.
- Exceptionally well-organized and detail-oriented.
- Unusual ability to elicit confidence and build rapport.

RELEVANT ACCOMPLISHMENTS

As Executive Assistant at Coltrane, Stiverson, et. al.:

- Managed all personal and business affairs for a federal judge who had chosen to return to private practice, including estate administration upon his death:
  - Effectively maintained the trial practice of a law firm partner, including case preparation and legal research.
  - Monitored investment portfolio and managed accounts for all personal expenses, including two homes and three children in college.
  - Served as liaison between financial institutions and family members, estate and tax attorneys, ensuring correct distribution of funds and resolution of accounts.
  - Arranged for continued medical care throughout 14-month illness.

As Executive Assistant to the chair of the board of Lindley Supply, a premier East Coast linen and textile supply company:

- Represented principal owner in numerous brainstorming sessions with top management consultants to develop and implement specific programs to increase efficiency and productivity throughout the company.
- Researched and determined feasibility of potential marketing and cost-cutting ideas such as linen versus paper towels, and conversion of vehicles from diesel to gasoline.

As Executive Assistant to the Trustee of Robert Johnson Industries:

- Implemented decentralization to three satellite locations, a key move in the transformation of a near-bankrupt entity into a thriving business over two years:
  - Supervised the successful long-term relocation of management personnel and their families, effectively balancing company priorities with their personal needs.
  - Oversaw the transportation, purchase, and sale of office equipment and the hiring of local support staff.

WORK HISTORY

1990-94	**Legal Secretary**	Rona, Fillert, et. al., San Francisco, CA
1984-90	**Executive Assistant**	Coltrane, Stiverson, et. al., Cincinnati, OH
1981-83	**Executive Assistant**	Garber & McWilliams, Baltimore, MD
1979-81	**Executive Assistant**	Lindley Supply Corporation, Baltimore, MD
1973-79	**Executive Assistant**	Robert Johnson Industries, Baltimore, MD

EDUCATION

Current coursework in Business Administration, Laney College, Oakland, CA
Paralegal Certification, Maryland State University, Baltimore, MD

- Resume writer: Jenny Mish -

CORRINE R. ROBERTS
2000 S. Washington, #4
Berkeley, CA 94777
(510) 848-8484

Corrine is sick of the law office environment and would really like to move into sales, but she's a single parent and can't risk a cut in pay. She's hoping to find office work in a creative environment. —J.M.

OBJECTIVE

Office Manager or Administrative Assistant for a creative East Bay company.

HIGHLIGHTS

- Twelve years experience in office management and administrative support.
- Talented in problem solving and office system design.
- Skilled liaison between workers, clients, and other groups.
- Would make an outstanding sidekick for a creative individual.

RELEVANT EXPERIENCE

1992-present   *OFFICE MANAGER*
Law Offices of Sue Wilson, Berkeley CA
Ensured smooth administration of a high-pressure 11-person law office:
- Produced accurate financial reports and projection for owner.
- Streamlined numerous procedures to increase office efficiency and effectiveness:
  - Created Lotus spreadsheets to track complex insurance-related billings, and trust account records.
  - Significantly increased cash flow by adjusting billing cycle.
  - Reorganized bookkeeping and filing systems for increased clarity and ease of use.
- Conducted employee safety orientation and wrote employee safety manual to comply with SB 198 and OSHA guidelines.
- Coordinated maintenance of historic building which houses the Law Offices and four tenants.
- Researched and purchased computers, lighting, and other office equipment and approved the purchase of office supplies.

1987-91   *PRODUCTION COORDINATOR AND OFFICE MANAGER*
Chris Malouf Associates, Inc., Berkeley CA
Coordinated production and managed busy office of a six-person print consulting firm whose principal traveled extensively:
- Coordinated efforts of designers, materials suppliers, die cutters, and printers to smoothly produce credit cards, books, and promotional brochures on schedule.
  - Estimated production costs and solicited bids from vendors.
  - Served as liaison between corporate clients and vendors to coordinate schedules and production.
  - Reviewed work for accuracy and quality, and ensured compliance with corporate standards.
- Maintained high-pressure long-distance communication about many precise details by phone, fax, and Federal Express.
- Reviewed billing to account for all costs and billable hours.
- Supervised four-office support staff.

1986-87   *OFFICE MANAGER*
Biltmore Plaza Financial, San Francisco CA
Assisted President in establishing and operating a financial planning and real estate development office:
- Served as liaison between owners, investors, property managers, securities agencies, tenants, accountants, and lawyers through extensive phone contact daily.

1982-86   *ADMINISTRATIVE ASSISTANT*
Professional Accounting Financial Services, Oakland CA
Established all office systems and provided office support for a financial planning sales staff of seven.

EDUCATION

B.A., Theatre Arts and Dance, University of California, Santa Barbara

- Resume writer: Jenny Mish -

Randall St. James

8997 14 Street, Apt. #30, Oakland, CA 87099 **(510) 221-9315**

JOB OBJECTIVE: Word Processor for a law organization

SUMMARY OF QUALIFICATIONS

- Eight years as a fast, accurate word processor at one law firm.
- Familiar with legal terminology and litigation documents.
- Proficient in WordPerfect 5.1.
- Exceptional ability in grammar and spelling.
- Excellent attendance record.

PROFESSIONAL EXPERIENCE

1992-present *Legal Secretary*
PEARSON & MC DUFFIE, Oakland

- Typed coverage opinions quickly and accurately.
- Filed civil litigation papers in state and federal courts.
- Calendared documents.
- Performed proofreading.

1984-1992 *Word Processor*
FALMOUTH, HARRISON & MOORE, Oakland

- Transcribed tapes, deciphered handwritten notes, and word processed a large volume of detailed documents for this law firm.
    Material included:

Pleadings	Summaries of medical records
Correspondence	Witness statements
Summaries of depositions	Release agreements
Indexes of depositions	

- Recognized for accuracy, reliability, and speed.
- Performed light editing, relying on proficiency in spelling and grammar.

1983 *Secretary (part time)*
CONSORTIUM FOR INTERNATIONAL IRRIGATION LAW, Berkeley

- Typed correspondence and lengthy scientific proceedings of international conferences.
- Corrected grammar written by foreign-speaking scientists, while typing finished documents.

1983 *Secretary (part time)*
DENTAFORM, INC., San Francisco

- Typed correspondence and performed general clerical work for this firm which offered data processing services to dental insurance plans.
- Provided secretarial support for an office of 10 professionals.

EDUCATION

Business Administration, Vista College, Berkeley

- Resume writer: Susan Ireland -

6

TRADES

MATTHEW A. PARKER, PLUMBER
3056 Hillegass Ave. • Berkeley CA 94705
(510) 540-7750

Since Matt got all his experience on the job and is not a union plumber, he wanted enough detail so an employer could recognize his competence. *Compare this with Matt's music resume on page 165. These two resumes clearly show that you need different resumes for significantly different job goals.* —Y.P.

SUMMARY
- Over seven years quality experience in commercial, residential, remodeling, and solar installation and service.
- Very familiar with blueprints, layout, and local codes.
- Skilled in painting and carpentry.
- Cooperate well with co-workers and other trades.

EXPERIENCE

1986 - present	Plumber	THE SOLAR STATION, Oakland

Provided rough & finish plumbing, as subcontractor for scores of Bay Area contractors. For example:

- Nine-unit San Francisco townhouse project for ShelterBelt of Berkeley:
  ...supervised and coordinated two-month job ...dealt with inspectors ...tracked materials ...ran pipe ...drain waste and vent ...water ...gas ...rough ...finish ...water service ...catch basins ...street traps and vents ...sewer tie-ins ...rain leaders ...testing.

- Two new American Savings Banks for T.L. Jenkins Co. of Concord:
  ...all rough and finish plumbing ...handicap bathrooms ...roof drains ...floor drains ...urinals ...wall-hung toilets ...condensate drains ...floor sinks ...trap primers.

- City Blue Productions for Dome Construction of San Francisco:
  ...all ground work ...rough and finish ...handicap bathrooms ...urinals ...silver recovery PVC line ...roof drains ...floor sinks ...floor drains.

- Ten-unit apartments with one commercial space for Fitzmaurice Construction of Oakland:
  ...commercial, rough, and finish plumbing ...two 100-gal water heaters ...solar lines for future use ...recirculating pump ...water service ...sewer tie-in.

- Oakmont Memorial Mortuary for T.L. Jenkins Co. of Concord:
  ...remodeling rough and finish ...3" gas line in ground.

Provided new and replacement solar installations for local contractor:

- Installed new solar systems, both passive and active, and provided service.
  ...ran pipe ...installed hot water storage tanks (pumps) ...insulated and jacketed pipe ...built racks ...put down sleepers ...mounted panels and tanks ...ran sensor wires ...etc.

- Did a series of "tear-offs and put-backs" of large solar water heating systems throughout the Bay Area, plus small residential tear-offs/put-backs associated with roofing jobs.

1985-86	Plumber	MARSHALL FRAZIER PLUMBING, Oakland

- Installed all rough, finish, and service plumbing for a new 16-unit townhouse project, and for seven large single-family residences.

- Installed kitchen and bathroom plumbing for 20 units in a large commercial construction project, Vulcan Studios in Oakland.

- Did service work for two large hotels in downtown Oakland.

1983-85	Fry Cook	ROYAL CAFE; SMOKEY JOE'S; GIANT HAMBURGERS
1979-80	House Painter	SELF-EMPLOYED, Oneonta NY

1979	Plumber's Helper	ZIMMERMAN PLUMBING & HEATING, Oneonta NY

- Helped install new furnaces, duct work, and rough plumbing, and cleaned sewers.

- Resume written by Matt Parker & Yana Parker -

James Harding
P.O. Box 164
Medford, Oregon 97777
(503) 899-8999

Objective

Apprentice Plumber

Qualification Highlights

- Three years experience as a general helper in the plumbing industry.
- Dependable employee with common sense and a variety of skills.
- Current Class A TX CDL license.

Summary of Experience

- Installed and maintained underground utilities, making sure the connections were sound.
- Repaired and replaced ABS surface drain pipe, copper pipe and PVC pipe.
- Laid steel-coated pipe and polypropylene pipe for new construction.
- Accurately read blueprints and schematics to install according to plan.
- Developed skills in safely using a variety of power and pneumatic tools.
- Worked well with supervisors, coworkers, and customers.

Equipment Operated

- Pipe machine
- Hand tools, pipe wrench, chain touge, vises, soldering torches, irons
- Air hammer, air drill, hole haws
- Electric hammers, drill, band saws
- Ground prep tools: shovels, picks, sod spades, air spades
- Heavy trucks, Class 8

Work History

1991-1994	Haynes & Peters Plumbing, Laborer, Portland, Oregon
1985-1991	Long-haul Truck Driver, various lines, 48 states

Education

General Studies	Portland State College, Portland, Oregon

- Resume written by Dislocated Workers Project -

Roger Edmund
23 NE Sandpiper, Apt. D
Salem, Oregon 97060
(503) 434-4343

Objective

Marine Pipe Fitter

Highlights of Qualifications

- Progressive experience of over 10 years Marine Pipe Fitting.
- Excellent supervisory experience with up to 16 workers.
- Quality maintenance and operation of pipe bender.
- Highly adaptable at learning and understanding new procedures and techniques.

Experience and Accomplishments

- Performed certified brazing on Navy and commercial ship piping systems.
- Developed extensive knowledge and skill in pipe bending.
- Trained personnel on pipe bending procedures.
- Supervised in shop and on ships in the removal, fabrication, and installation of piping systems.
- Read blueprints and laid out work for shipboard piping systems.
- Maintained vested Pipe Fitter status 10 years with United Association of Plumbers and Pipe Fitters, Local 290.

Work Experience

1990 - 1994	Northwest Ship Repair Yards, Portland, OR	Pipe Fitter
1989 - 1990	Oregon West Incorporated, Portland, OR	Pipe Fitter
1985 - 1988	Oregon Marine, Portland, OR	Pipe Fitter/Supervisor
1981 - 1985	Bellingham Ship Repair, Portland, OR	Pipe Fitter

Education

Journey Certificate, Metal Trades Pipe Fitter, Oregon Bureau of Labor and Industries

Pipe Fitter apprenticeship (3 years), United Association of Plumbers and Pipe Fitters, Local 290, Oregon State Apprenticeship Programs, and Portland Community College

- Resume written by Dislocated Workers Project -

Richard Edelson

8080 SW 23rd Street
Portland, Oregon 97225
(503) 644-4646

Objective

- Pipe Fitter / Welder

An "Additional Accomplishments" section gives Richard a chance to show off his unique experience in the Navy.—Ed.

Professional Qualifications

- Over 20 years in the steel fabrication and repair industry.
- Experienced in layout and fabrication of metal structures.
- Work well under pressure to meet deadlines.
- Produced X-ray and UT quality welds.
- Analyzed blue prints and specifications of jobs.

Experience

- Regularly used oxygen-acetylene cutting and welding equipment, practices and techniques.
- Performed metal arc, MIG (GMAW), TIG and gas welding.
- Operated carbon-arc and plasma-arc equipment for gouging and cutting of materials.
- Skillfully used a variety of hand and power tools to accomplish tasks.
- Planned work and supervised a crew doing layout, fabrication and welding activities.
- Consulted with supervisors to resolve difficult installation and repair problems.

Additional Accomplishments

- Worked as a team member and supervised a crew that installed a vertical launch missile system on a US Navy ship.
- Directed a crew of workers, removing over 300 equipment foundations and installing all new foundations for the Combat Intelligence Command (CIC) on a US Navy ship.

Work History

1993 - present	Fitter / Welder	Pacific General, Portland, Oregon
1992 - present	Fitter / Welder	North State, Inc., Portland, Oregon
1985 - 1992	Leadman / Fitter / Welder	Cascade Marine, Portland, Oregon
1984 - 1985	Leadman / Maintenance / Fitter	P & Q Marine, Portland, Oregon
1978 - 1984	Leadman / Fitter / Welder	Zedlik Marine Repair, Portland, Oregon

Education

Associate Degree, Welding Technology	Portland Community College, Portland, Oregon
Engineering	Portland State University, Portland, Oregon
Electronic Technology	University of Portland, Portland, Oregon
NCO Candidate School	US Army; Honorable Discharge

- Resume written by Dislocated Workers Project -

Ken G. Donalds

2222 O'Farrell Street, #2
San Francisco, CA 95555
(415) 987-6543 (message)

Objective: A position as a Welder / Maintenance Mechanic
•Structural   •Plate   •Combination

Current American Welding Society Certifications:

•Shielded Metal Arc Welding, 1" test plate vertical and overhead.
•Flux Core Arc Welding (Innershield), 1" test plate vertical and overhead.
•No.11 Reinforcement Steel (Rebar), direct & indirect butt joint (stick) vertical.
•Vertical plug weld (stick).

Summary of Qualifications:

•Over 12 years experience.
•100% success rate in passing full-penetration UT inspection tests.
•Familiar with MIG and TIG welding.
•Knowledgeable in blueprint reading for welders.
•Excellent hand and eye coordination and a safe work record.
•Able to work with plates of any thickness.

Employment History:

1993-Present   **Precision Welding, San Francisco, CA.**
Journeyman: Performed layout, fabrication, and installation of rigid frames, base plates and connectors requiring full penetration welds. Skilled in oxy/acetylene cutting.

1991-1992   **City College of San Francisco, Full-time welding program student**

1981-1990   **Friedman Service Company, Brisbane, CA.**
Senior Service Technician: Welded thin gauge metals and handled materials using forklifts, bailers, trash compactors, pallet jacks, and tow motors. Performed preventative maintenance, lubricated and replaced parts on all supermarket equipment.

1976-1980   **Double "C" Shipyard, San Francisco, CA.**
Journeyman-Mechanic: Troubleshot and repaired all shipyard equipment including vehicles, bulldozers, backhoes, forklifts, hydraulic manlifts, pumps and compressors.

Education:

Combination Welding Certificate (4,116 total hours)
City College, John O'Connell Campus, San Francisco, CA

Quartermaster Heavy Equipment Repair Diploma
US Army Quartermaster School, Fort Lee, VA

References Available Upon Request

- Resume written by Roving Resume Writers -

PETER L. VOLPE
88 Propose Road
Shirley, NY 1167
(516) 987-6543

Job Objective: Position as Maintenance Mechanic

Professional Experience

Set Up, Maintenance and Repair

- Maintained and repaired machinery, assuming full responsibility that equipment was in good working order at all times.
- Machinery maintained: inserters, wrappers, printers, labelers, packers, heat sealing machines, bakery equipment, winding machines, commercial boilers, compressors, etc., including Scandia, Apex, Label Aire, Lehigh, Shanklin, and ITT equipment.
- Set up machinery for production.
- Developed extensive knowledge of hydraulics and pneumatics.

Design and Fabrication

- Designed and constructed catwalks and racks for machinery.
- Built, upgraded and repaired equipment; worked with engineers and read blueprints.

Welding

- Experience in MIG, TIG and Heli-Arc welding.
- Fit and welded high and low pressure steam lines, steel dikes, pipelines for oil, gas and kerosene tanks, etc.

Other Experience

- Good working knowledge of electrical, plumbing and heating trades.
- Experience as Lead Person in factory as well as overseeing jobs for subcontractors, including estimating and supervision of personnel.

Work History

1987-present	**Maintenance Mechanic** - Production and Packaging Electrosound Long Island, Hauppauge, NY
1987	**Maintenance Mechanic** - Bakery Machinery Entenmann's Bakery, Inc., Bay Shore, NY
1985-1988	**Welder, Fabricator** - Commercial Boiler Repair Surefire Welding Corporation, West Babylon, NY
1984-1985	**Welder** - Commercial Boiler Repair DP Boiler Repair and Welding, North Babylon, NY
1984	**Maintenance Mechanic** - Maintenance Department Steelflex Electro Corporation, Lindenhurst, NY
1978-1984	**Maintenance Mechanic** - Maintenance Department Fiberglass Resources Corporation, Farmingdale, NY

Education

Associate of Science Degree in Biotechnology
State University of New York at Farmingdale, NY, 1978

- Resume writer: Nancy Rosenberg -

KEITH BINKLER
555 NE Airport Blvd.
Portland OR 97218
(503) 281-7676

OBJECTIVE: Maintenance Mechanic

SUMMARY OF QUALIFICATIONS

- 11+ years experience in various aspects of machine maintenance and welding.
- Capable of designing and developing customized equipment using steel fabrication.
- Working knowledge of testing and tempering procedures for steel springs.
- Ability to pinpoint problems and initiate creative solutions.
- Demonstrated ability to adapt to new equipment and technology.
- Capable of supervising a five-member crew.

RELEVANT EXPERIENCE

- Troubleshot, repaired, and maintained all types of equipment, including:
  - drill and punch presses
  - hydraulic presses and rams
  - conveyor belts
  - high pressure water and sump pumps
  - blast and tempering furnaces
  - Dano drums used in composting system

  Heavy equipment:
  - forklift
  - Bobcat
  - front loaders
  - high lifts
  - pressure washers
- Working knowledge of mig, stick, tig, and gas welding on a variety of equipment.
- Used a variety of hand tools.
- Developed ability to read blueprints and complete layout.
- Fabricated patterns, jigs, coil springs, u-bolts, and all small parts for spring manufacturer.
- Maintained filtering system for hydraulic motor system.
- Supervised clean-up crew and logged completed maintenance.

WORK HISTORY

Pacific Compost Co., Portland, OR - **MAINTENANCE MECHANIC**	1993-1994
Bolt Spring Co., Portland, OR - **ASSEMBLY/MAINTENANCE MACHINIST**	1982-1993
Midas Muffler, Portland, OR - **INSTALLER/WELDER**	1979-1982
Quik Stop Automotive, Portland, OR - **INSTALLER/MECHANIC/WELDER**	1978-1979

EDUCATION

Mt. Hood Community College and Portland Community College
Communications/Intro to PCs, 1994

Portland Job Corps, Portland, OR
Welding/Machine Shop/High School Diploma

References available on request

- Resume written by Dislocated Workers Project -

Phil Beeson

3333 Fremont Ave.
Fremont, CA 33333
(510) 123-4567

A Master Craftsman, offering expertise in sheetmetal:
- Product design and development
- Production management

HIGHLIGHTS

- Lifelong interest in metal crafting, both professionally and as a hobby.
- Reputation among design professionals for creating products that meet specifications precisely.
- Ability to simplify manufacturing through design.
- Skilled problem solver.

PROFESSIONAL EXPERIENCE

PRODUCT DESIGN AND DEVELOPMENT
X-Y-Z and Strider Lighting
- Produced layout, prototypes, and tooling for a wide range of sheetmetal projects.
- Redesigned layouts to solve or prevent problems in design, manufacturing, and assembly.

PRODUCTION MANAGEMENT
X-Y-Z and Strider Lighting
- Established new production standards by fabricating or modifying equipment.
- Supervised 15 craftsmen involving scheduling, quality control, and problem solving.
- Produced accurate estimates based on time and materials.

TECHNICAL EXPERTISE
- Drafting: shop drawings and layouts by hand or on CAD system.
- Sheetmetal work: steel, stainless, aluminum, brass, bronze, copper.
- Machine work.
- Welding: TIG, MIG, arc, gas, silver solder, soft solder.
- Cabinetmaking: laminates, hardwoods.

WORK HISTORY

1989-present	**Journeyman Fixture Maker**	Strider Lighting, Pinole, CA
1985-89	**Production Manager, Research & Development**	X-Y-Z Corporation, Castro Valley, CA
1981-85	**Combat Engineer**	U.S. Marine Corps Reserve
1977-81	**Sheetmetalist, Machinist, Welder, Ironworker, Cabinetmaker**	X-Y-Z Corporation, Castro Valley, CA
1975-77	**Mechanic**	Fremont Motor Homes, Fremont, CA

EDUCATION

Design Engineering, Diablo Valley Community College, Richmond, CA
Coursework included: -CAD (Computer Aided Design) - Mechanical Drafting -Mathematics

- Resume writer: Susan Ireland -

HAROLD DANSON
9988 Rockridge Drive
Oakland CA 94609
(510) 987-6543

O B J E C T I V E

A position as MACHINIST.

H I G H L I G H T S

- Ten years experience as Machinist.
- Journeyman machinist, California licensed.
- Proven ability to independently handle specialized projects at remote worksites.
- Extremely broad experience with all kinds of machine tools and materials.
- Responsible, dependable, punctual; take pride in my work.

R E L E V A N T   S K I L L S   &   E X P E R I E N C E

GENERAL MACHINING

- Set up and operated: -lathes -mills -precision grinders -turret lathes
-horizontal and vertical boring mills -planers -slotters -shapers - NC machines
- Used fixtures such as: -dividing heads -indexing heads -vises -knees -angle plates
-taper attachments -rotary tables -steady and follow rests
- Performed precision measurement and layout using such instruments as:
-micrometers: inside, outside, pitch
-gauges: depth, surface, height, Mueller, ring, plug
-calipers: dial, vernier   -scales: 6" through 72"
-precision squares and protractors   -dial indicators
- Worked with documents: -blueprints -sketches -design memos -technical requirements
-military standards -Machinery Handbook

MATERIALS EXPERIENCE

- Machined a broad range of materials including:
-mild steel -HY-80 -high carbon steel -stainless steel -monel -brass
-nickel aluminum bronze -stellite -cobalt -titanium -aluminum -Delrin -Teflon

SPECIAL PROJECT

- As lead machinist assigned to work independently on 90-day submarine overhaul projects at remote sites:
- Planned and shipped all necessary tools to the job site.
- Acted as machinist-liaison, coordinating machining with the work of other trades.
- Designed and manufactured test equipment and special tooling needed for overhaul.
- Accomplished a variety of special setups with limited machine tools.

W O R K   H I S T O R Y

1993-94	*Student*	Solano Community College, Suisun CA - career exploration
	Part-time sales	(concurrent with school)
1992-93	*Machinist*	PUGET SOUND NAVAL SHIPYARD, Bremerton WA
1983-92	*Machinist*	MARE ISLAND NAVAL SHIPYARD, Vallejo CA

E D U C A T I O N

Four-year Machinist Apprenticeship: Mare Island Naval Shipyard, 1983-87

Solano Community College, Suisun CA, 1979
Major: Ship Building/Machine Tool Technology

- Resume writer: Yana Parker -

Carlos Neruda
Marine Machinist
4242 E. Toller Street
Portland, Oregon 97202
(503) 232-2322

Highlights of Qualifications

- Extensive experience as Marine Machinist.
- Hard worker, team player, fast learner.
- Excellent organizational skills.
- Loyal to goals and objectives of a company.
- Skilled at working with people with diverse backgrounds.

Professional Experience

Mechanical Skills

- Removed, repaired and installed shipboard machinery and equipment using hand tools and precision measuring instruments.
- Performed inspections and tests on shipboard propulsion, fluid delivery systems, piping, pumps and machinery.
- Evaluated sub-contractors' ability to follow Naval procedures.
- Coordinated with government agencies in scheduling inspections, tests and submissions of reports to assure a quality product.

Problem-Solving Skills

- Planned and installed a cable-operated emergency shut-down system on a U.S. Navy destroyer without benefit of engineering support.
- Planned a program of instrument testing for a sub-contractor to qualify for work on a U.S. Naval vessel.
- Coordinated the inspection of several shipboard systems to maximize production within time constraints.

Work Experience

1989 - present	Pacific Marine, Inc.	**Marine Machinist**
1985 - 1989	Bellingham Ship Repair	**Marine Machinist**
1984 - 1985	Pacific Marine, Inc.	**Quality Assurance Inspector**
1973 - 1984	Cascade Iron & Steel Corp.	**Marine Machinist Asst. Supt.**

Education

B.A., Liberal Arts, Portland State University, Portland, Oregon

- Resume written by Dislocated Workers Project -

Oliver W. Homestead

3838 N. Enfelt Ave.   Portland, OR 97217   (503) 282-2828

OBJECTIVE

Position as a Machinist

HIGHLIGHTS OF QUALIFICATIONS

- Creative, independent machinist/millwright, with strong mechanical aptitude.
- Fifteen years of experience in various aspects of machine repair and operation.
- Ability to work independently as well as a team player.
- Adept at "seeing" a problem and finding a solution.

RELEVANT EXPERIENCE

- Supervised and trained employees on the use of various equipment.
- Set up work schedules for machinists according to job priorities and machine size.
- Operated largest and newest CNC Super Profile Multi-Spindle Milling Machines.
- Troubleshot, repaired, and maintained heavy mill equipment.
- Developed hands-on knowledge of a variety of hand and power tools.
- Learned to skillfully read blueprints and schematics.
- Set up and operated a variety of machinery.
- Received three cash awards for production enhancement suggestions.
- Received ACE Award for performance and named "Employee of the Month."

EQUIPMENT OPERATED

- Lathes
- Milling Machines
- Radial Drill Press
- Horizontal Boring Mill

- Surface Grinders
- Key Seaters
- Cylindrical Grinder
- Fanuc M6

- GE Fanuc 15
- Allen Bradley 8600
- Cincinnati Millacron Control
- Mobile Cranes

WORK HISTORY

CNC MACHINIST, Boeing of Portland	1986-present
CNC MACHINIST, Western Iron Works	1985-1986
MACHINIST/MILLWRIGHT, Cascade Steel Mill Corporation	1974-1984

EDUCATION

Mt. Hood Community College - Career/Life Planning

Portland Community College - **Machine Technology**

- Resume written by Dislocated Workers Project -

HARRY F. WILLIAMS
7676 N. Mississippi
Portland, OR 97217
(503) 622-6222

OBJECTIVE
Millwright

SUMMARY
- Over 15 years experience as a millwright.
- Dependable, reliable, willing to work hard.
- Willing to try new things.
- Able to work independently or with a crew.

RELEVANT EXPERIENCE
- Set up and prepared equipment for daily use.
- Established scheduling priorities in order to meet production deadlines.
- Trained crew to run sawmill equipment safely and efficiently.
- Troubleshot and repaired equipment.
- Developed and implemented a productivity and safety improvement that saved the company $20,000 per year.

MACHINE ABILITIES
- Forklift
- Skrag
- Welding Equipment
- Planer
- Grader (Certified)

WORK HISTORY

Woodright Products, Troutsdale, OR	1994
Oceanside Lumber, Portland, OR	1991-1993
St. Tim's Forest Products, Portland, OR	1983-1991
J & B Lumber, Portland, OR	1974-1983

- Resume written by Dislocated Workers Project -

Trades

Jorge Vasquez
6969 Emerald Lane
Portland, OR 88888
505-555-5050

OBJECTIVE: Crew position in the Marine Trade

HIGHLIGHTS OF QUALIFICATIONS

* 6 years marine experience (>8000 hours) on tugs, 85' self-propelled barge, landing craft and fishing vessels.
* Diesel and hydraulic maintenance experience.
* Marine Emergency Duties I Certificate.
* Responsible and dependable.
* Skilled in handling the public with professionalism and sensitivity.

WORK HISTORY

92-94 Skipper, MV "7th Fjord," Quathiaski Cove.

- Operated and maintained freight delivery service to outer islands with 42' aluminum landing barge.

92-93 Deckhand/Loadmaster, MV "Forest Transporter," Campbell River.

- Coordinated freight and acted as deckhand on 85' self-propelled landing barge between North Arm and outer islands.
- Supervised and trained up to 8 people in salmon harvesting.

91-92 Skipper, MV "Partner," Heriot Bay.

- Owner/operator of 36' work boat and 40' barge.
- Provided construction and freight services to outer islands.

89-91 Deckhand, Various fishing vessels.

- Trolled west coast, underwater harvesting inside waters.

79-91 Telecommunications Technician, Whitehorse, Yukon.

- Serviced telephone and VHF radio equipment and data in the Yukon and western Arctic.

78-79 Radar Technician, Canadian Armed Forces.

EDUCATION & TRAINING

1994   Introduction to Computers, North Island College.

1993   Marine Emergency Duties I (NED 030), North Island College.

1992   VHF Radio License.

1978-91 Various Electronic & Telecommunications Courses.

- Resume writer: Katannya van Tyler -

Jeffrey G. Cardoza
295 Willow Falls Street
Woodland, CA 95695 916/667-0709

Objective: Position as Firefighter with a municipal fire department.

Education

A.S. Fire Technology, Columbia College, CA, 1991

Specialized Training - Certificates

Firefighter I, Columbia College, 1990
Emergency Medical Technician, Columbia College, 1989 *(Recertified 1993)*
Cardiopulmonary Resuscitation 1989-90-91-92-93

Advanced Forest Firefighter	1991	Basic Forest Firefighter	1989
Fire Prevention 1A	1989	Fire Prevention 1B	1989
Low Angle Rope Rescue	1990	Basic Rescue Systems I/Heavy Rescue	1990
Fire Control III	1990	Fire Control IV/Flammable Liquids	1989
Fire Ground Commander	1990		

Highlights of Qualifications

★ Experienced state firefighter and EMT-1A; respond rapidly/confidently in emergencies.
★ Organized teamworker and leader under critical and constantly changing variable.
★ Able to function at top performance throughout a 12-24 hr/4 on 3 off shift schedule.
★ Committed professional, constantly upgrading training; initiative, good judgement.
★ Excellent relations with the public and the community; dependable.
★ Mature lifestyle, compatible with emergency work.

Professional Work Experience

Firefighter *(volunteer)*	Woodland Fire Department	1992 - present
Firefighter	California Dept. of Forestry & Fire Protection	1991 - 1993
Firefighter Captain *(appointed by Chief)*	Columbia College Fire Department	1991
Firefighter Lieutenant	Columbia College Fire Department	1990
Firefighter	Columbia College Fire Department	1989

Relevant Skills

Supervision & Leadership

- Supervised/trained 5 4-person fire teams in safety procedures, apparatus operations, fire prevention and protection/rescue techniques, policies and procedures, to protect and assure safety of public.
- Led/directed 3-person response crew in fire, medical and rescue emergencies effectively handling any emergency.
- Provided search and rescue guidance to new trainees, lowering liability rate to crew and victims.

Prevention - Control - Evaluation

- Participated in response to statewide fires of massive intensity up to 2 weeks and covering an area up to 150,000+ sq. acres.
- Performed specific duties as outlined by Fire Fighting Officer in charge.
- Experienced in ventilation techniques, equipment use, and salvaging building and contents.
- Evaluated building plans and contents for possible hazards.
- Provided mutual assistance and aid to town via campus fire department.
- Participated in educating the campus and community through fire prevention/safety programs and residential inspections.
- Assisted in building inspections, hydrant and extinguisher maintenance.
- Monitored/maintained maintenance/repairs of engines, equipment, and station.

Administration

- Drafted objective and factual fire incident reports.
- Reviewed fire science literature to keep abreast of technological developments and administrative practices and policies.

- Resume written by Karen Staggs -

Trades

LUCY SMITH
BOOKBINDER
4224 Southeast 26th St.
Portland, Oregon 97202
(503) 287-8787

SUMMARY OF QUALIFICATIONS

- 15 years experience in the printing industry.
- Resourceful and committed, can be counted on to get the job done.
- Equally effective working in self-managed projects and as a member of the team.
- Sincerely enjoy helping people and willing to go the extra mile.

MACHINERY KNOWLEDGE

- Shrink-wrap
- Stitcher
- Multi Drill
- Folder
- ABDick Press
- Bindery Equipment
- Cutter
- Address-o-graph
- 16-Bin Collator

BOOKBINDER EXPERIENCE

- Successfully handled customer orders, ensuring they were properly packaged and shipped.
- Accurately maintained shipping and delivery records.
- Handled customer inquiries and complaints; successfully resolved problems involving shipping delays and damages.
- Reorganized shipping department, making it more cost effective.
- Reviewed products monthly to assure that inventory levels were maintained.
- Trained new and temporary employees.
- Coordinated bindery jobs to assure timely completion.

WORK HISTORY

WILSON'S PRECISION PRINTING   1978-1994

Journey Level Bookbinder II, 1988-1994
Journey Level Bookbinder I, 1984-1988
Apprentice Bookbinder, 1978-1984

COMMUNITY SERVICE

Volunteered at St. Joseph Nursing Home, Meals-on-Wheels Program, and Portland Community College's ESL Program.

EDUCATION

Mt. Hood Community College and Portland Community College, 1994
Certificates in: •Business Communications •Customer Service
•Intro to Micro Computers   •Career Life Planning

- Resume written by Dislocated Workers Project -

PRAWIN PARBHUBHAI
SIGNPAINTER

1510 Lexington Ave., Apt. B
El Cerrito, CA 94530
(510) 215-0368

HIGHLIGHTS

- Seventeen years of experience handpainting small and large promotional signs.
- Highly skilled in many styles of lettering and graphics.
- Competent and creative in designing signs to attract new customers.
- Able to construct high-quality signboards and mounting fixtures.
- Reliable, honest, and friendly.

SIGNPAINTING ACCOMPLISHMENTS

- Attracted customers for over a thousand small businesses with holiday and special promotion window signs.
- Designed and screenprinted posters, showcards, tickets, and banners, increasing sales for hundreds of special events and promotions. For example:
  - Produced 300 holiday greeting posters for Morris-Hedstrom stores throughout Fiji.
  - Produced dozens of tickets daily for Morris-Hedstrom supermarkets, describing items, sales, and prices on 10"X 15" signs.
  - Screenprinted 7,000 logos on tee-shirts for Coca-Cola Company.
- Designed and handpainted 250 road signs for Public Works Department in Fiji providing drivers with clear information and directions.
- Designed Cutty Sark logo used throughout Fiji, and painted 30-foot mural on distributor's wall announcing this product.
- Designed and cut wood and Styrofoam to produce letters which jump out from walls to attract attention for many small businesses in Fiji.
- Built sheetmetal, Plexiglass, and wooden stand-alone sidewalk signs, exterior hanging signs, frames, and other signboards to effectively support thousands of advertisements.
- Painted 20-foot lettering on seven British Petroleum oil tankers to clearly identify them from great distances.

RELATED ACCOMPLISHMENTS

- Painted dragon murals on 14 interior walls of Golden Dragon Night Club, decorating one of the most famous night clubs in Fiji.
- Painted 6 ' x 4' oil portrait of Queen Elizabeth II to honor her during her 1976 visit to Fiji.
- Designed and produced Citibank float for annual Hibiscus Festival in Fiji.
- Spongeprinted and blockprinted designs by hand on clothing for Jack and Harry Company in Suva, Fiji.

WORK HISTORY

1990-present	**Signpainter**	RAPHAEL LUMBER, San Raphael, CA
1975-89	**Signpainter**	FREELANCE ADVERTISING, Suva, Fiji
1980-89	**Driver**	MINISTRY OF EDUCATION, Suva, Fiji
1975-80	**Signpainter**	MORRIS-HEDSTROM LIMITED, Suva, Fiji

- Resume writer: Jenny Mish -

Phillip Hoffman

151515 SW Roundtree Court
Beaverton, OR 97007
(503) 454-6676

Position Desired: Senior Mechanical Designer

HIGHLIGHTS

- Able to develop good working relationships with all levels of people and departments within an organization.
- Proven ability to learn new areas of responsibility and adapt to change.
- Strong skills in oral communication, decision-making, and negotiation.
- Able to coordinate facility planning, selection, design, and installation of equipment.
- Skilled at monitoring construction practices with emphasis on high quality.

RELEVANT EXPERIENCE

- Completed design, layout and installation of $150 million paper machine, including major equipment and piping.
- Successfully used Autocad as primary design and drafting tool.
- Established quality guidelines for construction practices and installation, resulting in higher efficiency on time and costs.
- Served as mechanical engineering area leader, including supervision of design and installation, goal setting, and performance evaluations for 5 designers and 4 drafters.

AREAS OF EXPERIENCE

- Equipment Layout
- Process Piping Design
- Building Air Systems
- Fire Protection
- Scheduling

- HVAC
- Plumbing
- Structural Layout
- Sewers
- Expediting

- Continued -

Phillip Hoffman

EMPLOYMENT HISTORY

1990 - Present	Senior Piping Designer	Cascade Industries Portland, OR
1989 - 1990	Project Coordinator	P.R. Schmidt & Associates Oregon City, OR
1988- 1989	Senior Mechanical Designer	Pacific Engineering Portland, OR
1985 - 1988	Designer/Construction Coordinator	Kishoff Construction Denver, CO
1982 - 1985	Senior Designer	Harvest International Portland, OR
1980 - 1982	Designer	Rothburn-Buckley Industries Portland, OR

EDUCATION & TRAINING

Mt. Hood Community College
Engineering Design/Drafting Technology

Continued education in computer design and drafting.

Member of American Society of Plumbers/Engineers since 1983.

> Phillip paints the picture of a highly skilled mechanical designer by the way he describes his accomplishments in his "Relevant Experience" section. Separately listing the areas of experience makes his strengths clearly stand out. —Ed.

- Resume written by Dislocated Workers Project -

JOSEPH T. FERNANDEZ

2530 Martel Street
Oakland, CA 94607
(510) 444-1782

OBJECTIVE

Cabinetmaker with major design responsibility.

SUMMARY

I am a self-taught, highly self-motivated custom cabinetmaker and small business owner. Starting with little more than a love of craft and a fondness for wood, I have grown to become a highly skilled woodworker with the ability to design and detail all types of residential cabinetry.

In recent years, my focus has been on the design and planning of larger, more complex projects. My work has predominantly involved kitchen and bathroom projects, but has also included a wide variety of built-in cabinets and custom-designed furniture.

A commitment to detail is central to my work in construction and installation, as well as design. I believe the time and effort spent producing quality now will be repaid many times in the future as demonstrated by the whole-hearted recommendations and referrals from satisfied clients.

QUALIFICATIONS

- Over 19 years experience in the design and construction of residential cabinetry and furniture.
- Skilled project and personnel manager.
- Ability to read and develop architectural plans.
- Strong verbal and written communication skills, including ability to elicit, define and successfully meet client needs.
- Knowledge of computer systems and business/cabinetmaking software.
- Firm understanding of small business organization including bookkeeping, record keeping and cost analysis.

- Continued -

CAREER HIGHLIGHTS

- Management responsibility for 25+ employees, including hiring, scheduling and supervision, 1965 - 1970.
- Designed, built and installed first kitchen project, 1973.
- Employed as union Journeyman Cabinetmaker, 1976.
- Constructed single family residence from foundation to finish, 1979.
- Construction Foreman for commercial renovation and remodeling projects, 1980.
- Designed and built over 20 custom beds, 1981 - 1989.
- Complete design and construction responsibility for major kitchen remodels, 1987, 1989, 1991.
- Project Coordinator with design responsibility for $30,000 new house cabinet project, 1988.
- Five kitchen remodels with major design responsibility, 1991 - 1992.

EXPERIENCE

Cabinetmaker, Joseph Fernandez Custom Woodworking, Oakland, CA
1984 - present: Design and construction of custom cabinets

Carpenter/Cabinetmaker, James Cornell Construction, Berkeley, CA
1976 - 1984: All phases of home construction and remodeling

Journeyman Cabinetmaker, Builders Cabinets, Oakland, CA
1976: Assembly bench

Cabinetmaker, Joseph Fernandez Custom Woodworking, Oakland, CA
1972 - 1976: Design and construction of custom cabinets

Joseph writes beautifully, and I incorporated some of his resume "homework" into the final document, which straddles the line between brochure and resume, emphasizing his extensive experience and quality orientation. —L.A.

REFERENCES

Available upon request

- Resume writer: Laila Atallah -

7

WAREHOUSE, MANUFACTURING, AND ELECTRONICS

Warehouse, Mfg., & Electronics

MARTIN Q. DROGAN

322 Fortieth Ave.
Rockplace, CA 94222
(512) 123-4567 or 666-3456 (messages)

Objective: Position as a warehouse worker and/or driver

HIGHLIGHTS OF QUALIFICATIONS

- Experience as a warehouse worker with a major firm.
- Sharp and creative in solving problems; great mechanical aptitude.
- Extensive experience and knowledge of warehouse operations and moving equipment.
- Hard worker, follow instructions easily, work well under pressure.
- Possess own tools and equipment.
- Volunteer experience in community service agencies

RELEVANT EXPERIENCE AND SKILLS

Warehouse/Inventory

- Supervised the loading and unloading of goods, making sure that items were handled with care and placed accurately in the warehouse.
- Prepared, wrapped, weighed, and loaded items for shipping according to packing slips.
- Monitored inventory paperwork and ordering, to keep warehouse fully stocked at all times.
- Operated a forklift extensively and safely, transporting heavy loads of paper within the warehouse.

Driver/Mover

- Operated dollies, safe-jacks, book-carts, tubs, piano dollies, and other moving equipment, using the right equipment for each job.
- Drove bob-tail truck; working towards possession of Class 1 (A) Driver's License.
- Currently employed part-time by a San Francisco moving firm:
    - Load and unload large and small furniture, books, delicate items, wardrobes, etc.
    - Pack truck so that road bumps and shifts won't damage goods.
    - Work with customers to treat special items special.

Mechanical

- Took apart and fixed a wide variety of mechanical devices including appliances, small engines, etc.
- Did maintenance, troubleshooting, and repair on cars and trucks.

RECENT EMPLOYMENT HISTORY

1992-Present	Mover/Installer	Fast Action Movers, Sebastopol
1992-1993	Supervisor/Cook	Haynes Family Center, Crosstown
1990-1991	Weight Trainer	Boys Clubs of America, Crosstown

OTHER RELATED WORK EXPERIENCE

2 years	Warehouse Worker	Tri-City Paper, Sebastopol
2 years	Carpenter	Solid Action Construction, Crosstown
3 years	Mover	Felix Trucking, Jump City
5 years	Construction Worker/Foreman	Pine Ridge Construction, Taylorville

EDUCATION AND TRAINING

Richardsville College, Richardsville, Psychology Major, 1977-78
Peterson School of Industry, Crosstown High School Diploma, Culinary Arts Major, 1970-76

- Resume written by Roving Resume Writers -

DONALD H. SMELTZER, JR.

260 27th Street SW · Naples, Florida 33964 · (813) 455-9305

Objective: Warehouse/Inventory Control

PROFILE

Over 19 years stable employment history, utilizing many talents in variety of fields. Obtained broad scope of shop experience for a major manufacturer of construction and farm equipment parts, demonstrating loyalty until terminating due to plant closing.

STRENGTHS

★ Fast learner with a wide range of practical skills.
★ Adept at performing routine inventory control warehouse functions - experienced at handling shipping and receiving.
★ Knowledgeable with industrial equipment and manufacturing processes.
★ Skilled machine operator - wide background of experience on numerous machines.
★ Proven track record of performing with little or no supervision.

EMPLOYMENT HISTORY

CASE IH, East Moline, ILLINOIS, September 1990 to April 1991
Machine Operator
- Maintain quality control in various areas of production.
- Operate numerous machines, i.e., drills, mills, hones, lathes and grinders, to ensure economic and timely production of company products.

WEIGOLD & SONS AIR CONDITIONING, INC., Naples, Florida, 1989 to 1990
Warehouse Inventory Control
- Managed and preserved organization of company products and equipment stored in warehouse.
- Monitored incoming and outgoing shipments, facilitating efficiency in delivering sold goods and acquiring new inventory.

AQUALETIC SWIM CLUB, Rock Island, Illinois, 1979 to 1989
Seasonal Maintenance Worker
- Responsible for all aspects of maintenance on 3 outdoor swim pools including plumbing, electrical, carpentry and cement upkeep/repairs.
- Assisted Manager in club operations - conducted facility tours, completed membership paperwork, responded to telephone inquiries.

CASE IH, Rock Island, Illinois, 1972 to 1988
Production Worker
- Performed multiple jobs during term of employment, obtaining numerous skills:
  - Operated various machines
  - Used holding devices
  - Assembled component parts
  - Performed set-ups
  - Worked with hydraulic cylinders
  - Operated forklift

MILITARY

VIETNAM VETERAN - HONORABLE DISCHARGE
Ft. Riley, Kansas

> Here is a very strong resume design that's easy to scan. The use of bold-face type plus large letters for headings results in a crisp, clean, high-contrast look. (Note: This resume was current in 1991.) —Ed.

EDUCATION/TRAINING

BLACK HAWK COLLEGE, Moline, Illinois
Introduction to Numerical Control Machining

Warehouse, Mfg., & Electronics

DEIDRE GOLDEN
4545 N. Babcock
Portland, OR 97217
(503) 283-8333

OBJECTIVE: Position in Shipping and Receiving

PROFESSIONAL EXPERIENCE

WAREHOUSE / SHIPPING / RECEIVING

- Shipped high volume of orders daily; followed all procedures and kept good records.

- Worked with a team of four people to have better quality control in receiving; established a control system which is still in place.

- Set up a customer service phone line direct to staff in the warehouse receiving area.

SUPERVISION

- Advanced through the ranks to manage 12 people in hospital central supply, ensuring areas were covered and finished in a timely matter.

- Supervised people of various ethnic backgrounds, helping them deal with their personal and work problems so that the tasks at hand could be accomplished with little interference while on the job.

- Took management classes in effectively dealing with problems that arise among staff.

WORK HISTORY

WAREHOUSE / SHIPPING / RECEIVING, 1990-1994
    Adidas, Inc., Beaverton, OR -

ASSISTANT TO MANAGER IN CENTRAL SUPPLY, 1979-1989
    St. Joseph's Hospital, Portland, OR -

- Resume written by Dislocated Workers Project -

Paul Crouthamel

(510) 665-6655

1352 Ballena Blvd., #212
Alameda, CA 94501

JOB OBJECTIVE: Inventory Controller or Inventory Control Supervisor

SUMMARY OF QUALIFICATIONS

- 12 years' experience in Inventory Control, including seven years of supervision.
- Demonstrated record of accuracy.
- Excel in organizing and coaching personnel to work effectively in a team.
- Committed team player in supporting company objectives.

PROFESSIONAL ACCOMPLISHMENTS

INVENTORY CONTROL

- Organized and managed five large stock areas each comprising up to 10,000 line items; maintained excellent accuracy ratings.
- Coordinated parts-kitting work centers, frequently juggling a variety of tasks simultaneously.
- Initiated cycle counting, greatly improving inventory integrity.
- Worked with computer programmers to develop customized data base applications. Proficient with Lotus 1-2-3.
- Facilitated materials expediting, involving status checking and progressing.

SUPERVISION

- Supervised up to 26 inventory controllers and electronics technicians.
- Trained new personnel, organized work routines, and successfully promoted team unity among a diverse staff.
- Solved problems on a daily basis, working closely with customers and staff.

WORK HISTORY

1985-present	Lear Siegler Management Services Corp., Alameda	Site Supervisor (1989-present) Leadman (1987-1989) Sr. Supply Specialist (1985-1987)
1983-1985	Naval Air Rework Facility, San Diego	Production Control Assistant

EDUCATION

A.S.   Business Administration, anticipated 1995
College of Alameda, Alameda, CA

- Resume writer: Susan Ireland -

Warehouse, Mfg., & Electronics

BRIAN HAUSMAN

3004 Turner Blvd., Apt. 7
Oakland CA 94605
(415) 909-6666

Objective: New position with Hillside Press as
Asst. to Warehouse Manager/Liaison between Warehouse & Management

SUMMARY

★ 7 years experience with Hillside Press; record of loyalty and dependability.
★ Hardworking, ambitious, willing to learn.
★ Able to view problems in a positive way, and propose solutions to streamline operations and improve working conditions.
★ Excellent working relations with warehouse staff; skill and experience as liaison between warehouse and office.

PROPOSALS FOR IMPROVEMENT

ASSISTING MANAGEMENT

- Establish uniform quantity of books-per-box, allowing for:
  - efficient stacking and shipping
  - more accurate inventory
  - eliminating damage to books.
- Establish uniform labeling of boxes from printer.
- Install computer terminal at warehouse for immediate update of inventory.

COMMUNICATION / LIAISON

- Hold monthly joint meetings of warehouse and office management to:
  - keep warehouse staff fully informed about new titles
  - anticipate and prepare for changes in workload
  - maintain fullest communication between warehouse and management
  - update warehouse staff on changes in office personnel and job responsibilities
  - discuss shipping and packing problems and develop solutions.
- Hold quarterly meetings of all company personnel to improve morale and provide opportunity for staff to present problems for discussion.
- Involve warehouse staff in interviewing and hiring process to assure that new employees have adequate experience, valid driving license, & good work attitude.

EMPLOYMENT HISTORY

1989-present	Assistant Foreman	Warehouse, HILLSIDE PRESS
1987-89	Warehouseman	Warehouse, HILLSIDE PRESS
1986-87	Assistant Foreman	DATALINE COMPUTERS, Hayward
1985-86	Co-Owner/Gardener	MAGIC GARDENER, Oakland

EDUCATION

Chabot College, 1986

- Resume writer: Yana Parker -

JOHN L. BARBER
3 North Stevens Place
Hazlet, New Jersey
(908) 264-8496

John's background is unusual these days: he has worked virtually all his adult life for one employer, in a number of different roles. (Note: This resume was written in 1991.) —J.R.

OBJECTIVE

Management position in warehousing.

HIGHLIGHTS

- 17 years diversified experience in warehousing: progressing from labor to management.
- Exceptional interpersonal skills; diplomatic and effective with customer relations.
- Completely versatile in a warehouse environment: able to perform any task.
- High energy, self-starter who takes great pride in work.

RELEVANT EXPERIENCE

1972-Present   **Assistant Operations Manager**   JOSEPH CORY WAREHOUSE, INC., Elizabeth, NJ

Management
- As one of 3 Assistant Operations Managers, ensured the smooth work flow of over 700,000 square foot warehouse with multi-million dollar furniture inventory:
  - managed 17 supervisory personnel and 160 union employees
  - ensured compliance with all union regulations   - dispatched and routed up to 110 trucks daily
- Account executive for Seaman Furniture, the 22-store major client of the warehouse:
  - handled union disciplinary actions for violations, completing all paperwork and presenting cases before shop steward and offending employees.
  - managed the floor boss, 16 warehousemen and shop staff, 6 office employees.
- Account executive for K/Dee Imports:
  - directed shop prep and assembly of merchandise, increasing productivity by 25% in two months.
- Floor boss for an entire 120,000 square foot floor in the warehouse:
  - supervised and delegated work to 7 warehousemen.
  - directed the proper loading and inspection of up to 25 trucks daily, checked drivers' manifests.
  - resolved inventory problems by locating or accounting for missing merchandise.
  - performed manual tasks when there was insufficient staff available for the day's activities.

Communication/Problem Resolution
- Settled account problems with corporate representatives and management of Seaman Furniture, Barney's Furniture, and Country Furniture.
- Resolved manufacturing problems regarding damaged merchandise and incomplete deliveries, dealing with factory representatives and CEOs from more than 40 factories.
- Resolved a wide range of delivery problems, from delivery cancellations to lack of payment.
- Successfully resolved difficult customer complaints in person to ensure complete satisfaction, especially effective with problems that could not be resolved by the retail store or manufacturer.
- Maintained good rapport with union employees.

Labor Skills
- Delivered merchandise promptly to customers and collected payments.
- As warehouseman, efficiently maintained 50,000 square foot warehouse area:
  - kept stock neatly organized   - accurately filled orders   - received deliveries from manufacturers
- Organized 10,000 square foot area to uncrate furniture and prepare it for stock:
  - established new procedures for uncrating 1,200 pieces of furniture per day.
  - operated machinery to bail cardboard for recycling.

EDUCATION

Business Management, BROOKDALE COMMUNITY COLLEGE

- Resume writer: Judi Robinovitz -

Warehouse, Mfg., & Electronics

REBECCA VANESS

2707 Benvenue Ave.
Oakland CA 94606
(415) 313-0854

Objective: Position as Production Assistant
with a clothing manufacturer, wholesaler or design house.

HIGHLIGHTS OF QUALIFICATIONS

- Experience with all aspects of garment production.
- Hands-on knowledge of sewing and pattern development.
- Effective and experienced sample room supervisor; special talent for bridging communication barriers.
- Proven ability to assume increasing responsibility.
- Committed to maintaining exacting standards.

RELEVANT EXPERIENCE

Production/Engineering
- Coordinated sample room activity:
  -maintained wide variety of sample yardage to meet current and on-going needs of merchandisers and engineering department;
  -monitored and replenished supplies;
  -maintained records of all lines in production for referral of merchandisers.

Supervision/Project Coordination
- Balanced work flow of pattern makers, sample makers, cutter, and merchandisers according to established deadlines and production considerations.
- Promoted cooperative and productive working environment:
  -assessed needs and abilities of each person;
  -maintained an overview of each project;
  -supported staff by assuming appropriate responsibility.
- Negotiated and established realistic deadlines.

Quality Control
- Inspected garments, checking for:
  -correct seam construction, finish stitching and trims
  -appropriate packaging   -fabric quality.
- Measured first-production and counter samples, comparing with specifications.

EMPLOYMENT HISTORY

1992-present	*Design Room Assistant*	BAY CITY UNIQUE CREATIONS (private label design firm)
1985-92	*Boutique Seamstress*	Self-employed, part-time
1983-85	*Cutter/Seamstress*	DAY'S CUSTOM UPHOLSTERY, Spokane WA
1981-83	*Seamstress/Designer*	Free-lance, concurrent w/travel in Europe
1980-81	*Boutique Seamstress*	NAPOLEON & JOSEPHINE'S boutique, Berkeley

Language skills: familiar with Spanish, French, Greek, German

- Resume writer: Yana Parker -

GAIL POWELL

913 Stewart Street
Santa Rosa CA 95404
(707) 537-9374

Gail is moving to a new city, and wants to get into a somewhat different line of work, using her dexterity with machines at a place like Hewlett-Packard. —Y.P.

Objective: Position with Hewlett-Packard in assembly, inspection, lab assisting, fabrication, or material handling.

SUMMARY OF QUALIFICATIONS

★ Over 15 years experience in manufacturing assembly, machine operation, and inspection, meeting high standards of quality and productivity.

★ Special talent with machines; easily learn to operate new equipment.

★ Excellent eyesight and dexterity. Physically strong, able to lift 50 lb.

★ Maintain good working relations with co-workers.

★ Reliable, honest and conscientious; outstanding record of attendance.

RELEVANT EXPERIENCE

1993-present   *Sewing Machine Operator & Customer Service*
PENINSULA CANVAS, Redwood City CA, custom boat covers
- Operated sewing machine (both single & double-needle), **producing custom boat covers to specifications** of the pattern maker.
- Produced other custom products **to customer's specifications** for dimensions, materials, color, with careful attention to **cost-effectiveness** in production.
- **Operated hand tools** such as fastener setters, measuring tools, hot-knife, etc.
- Directly worked with customers, taking incoming calls and orders, billing, and **assisting customers** in selecting products and materials.

1988-93   *Production Coordinator/Supervisor, & Sewing Machine Operator*
GIANOLA & SONS, Sausalito CA, custom boat covers & awnings,
- **Hired and trained** sewing machine operators, relaying complex design details.
- Monitored production **quality control.**
- Served as **liaison** between management and employees on working conditions.
- Oversaw **stock control.**
- **Operated sewing machine** to produce custom boat covers, awnings, and other custom products to one-of-a-kind specifications.

1987-88   *Production Coordinator & Sewing Machine Operator*
ANCHOR AWNING CO., Decatur GA
- **Trained** machine operators.
- **Fabricated and assembled** awnings.

1982-87   *Co-owner/Operator*
INDUSTRIAL SEWING Inc., Eugene, OR
- Established (with two others) a freelance industrial sewing business.

1978-82   *Co-owner/Operator*
BURLEY DESIGN CO-OP, Eugene, OR
- **Original member of manufacturing co-op** (still in operation) producing bike bags, backpacks, rain gear, and yurts.

- Resume writer: Yana Parker -

Warehouse, Mfg., & Electronics

LESLIE FOULK
1200 SE 140th
Portland, OR 97233
(503) 258-422

OBJECTIVE

A position in assembly and production

HIGHLIGHTS

- Seven years experience in assembly/production work.
- Proven ability to work with others to achieve a goal.
- Demonstrated ability to produce high volume and to developed knowledge and skills.
- Knowledge of federal safety and quality regulations.

RELEVANT EXPERIENCE

ACUFINE PARTS CASTING   1989-1994
Wax Assembler

Assembled wax components by welding various wax supplies to produce detailed medical,
aviation, and other products.
- Worked closely with others on a self-directed team (JIT).
- Used gauges and other measuring devices to produce visually pleasing, accurate, and
  proportionate patterns.
- Mastered precision detailed tools such as torches, soldering irons, mirrors, lights, and
  various scrapers and scalpels.
- Achieved high volume productivity (120%-150% recorded and documented).
- Completed training and developed skill in inspecting products for quality and defects.

COLONIAL BATHWARE   1988-1989
Bathware Assembler/Warehouse

Performed assembly operations to mass-produce quality bath products.
- Packaged high volume off conveyor belt.
- Inventoried supplies for fiscal budget.
- Prepared and packaged products for shipping.
- Documented and filled invoices for bathware.

ATLANTA DIALYSIS CENTER   1987-1988
Reuse Technician

Cleaned, sterilized, and ensured general quality of dialyzers (artificial kidneys).
- Closely monitored and maintained dialysis machines for proper levels of acid,
  bicarbonate, and water, which were crucial for patient safety.
- Properly packaged and discarded hazardous waste materials.
- Stocked floor with necessary supplies and recorded all supply transactions in inventory log.
- Filed patient records and documented day and time of patient dialysis cycle.

EDUCATION

Mount Hood Community College, 1994

- Resume written by Dislocated Workers Project -

DIANE WARNOCK
12345 S.E. Creek Court
Portland, Oregon 97233
(503) 454-4545

OBJECTIVE

Production Supervisor / Manager Position

HIGHLIGHTS OF QUALIFICATIONS

- Fourteen years professional experience in manufacturing/packaging.
- Committed to a total quality control system.
- Able to organize flow of people and materials on a daily basis.
- Successful record analyzing and interpreting unforeseen problems.
- Able to work under pressure efficiently and carefully.

PROFESSIONAL EXPERIENCE

Supervision

- Planned and scheduled people and materials, delegating work effectively.
- Encouraged a conscientious effort to work with people in a team-oriented process. to produce an attractive salable product.
- Supervised difficult people with empathy.
- Diagnosed production needs and problems.

Quality Assurance

- Designed and implemented effective quality control programs.
- Rewrote procedures and operations simply and clearly.
- Tested all materials to chemical laboratory specs by reading gauges and instruments.
- Wrote new formulas for the blending department.
- Maintained accurate and detailed numerical records.

Training Skills

- Trained new employees in quality control, warehousing, and packaging.
- Explained difficult ideas and concepts in a way that is easy to understand.
- Presented written and spoken information in a logical step-by-step fashion that built a solid foundation for future learning.
- Assessed learning styles of individuals to tailor the training to their needs.

EMPLOYMENT HISTORY

GREENBRAE DISTILLERIES, Portland (1980-94)

Quality Control and Blending Supervisor	1985-94
Warehouse Worker	1982-85
Production Line Worker	1980-82

References available on request

- Resume written by Dislocated Workers Project -

Warehouse, Mfg., & Electronics

DAVID HELLER

602 Alcatraz Avenue
Oakland CA
653-9999

Current Job Objective: a position as electronics assembler
(Future goal: electronics technician)

QUALIFICATIONS & EXPERIENCE

- Rebuilt and repaired tape recorders, stereo receivers, TVs, CDs, and car radios:
    - Assembled and disassembled dozens of units.
    - Identified, tested, and replaced components.
    - Cleaned and serviced equipment.
    - Aligned tuned circuits in radios.

- Successfully completed TV and Radio Repair class at community college:
    - Studied widely applicable electronics theory.
    - Learned numerous test procedures and repair techniques.
    - Practiced hands-on diagnosis and repair of equipment.

- Technical skills include:
    - Soldering
    - Component identification (color coding)
    - Reading schematics
    - Using oscilloscopes, voltmeters, signal generators, and other test equipment.

- Very strong interest in electronics; I spend much of my spare time on:
    - Reading and studying electronics (Popular Electronics and many books on the subject).
    - Troubleshooting, exploring, and redesigning circuitry.

EMPLOYMENT HISTORY

1993-present	Freelance Auto Mechanics and Electronics Repair
1993-94	Assembler & Driver - Miracle Mountain Hot Tubs, Berkeley CA
1991-92	Fountain person - Mercer's Ice Cream, Berkeley CA
1989-90	Newspaper Routeperson - San Francisco Chronicle (while in school)

EDUCATION

Laney College - TV and Radio Repair - Fall 1993
Berkeley High School & Berkeley Adult School - Equivalency certificate 1994

Other interests: Hiking, bicycling, chess, shortwave broadcasts

- Resume writer: Yana Parker -

STEPHEN SILVER
9999 Mountain Road
Claremont CA 94444
(510) 123-4567

Just out of high school, Stephen wanted more than anything else to work at Apple Computer, but he didn't have any directly relevant experience. We looked at descriptions of entry-level jobs at Apple, and put together a resume showing the most relevant skills gained in a variety of ways. —Y.P.

Current job objective: Entry position with a computer manufacturer.
Longer-term goal: Position in advertising, sales, and marketing of computer products.

SUMMARY

- Energetic, hard working, willing to learn and accept constructive criticism.
- Strong motivation for advancing in a career.
- Enjoy contributing to a team effort and creating a good working environment.
- Basic understanding of the Macintosh computer.

RELEVANT SKILLS & EXPERIENCE

Maintenance Skills
- As carpenter's helper:
  -painted interior walls -measured and cut lumber -helped with framing
  -operated power tools (saws, drills, sanders).
- Did basic home maintenance:
  -rewired lamps -repaired plumbing and appliance -built shelves.
- Completed classes in:
  -electronics (built a TV scrambler from a circuit board)
  -architectural drafting   -basic carpentry.

Office Support Skills
- Assisted in inventory control and priced merchandise, as stock clerk at Jorgensen's Market.
- Cashiered at Jorgensen's, computing and handling large sums of money; answered phones as needed.
- Completed class in Marketing:
  -invented unique products
  -developed simulated marketing strategies.

Computer Familiarity
- Basic understanding of Macintosh programs, MacWrite and MacPaint.

WORK HISTORY

Oct. 1993-present	**Stock Clerk/Cashier**	JORGENSEN'S MARKET, Claremont CA
Summer 1991*	**Valet Parking Asst.**	MENLO COUNTRY CLUB, Claremont CA
(* while in school)	Plus short-term jobs: Carpenter's Helper, Waiter, Busboy, Stockwork.	

EDUCATION

Claremont High School, Claremont CA, 1993

- Resume writer: Yana Parker -

Sam Kramer

(510) 771-0942

52 Forest Haven Road
Emeryville, CA 94910

JOB OBJECTIVE: Computer/Communications Technician

SUMMARY OF QUALIFICATIONS

- 14 years experience as hardware technician for top electronics firms.
- Specialist in data communications and electro-mechanical devices.
- Excellent troubleshooter and problem solver.
- Versatility with wide range of equipment.

PROFESSIONAL ACCOMPLISHMENTS

1986-present   Customer Service Engineer   Digital Equipment Corp., San Francisco

- Managed 45 accounts at a time, offering remedial and ongoing service for DEC and non-DEC systems.

- Took over the maintenance of 36 PDP 11-70's, 40 disk drives, 12 tape drives, and various data communication interfaces at Bank of America Data Center/Money Transfer System.
  - Identified major problems due to lack of service.
  - Provided thorough emergency repair to correct system malfunctions within six months.
  - Scheduled ongoing maintenance that successfully reduced amount of down-time, saving the bank substantially through timely transfer of funds.

- Stepped in and restored third party, vendor hardware for the City and County of San Francisco, bringing equipment up to specified preventive maintenance levels within eight months. Equipment included:

3 PDP 11-70's	2 Kennedy 9300 tape drive sub systems
10 CDC 9766 disk drives	Storage Technology tape drive

- Built a reputation as the district resource for PDP 8 troubleshooting and maintenance. Large accounts included:
  - San Francisco Fire Department Communications Center
  - West Coast Life Insurance Company

- Performed on-the-job training for new technicians, focusing on accurate identification of problems and implementation of long-term solutions.

1980-1986   Field Service Engineer   Bunker Ramo Corp., San Francisco

- Performed troubleshooting for Bank Control Systems (BCS-90) at Bank of America, Sanwa Bank, and Hibernia Bank. Promoted to Field Installer within first year.

- Installed all BCS-90's for Bank of America in Northern California; worked closely with Pacific Bell technicians to interface equipment with telephone lines.

EDUCATION

Technical Training, United Electronics Institute, Oklahoma City

- Resume writer: Susan Ireland -

SHAWN C. McGUIRE

2610 W. 7TH Street • Chester, Pennsylvania 19013 • (215) 555-1234

OBJECTIVE: A position as a *Computer Technician*.

SUMMARY OF SKILLS

◆ Trained and skilled as a Certified Computer Repair Technician.
◆ Experience in troubleshooting a variety of computer hardware and software.
◆ Skilled in quickly diagnosing and analyzing technical problems on 8088s to 486s.
◆ Committed to working with the computer until the problem has been corrected.
◆ Excellent team player, yet confident in my own technical abilities.
◆ Willing to relocate.

PROFESSIONAL EXPERIENCE

Bench Technician
Independent Computer Support Services; Wayne, Pennsylvania   1993 - 1994
• Repair all types of IBM equipment; i.e., PS/1 computers, PCs, laser printers.
• Install hard drives, floppy drives, copy boards, network boards and diagnostic boards.
• Run diagnostics on LAN diagnostic cards.
• Repair amplifier boards for printers.
• Work on low voltage and micro-uninterrupted power supplies.
• Ensure that all equipment is running properly before it leaves my station.
• Troubleshoot hardware/software conflicts on all types of computers up to 486s.
• Work with virus protection utilities; have a working knowledge of Pentium.
• Configure systems to the customers specifications.

Hydro-Blaster
Broadbents Company Contractors; Essington, Pennsylvania   1992 - 1993
• Maintained machinery to ensure it was working properly and was available when needed.
• Cleaned and inspected industrial building sites.
• Processed inventory pickups and drop offs.

Maintenance Worker
Chester Upland School District; Chester, Pennsylvania   1992
• Assisted electricians, troubleshooting and repairing electrical problems throughout the school.
• Restocked inventory in the stockroom to guarantee supplies were available when needed.

■ SOFTWARE SKILLS
MS/DOS ver. 1.0 - 6.0 ◆ Check It PRO ◆ Norton 7 Utilities
PC Tools Utilities ◆ ARCnet Novell

EDUCATION

Certificate in Computer Repair Technology; RETS Educational Center - Broomall, PA, 1993

- Resume writer: Wanda Jenkins -

Warehouse, Mfg., & Electronics

DOUGLAS E. LECTRONIC

433 Martin Street
Spurious, CA 94808
(415) 555-1213

Objective: **Service Manager or Field Service Manager**
for the installation/repair of electronic or electro-mechanical equipment

HIGHLIGHTS OF QUALIFICATIONS

★ Take full responsibility for customer satisfaction, with personal commitment to getting the job done right the first time.

★ Demonstrated record of success in positions of responsibility, including eight years of supervisory experience.

★ Accomplished in repair work on a wide variety of equipment, both in-house and in the field.

★ Flexible; work independently; available for on-call and shift work.

RELEVANT SKILLS & EXPERIENCE

CUSTOMER SERVICE
• As owner of Dexter's TV, created an effective approach to customer service, based on:
...developing a one-on-one relationship with the client;
...being willing to "go the extra mile," taking personal responsibility for seeing that the client is fully satisfied;
...being available at virtually any hour to assist the customer.

FIELD SUPERVISION
• Supervised Lundy technicians in maintenance and repair of check processing equipment for the banking industry.
• Served as Site Supervisor for the installation, modification, and maintenance of Sprint's telephone switching equipment at 7 different sites throughout the West.
• Supervised Telecom field engineers, installing and maintaining computers and electro-mechanical learning aids in public and private schools.

TECHNICAL EXPERTISE
• Installed and repaired equipment in diverse fields: ...schools ...banks
...aerospace ...retail consumers ...private industry ...telecommunications.
• Quality Assurance: monitored Lundy's aerospace manufacturing processes, and tested final products, for compliance with requirements of NASA and Dept. of Defense.
• Familiar with repair and installation of: ...minicomputers ...computer peripherals
...teletype ...optical sensing equipment ...UPS equipment ...OCR & MICR equipment.
• Certified in NASA soldering.

EMPLOYMENT HISTORY

1984-present	Senior Engineer	U.S. SPRINT, Burlingame CA
1978-84	Site Supervisor	NORTHERN TELECOM, Texas/California
1975-78	District Supervisor	LUNDY ELECTRONICS & SYSTEMS, INC., Charlotte NC
1973-75	Owner/Partner	DEXTER'S TV (retail sales/service), Larkspur CA
1971-73	Field Service Mgr	THOMAS A. EDISON INDUSTRIES LAB, W. Orange NJ

EDUCATION

Electrical Engineering - three years undergrad studies
US Army, Field Radio Repair

- Resume writer: Yana Parker -

John Reed

1938 Taylor Street
San Francisco CA 94133
(415) 673-7071

A waiter for 20 years, John aims for a major career change, BACK to an earlier interest in electronics. He'll use this DRAFT RESUME for some "Information Interviewing" to explore how he could gain entry into the field and apply his experience and training from 20 years ago. —Y.P.

Objective: Entry level position as electronics engineering technician, involving field service and/or research and development.

HIGHLIGHTS OF QUALIFICATIONS

★ Very strong commitment to developing a career in electronics.

★ Productive and responsible; willing to learn and handle any tasks needed.

★ Skill in tracing schematic diagrams, analyzing circuits and troubleshooting problems.
  -Heald College training as Electronics Engineering Technician.
  -2 years as Army radio mechanic and instructor in radio repair.

★ Over 20 years experience in successfully dealing with customers.

★ Able to represent a company with a professional appearance and manner.

RELEVANT SKILLS & EXPERIENCE

ELECTRONICS KNOWLEDGE
- Completed 2-year course at Heald College, in Electronics Engineering Technology:
- Completed math, physics and drafting courses at City College:
  -Algebra -Geometry -Trigonometry -Calculus -Physics -Drafting
- Taught radio repair in US Army Signal Corps.
- **Rebuilt and rewired** electrical home appliances.
- **Replaced portion of house wiring**, bringing it up to code.

TROUBLESHOOTING/RESEARCH
- **Researched** in technical manuals and consulted with professionals in the field, to resolve technical problems in home/auto repair; experience in use of hand tools in woodworking and metalworking.
- **Diagnosed problems** in home electronics: TVs, radios, disc players, tape decks.

CUSTOMER RELATIONS
- Developed a successful, professional approach to providing **top-quality customer service**, consistently applying these principles:
  -Create atmosphere that encourages the customer to freely express complaints.
  -Thoroughly and tactfully research the potential solutions to their problem.
  -Get feedback to be sure the customer is, in fact, satisfied with the results.

EMPLOYMENT HISTORY

1974-present	**Waiter** MONROE'S RESTAURANT, San Francisco
1989-93	**Consultant** to Restaurant Management Part-time (concurrent with above); advising management on personnel problems and professional standards in restaurant service.
1972-74	**Field Radio Repairman & Instructor** U.S. ARMY SIGNAL CORP

EDUCATION & TRAINING
Graduate, HEALD COLLEGE, Electronics Engineering Technician
US ARMY, Field Radio Repair

- Resume writer: Yana Parker -

Warehouse, Mfg., & Electronics

John LaMotte

6035 Buena Vista Ave., Oakland CA 94618
510-555-5555

OBJECTIVE: Electronics Technician.

HIGHLIGHTS

- Over ten years successful experience in troubleshooting and repair.
- Recent Computer Electronics Technology graduate with Highest Honors.
- Worked to finance 100% of education and living expenses.
- Never injured on a job.

PROBLEM-SOLVING ACCOMPLISHMENTS

COMPUTERS

Repaired dozens of personal computers at Merritt College:

- Visually inspected components, jumpers, and switches to assess configurations and determine proper installation.
- Identified malfunctions and traced causes of errors using diagnostics software, logic diagrams, and electronic testing.
- Determined cost-efficiency of component-level repair vs. board replacement, and replaced parts appropriately.
- Reinstalled, replaced, or reconfigured software as needed, and e-tested equipment.

ELECTRONIC AND MECHANICAL EQUIPMENT

Performed preventative maintenance, troubleshooting, and repair of mechanical and electronic components in several settings:

- Repaired numerous consumer electronics and appliances, and performed automotive circuit testing on a freelance basis.
- Maintained and repaired all equipment for eight Desert Petroleum service stations.
  - Identified and repaired electronic pump circuit and console problems.
  - Fixed lighting, plumbing, air compressors, and maintained buildings.
- Inspected wear, cleaned equipment, and ensured proper functioning of automatic and manual tooling at Moulton's.
  - Conducted component-level diagnosis and repair of electronic tooling.
  - Set up, adjusted, and maintained complex pneumatic equipment.

RELATED SKILLS

- Acquired theoretical understanding of various personal computers and peripherals in lectures, readings, and discussions at Merritt College.
- Read and interpreted schematic diagrams for hundreds of electrical systems in school and while repairing equipment.
- Upgraded building electrical system to support automated tooling at Moulton's manufacturing facility.
- As a carpenter, framed houses, and designed and built projects such as decks and stairs.
- Received awards for volunteer fire fighting and animal rescue during the 1991 Oakland-Berkeley hills firestorm.

EDUCATION

A.S., Computer Electronics Technology, 1994, Merritt College, Oakland CA
- Graduated with Highest Honors, GPA 3.78

RELEVANT WORK HISTORY

1991-present	Freelance Electronics Repair & Carpentry	
1991-94	Full-Time Student	
1985-90	Machine Operator	MOULTON'S, Castro Valley CA
1979-85	Area Manager & Station Manager	DESERT PETROLEUM, East Bay Area, CA

- Resume writer: Jenny Mish -

DAVID BORUNDY
5005 E. Paradise Dr.   602-996-1111   Scottsdale, AZ 85258

OBJECTIVE: Entry-level position in fiber optic applications.

RELEVANT SKILLS AND EXPERIENCE

ELECTRONICS KNOWLEDGE
* Repaired and assembled telephone answering devices.
* Reliably assembled and soldered work as independent contractor:
  - Worked on bank card terminals, printed circuit boards, pressure sensitive modules, and custom test cable assemblies.
* Rewired entire vehicle, including lights, gauges, radio, and ignition.
* Rebuilt and rewired electrical home appliances.
* Read blueprints and became familiar with electrical wiring for residential and commercial buildings.

TROUBLESHOOTING and RESEARCH
* Researched in technical manuals and consulted with professionals in the field to resolve technical problems in home/auto/motorcycle repair.
* Diagnosed and solved problems in home electronics:
  - Installed and repaired indoor/outdoor lighting, small appliances, and wiring of audio/video components.

EYE/HAND COORDINATION and MANUAL DEXTERITY
* Precisely cut and installed carpet in boats after laying necessary wires.
* Accumulated extensive experience in handling tools.
* Served as Master Helmsman for ship, a position requiring extreme concentration and accuracy.

EMPLOYMENT HISTORY

1994-present	Electronics Repair Specialist	Goldstar / TAD Temporaries
1990-present	Electronic Assembly	Independent Contractor
1993-94	Delivery/Service Medical Beds	Craftmatic Pacific
1991-93	Security	Scottsdale Racquet Club
1990-91	Marine Carpet Installation	Sea Ray Boats
1989-90	Landscaping	Scottsdale Ranch Assoc.
1985-90	Boatswains Mate, 3rd Class	U.S. Navy

EDUCATION

Phoenix Institute of Technology - Diploma in Architectural Drafting - 1993
Northwest Schools - Heavy Equipment Operation and Maintenance - 1985

- Resume writer: Claudia Jordan -

Warehouse, Mfg., & Electronics

STEVEN W. PINSKI
432 NE 38th Street
Portland, Oregon 97218
(503) 281-2828

OBJECTIVE

Technical or supervisory position in powder coat paint process development

HIGHLIGHTS OF QUALIFICATIONS

- Well grounded in coating processes and techniques.
- Committed to continual coat and quality improvement.
- Independent self-starter; disciplined, cooperative, and a supportive team member.

PROFESSIONAL SKILLS

Process Development
- Pioneered powder coating in unique applications for high quality cosmetic and functional finishes.
- Created and refined equipment and processes to continually improve quality and efficiency.
- Tripled productivity while dramatically reducing rejects.
- Led engineering staff in facility design and process evaluation.

Production and Quality Assurance
- Applied various coatings: catalyzed, baked, high solids, waterbase, powder coat, etc.
- Operated and maintained many application systems: airless, conventional, electrostatic spray and disc, dip coat, roller coat, conveyorized, etc.
- Evaluated coatings for color, gloss, thickness, hardness, adhesion, abrasion and impact resistance.
- Maintained quality assurance inspection of all incoming material and outgoing finished products.

Supervision and Training
- Led multi-shift production powder coat operation.
- Supervised crew for automated operations.
- Facilitated engineering project teams.
- Delivered short- and long-term trainings in coating process and industry practices.

WORK HISTORY

COATINGS TECHNICIAN - Duratek Manufacturing	1982-1994
PRODUCTION SPRAY PAINTER - Draper Industries	1980-1982
PAINTER/PLATER - Allied Brass	1979-1980
LEAD OPERATOR; PAINT - Jones & Hopkins Furniture	1975-1979
LEAD OPERATOR; PLATING - Summer Products	1974-1975

EDUCATION AND TRAINING

University of Portland, Portland Community College - 90 hours Engineering studies

Industrial Paint Processes, Statistical Process Controls, & Color Lab Technician Training

- Resume written by Dislocated Workers Project -

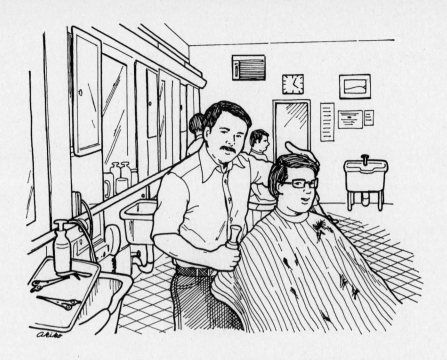

8
MIXED BAG

Marvin Morris
989 Athol Avenue, #404
Minneapolis, MN 55434
(612) 844-8484

OBJECTIVE

Proposal to receive credit through the University of Minnesota for experience in Grievance Handling

SUMMARY OF QUALIFICATIONS

- Four years as General President/Administrative Officer for Minneapolis Local American Postal Workers Union.
- Organizer of Grievance Handling training programs.
- Counselor to over 600 workers regarding grievances.
- Knowledge of labor laws and union contracts.

GRIEVANCE HANDLING ACCOMPLISHMENTS

As General President/Administrative Officer of Minneapolis Local American Postal Workers Union, 1983 to 1987:

COUNSELING

- Individually advised over 600 union members at risk of losing their jobs for reasons such as:
  Absenteeism
  Failure to pass requalification tests
  Conflicts with management and/or co-workers
  Contract interpretation
  Childcare and employment conflicts
  Alcohol and drug abuse related problems
  Disability
- Made government agency referrals for cases involving Equal Employment Opportunity complaints and other situations requiring strict confidentiality.
- Fought and won over 300 cases of employee discharges, working closely with national officers and the union's attorneys.
- Negotiated with management to resolve numerous cases outside of arbitration. Earned respect from management as a fair and credible mediator.
- Developed a contractual agreement, protecting employees from losing their preferred shift assignments when requesting, long-term light-duty positions.

TRAINING

- Served as the union's Director of Research and Education, offering programs to educate members in grievance handling, thus promoting the union's image as an organization dedicated to healthy management-labor relations.
- Organized ongoing Grievance Handling Training Program for officers, stewards, and members. Subjects included:
  Grievance Writing
  Role Playing of Grievances
  Perceptions of Grievance Problems
  Arbitration Preparations - Role of the Stewards in the Process
  Leadership of Stewards and Officers

(Continued)

- Developed and taught monthly classes on:
    - Contract Procedures and Interpretations
    - Human Relations
    - Union Organization
    - Occupation Safety and Health
    - Legislation
    - Equal Employment Opportunity
- Designed and administered tests.

WORK HISTORY

1983-1987	**General President/ Administrative Officer**	MINNEAPOLIS LOCAL AMERICAN POSTAL WORKERS UNION, Minneapolis, MN
1956-1983 & 1987-1993	**Transit Mail Expediter**	U.S. POSTAL SERVICE, Minneapolis, MN
1994-present	**Full-time Student**	UNIVERSITY OF MINNESOTA, Minneapolis, MN

> Marvin used this resume successfully to get school credit for some of his work experience. Notice the sequence of entries in the "Work History" section to emphasize the work he wants to get credit for. —S.I.
>
> P.S. Ordinarily we would NOT go as far back as the 1950s on a resume because that might invite age discrimination, but it is appropriate on this resume, where the aim is to get full college credit for a long work history.

- Resume writer: Susan Ireland -

JOHN GOMEZ

P.O. Box 1148, San Leandro, CA 94577

Home: (510) 352-6953 • Work: (510) 678-4259

OBJECTIVE

Internal Organizer for the AFL-CIO

HIGHLIGHTS

- Skilled at making alliances with workers and recruiting members.
- Experienced at organizing actions.
- Willing to relocate and work long, irregular hours.
- Current employer is willing to give me a leave-of-absence to participate in the program.

RELEVANT ACCOMPLISHMENTS

1971-present **Warehouseman** Lucky Stores, Inc., San Leandro, CA

RECRUITING

- Promoted the union by distributing pamphlets and showing my labor memorabilia dating from the 1800s (the largest private collection in California) at labor shows, schools, and fairgrounds.
- Recruited members from non-union trucking companies, spending time off the job explaining the benefits of membership.
- Publicly petitioned signatures for Democratic Party initiatives.

ORGANIZING ACTIONS

- Represented the area for the Coors Boycott Committee.
- Served as Captain in the Safeway boycott.
  - Hired an airplane to fly over the Oakland Coliseum, carrying the message "Boycott Safeway."
  - Got banners made.
  - Enforced schedules for picketers throughout the Bay Area.
- Participated in at least 50 strikes, boycotts, and informational pickets over the past 25 years.

TRAINING

- Logged in over 220 hours as on-the-job trainer of OSHA laws and forklift safety.

EDUCATION AND TRAINING

Organizing Techniques I
George Meany Center for Labor Studies, Silver Springs, MD

AFL-CIO Union Counseling Course
AFL-CIO Community Services and Santa Clara Central Labor Council

OSHA & Forklift Instructor Certification #1320
Ives & Associates and Safety Center of California

Teamster Support Volunteer Certification, Oakland, CA

Labor Studies Program, Laney College, Oakland, CA

- Resume writer: Susan Ireland -

Marty Robinson
42 Antelope Avenue
Hayward, CA 97881
(510) 360-4776

OBJECTIVE

Field Representative for Local 510

DEMONSTRATED EFFECTIVENESS

- Effectively negotiated and arbitrated grievances and contracts.
  - Served on three contract negotiating committees, each strengthening the union shop.
  - Codeveloped first steward training classes for Local 510.
  - Enforced collective bargaining agreements, health and safety standards, and grievance procedures as Rotating Floor Steward or Permanent Shop Steward since 1976.
- Chaired strike committees in 1989 and 1992, developing picketing plans, choosing picket captains, and informing membership of legal behavior on the picket line.
- Codeveloped and led Local 510 affirmative action workshops, using bilingual and biculturals skills to stress commonalties among people.
- Conducted training and strategy sessions for U. C. labor and academic professionals, resulting in Partnership Programs.

WORK HISTORY

1973-present **Journeyman Installer**
SIGN, DISPLAY, AND ALLIED CRAFTS, LOCAL 510, I.B.P.A.T.

1990 **Primary Campaign Manager**
WILSON RILES, JR., MAYORAL CANDIDATE, OAKLAND

1987-90 **Teacher (World Cultures/Spanish/Bilingual)**
OAKLAND UNIFIED SCHOOL DISTRICT

EDUCATION

B.A., Comparative Culture, University of California, Irvine, 1973

Graduate Studies, Latin American Culture, Stanford University

MEMBERSHIPS

Alameda County Central Labor Council
Local 510 Political Action Committee
Oakland Direct Action Committee
Former Member, A.P.R.I & C.B. T.U.

- Resume writer: Susan Ireland -

Mixed Bag

BONNIE CORNING
77 Rotterdam Road
New York, NY 10045
(212) 565-5656

OBJECTIVE

General Organizer/International Representative

HIGHLIGHTS

- Over 13 years as Representative for International Brotherhood of Teamsters; over 2 years as International Representative.
- Expertise in labor aspects of complex legal activities, including:

Merger/acquisitions	Collective bargaining
Employee stock ownership plans	Seniority integration
Community action campaigns	Strike coordination

- Proven ability to organize members.
- Effective negotiator of collective bargaining agreements and relocation agreements.
- Advocate of employee rights and adjudicator of labor/management disputes on various boards of adjustment.

PROFESSIONAL EXPERIENCE

REPRESENTATION

- Administered collective bargaining provisions for 7 contracts at over 15 locations for more than 1000 members in numerous crafts.
- Chaired Atlantic Air negotiations.
- Adjudicated labor/management disputes as Chair of Atlantic Air System Board of Adjustment and Continental Eastern Field Board of Adjustment.
- Served as Chair of Continental/National Grievance Board of Adjustment, successfully adjudicating over 200 cases.
- Chaired Continental/National Seniority Integration Committee, developing consensus.
- Served as Employee Advocate at all levels of dispute including arbitration.
- Prepared and testified for class and craft hearings before National Mediation Board.
- Managed a 6-week strike at Continental in New York.

ORGANIZING

- Organized for major airline campaigns, involving 1000s of employees at multiple cities nationwide; served at all levels including Campaign Coordinator, Regional Coordinator, and Field Representative. Campaigns included:

  American Airlines · Atlantic Air · Continental/Texas International
  Pan Am/National Merger · PSA/USAir
- Saved 200 Continental jobs through effective community action campaign.

WORK HISTORY

1993-present	Columbia University	**Labor/Community Liaison**
1981-93	International Brotherhood of Teamsters	**Representative, Local # 323 and #457**
		International Representative

EDUCATION

Liberal Arts, University of Milwaukee
Numerous seminars on labor issues

RELEVANT PRESENTATIONS

Instructor, Corporate Campaigns, Summer Institute for Union Women, SUNY, Albany

Panel member, E.S.O.P Seminar, Columbia University

Workshop Leader, Organizing Clerical Workers, I.B.T. Women's Conference

- Resume writer: Susan Ireland -

Ken Briggs

417 Christopher Road
Springstown, B.C. 4W5 W5W
(709) 797-7979

Job Objective: Entry-level position working with animals.

PERSONAL QUALIFICATIONS

- 13 years experience in horse, cat, and dog care.
- Two years paid work with animals.
- Receptionist experience.
- Dependable, hard worker.

RELEVANT EXPERIENCE

1993-94: FISH FEEDER - Pacific Aqua Farms, Campbell River, B.C.

- Carried out daily feeding program for ten pens of farmed fish.
- Learned by observation to recognize health problems of fish, and adjusted water, temperature, and food to help them stay healthy.

1992: KENNEL WORKER and RECEPTIONIST- Nanaimo Society for the Prevention of Cruelty to Animals (S.P.C.A.), Nanaimo, B.C.

KENNEL WORKER
- Maintained Cat Room in clean and orderly condition.
- Fed and watered animals and monitored for signs of illness.
- Under veterinary supervision, injected animals with required medicines and immunizations.

RECEPTIONIST
- Trained volunteers in animal care procedures at S.P.C.A.
- Assisted customers in filling out forms.
- Answered telephone, directing information inquiries.

1981-94: HOME ANIMAL CARE

- Tended my personal horse every day for 13 years, cared for pet dogs and cats over several years, and assisted in care of breeder dogs (a family business.)
- Fed, bathed, groomed, and exercised animals to maintain health.
- Nursed animals through injuries, illnesses, and pregnancy, seeking veterinary assistance when needed.

References available on request

- Resume writer: Cory Beneker -

Mixed Bag

John L. Mailer

201 Sixth Street
San Francisco, CA 94111
(415) 444-4444

OBJECTIVE: A position in mail services.

SUMMARY

- Over twenty years U.S. Postal Service experience.
- Prompt and dependable with a very steady work history.
- Easily assume responsibility, work with minimum supervision
- Quick learner; easily adapted to Post Office computerization.
- Pleasant straightforward approach; work well with others.

RELEVANT SKILLS

Mail Room Operations
- Knowledgeable and efficient in all phases of mail and package handling:

  -Sorting   -Bulk Mailings
  -Weighing   -Window Services
  -Deliveries   -Inventory Control
  -Issuing Receipts   -Record Keeping

Mail Room Management
- Kept accurate records and billed Business Reply Mail accounts.
- Temporarily assumed Postmaster responsibilities of a U.S. Post Office servicing over 15,000 households and businesses.

  -Managed over $50,000 in postal service funds and inventory.
  -Scheduled staff of ten employees.
  -Accurately kept books and financial records.
  -Ensured customer and staff safety and physical plant upkeep.

WORK HISTORY

Volunteer	*Lutheran Community Services*, San Francisco	1994-present
Courtesy Clerk	*Jones Food and Drug*, Las Vegas, NV	1993
Laborer	*Local Union 448*, Wood River, IL	1992-1993
Postal Employee	*U. S. Postal Service*, Wood River, IL	1968-1992

EDUCATION

Postal Employee Development Courses (PEDC), St. Louis, MO
Training included: Customer Service and Bulk Mailing
Johnson City Community High School Graduate
Studied Math and Science

- Resume written by Roving Resume Writers -

DENNIS E. JONES

3344 Wilbur Street, Richmond CA , 94804
Tel. (510) 544-5444

OBJECTIVE: A Position in Mail Room Operations

SUMMARY of QUALIFICATIONS

- 14 years of mail room and letter carrier experience for U.S. Postal Service, including 6 years supervising mail handlers, letter carriers and clerical staff.
- Able to accurately sort up to 600 pieces of mail per hour; work well under pressure.
- Perfect safety record during entire career in mail services; take safety procedures seriously.
- A team player who works well with others.
- A self-motivated hard driver; dedicated to getting the job done.

RELEVANT SKILLS

Mail Room Operations

- Skilled in all phases of mail room operations, including:
  - Sorting
  - Deliveries
  - Record Keeping
  - Issuing Receipts
  - Inventory Control

- Safely operated such mail-handling equipment as:
  - Letter Sorting Machines (LSM)
  - Flat Sorting Machines (FSM)
  - Optical Character Readers (OCR)
  - Delivery Bar Code Systems (DBC)

Supervision

- As supervisor of mail handlers, letter carriers and clerks:
  - Accurately kept employees' time sheets and attendance records;
  - Administered quality control checks of employees' work and maintained quality control log;
  - Monitored staff compliance with safety procedures, completing necessary safety records;
  - Motivated and encouraged staff members regarding attendance, work performance and adherance to organization policies when needed.

Mail Delivery

- Delivered mail to up to 500 households daily, with accuracy and energy.
- Responsibly carried accountable mail items such as CODs, certified mail, and registered mail.
- Kept records of address changes and promptly forwarded mail to new addresses.
- Ensured mailboxes were properly labelled and mail picked up on time.

EMPLOYMENT HISTORY

United States Postal Service, San Francisco	1980-Present
Mail Room Supervisor, Mail Handler, Letter Carrier	
United States Navy, San Francisco	1975-79
Electronics Technician	

EDUCATION and TRAINING

United States Postal Service's Postal Employee Development Courses:
- First-Aid and CPR
- Equipment Operations
- Leadership and Supervision

City College of San Francisco, San Francisco
  A.A. Degree - General Education

- Resume written by Roving Resume Writers -

Mixed Bag

Vince R. Tineberg
857 Belview Street
San Francisco CA 94444
415-777-9999

OBJECTIVE

Advertising Sales for a TV or radio station.

SUMMARY OF QUALIFICATIONS

- Four years experience producing satisfied customers.
- Track record in winning customer trust.
- Unusual commitment to excellence in all I do.

RELEVANT ACCOMPLISHMENTS

As Classic Motorcycle Broker:

- Matched customers with vehicles, consistently winning the trust of customers who appreciated my honesty.
  - Wrote and placed ads which successfully attracted potential buyers.
  - Asked questions and identified buyer's needs and preferences in order to locate a perfect match.
  - Called on network of potential suppliers to find an appropriate motorcycle.
  - Expanded network through cold-calling, and maintained index card file to keep track of detailed supplier information.
  - Filled customer needs within their time limits, and seized opportunities without delay.
- Negotiated numerous agreements to buy and sell motorcycles.
  - Acquired equipment at unusually low prices.
  - Consistently produced a sense of satisfaction for all parties concerned.
  - Never received a complaint from a buyer or seller.

As Driver & Dispatcher:

- Established excellent rapport with customers and co-workers, and presented an unusually clean appearance.
  - Kept cab immaculate and wore white shirt with black coat, tie, and hat.
  - Earned the respect of long-time drivers by learning a new city in less than a month, and maintained their support after a highly unusual promotion to dispatcher after less than a year.
  - Quickly sensed customer's mood and social tone, responding precisely and appropriately with friendliness or distance.
- Juggled 70 drivers to respond quickly to cab requests throughout San Francisco, ensuring that loyal customers received preferential treatment.

WORK HISTORY

1992-present	**Classic Motorcycle Broker**	BELVIEW DREAMER, San Francisco CA
1991-93	**Dispatcher & Driver**	APPLE CAB COMPANY, San Francisco CA
1989-91	**Fishing Boat Deck Boss**	ALASKAN EMERALD, Swiss Harbor AK

- Resume writer: Jenny Mish -

Bill Gates

7890 Wakuset Street
Prince Rupert, BC 2W4 L9F
407-744-4070

Bill was a recovering alcoholic who wanted to use his experience to help other members of his band (tribe) in their struggles with alcohol. Fortunately, his personal experience prepared him for the job better than any degree. (For non-Canadian readers, "counselling" is spelled with two l's in Canada. —Ed.

JOB OBJECTIVE: Drug and Alcohol Counsellor

RELEVANT EXPERIENCE

Counselling
- Provided firm and supportive drug and alcohol counselling for families and individuals, and counselled people on the street with addiction problems.
- Referred clients to inpatient treatment programs when needed, and provided introductory and follow-up counselling to extend its effectiveness.
- Arranged three A.A. meetings per week for people in recovery.

Work with Youth
- Shared personal experiences in schools, helping students to understand their parents' background.
- Showed students from Grades 5-12 video tapes on alcohol and drug issues, and organized follow-up "talking circles" so they could talk about their families.

Community Planning
- Maintained contact with the following groups to coordinate information and programs:
police	probation officers	teachers	family members
band members	hospital staff	holistic health teams.	
- Distributed information throughout the community to increase public awareness of drug and alcohol issues using local television, newsletters, and posters.
- Organized and presented drug and alcohol prevention workshops for various groups and the community-at-large.

Administration
- Assisted in the development of funding applications for drug and alcohol programs.
- Kept track of visitors to the community on behalf of the local Band.
- Maintained client files and wrote regular reports to the Medical Services Branch in Vancouver.

EDUCATION

1993 **Counsellor Intervention Training, Personal Growth and Roles of Helpers, Assisting Arthritis Patients, and Health and Human Services Programming,** Sal'i'shan Institute Society, Penticton, BC.

1991 **G.E.D. Grade 12 Equivalency Degree,** Carihi High School, Campbell River, BC.

RELEVANT WORK HISTORY

1992-94 **Drug and Alcohol Counsellor,** Heiltsuk Band Council, Bella Bella, BC.

1991-Present **Volunteer Street Worker,** North Island Drug and Alcohol Information Society, throughout BC coast area.

Other experience in Fish Processing, Commercial Fishing, and Logging.

- Resume writer: Cory Beneker -

Al Murfield
330 S. Becker #222
Santa Monica, CA 99999
434-4343

OBJECTIVE

A position as Living Skills Instructor for the Transition Service Agency.

HIGHLIGHTS

- Over ten years experience empowering individuals for independent living.
- Experienced peer counselor and highly praised supervisor.
- Keen judgment in designing personalized challenges and following them through to success.

RELEVANT SKILLS & EXPERIENCE

INDEPENDENT LIVING SKILLS

- As a Personal Care Attendant, helped three patients recover living skills:
  - Retaught basic skills such as dressing, hygiene, laundry, housekeeping, cooking, reading, and math.
  - Arranged for proper medical and psychological care, keeping appointments and following prescriptions and other treatment instructions.
  - Coached skill development in employment preparation and job search, securing driver's license, attending to income taxes and pending legal and insurance actions.
  - Researched and arranged for additional services such as a stroke recovery support group and displaced homemaker's networking, securing wheelchairs and walkers when needed.
- As a volunteer Physical Therapy Aide, created and implemented recreational activities to exercise specific muscle groups for patients recovering from accidents and illnesses.
- As Guest Information Coordinator for a 200-bed youth hostel, provided basic information to international travelers unfamiliar with common American customs and laws.
  - Provided bus schedules, shopping information, and accompanied group tours of local museums and other places of interest.

PEER COUNSELING SKILLS

- Provided up to 20 hours per week in volunteer peer counseling and informational support for the Shanti Foundation and The Center:
  - Provided short-term and open-ended one-on-one counseling, managing 6-8 cases with weekly clinical supervision.
  - Cofacilitated weekly peer counseling and health education groups.
  - Received 110 hours of initial training, and additional monthly seminars in:

Effective Communication	Facilitation Skills	Addictions
Identity Formation	Crisis Intervention	Grief & Loss
Cross-Cultural Issues	Domestic Violence	Sexual Abuse
Post-Traumatic Stress Disorder		

  - Kept clear records of all activities, including progress reports and written assessments, ensuring that clinical supervisors, doctors, and management personnel could effectively monitor services provided.
  - Assessed needs and provided referrals, matching people with other agencies and in-house services such as a food & clothing bank and in-home care.

- Continued -

SUPERVISORY AND TRAINING SKILLS

- Trained and supervised dozens of customer service workers in three resort hotel management positions, receiving frequent praise for skill in managing people. For example:
  - Supervised 24 employees at two Glacier National Park hotels, creating weekly schedules, providing performance feedback, and building strong cooperative teams.
    - Identified current skills levels and assigned tasks to progressively challenge employees and build skills in customer service, record keeping, and accounting.
    - Provided leadership for young workers, such as a clerk who became a front office manager.
  - Served as safety coordinator, training staff in emergency procedures, identifying and reducing hazards, and complying with guidelines.
- As a senior volunteer, mentored new volunteer counselors for Shanti and The Center.

WORK HISTORY

1981-91	**Personal Care Attendant**	INDEPENDENTLY, Irvine & Los Angeles, CA
1992-93	**Volunteer Peer Counselor**	SHANTI FOUNDATION & THE CENTER, Los Angeles, CA
1992-93	**Guest Information Coordinator**	AMERICAN YOUTH HOSTEL, Santa Monica, CA
1992	**Volunteer Physical Therapy Aide**	INDEPENDENTLY, Santa Monica, CA
1991 & 1993	**Office Manager & Night Auditor**	GLACIER PARK INC., Glacier National Park, MT
1991-93	**Front Office Supervisor**	LOEWS SANTA MONICA BEACH HOTEL, CA

EDUCATION

35 hours of A.A. coursework, Santa Monica Community College, including:

Psychology	Interpersonal Communication
Academic Survival	Eliminating Self-Defeating Behaviors

Compare this with Al's very different resume in the "Food Service" chapter! Here we relied entirely on Al's volunteer work to market him for a career change. Notice how we reversed the usual chronology of dates to further de-emphasize the hotel work. —J.M.

- Resume writer: Jenny Mish -

Mixed Bag

Autumn Diego

415-924-1325

23 Robin's Nest Rd.
San Rafael, CA 95555

JOB OBJECTIVE: Nutritional and herbal consultant with a comprehensive holistic healing center in the Bay Area.

SUMMARY OF QUALIFICATIONS

- Four years experience as a nutritional consultant.
- Certified Nutritionist and Herbal Practitioner.
- Empathetic and intuitive listener.
- Detail-oriented and well organized.
- Moderately fluent in Spanish.

TRAINING AND EDUCATION

National Institute of Nutritional Education
  Nutritionist Training in progress

Berkeley Institute of Chinese Herbology
  Intensive Introduction to Chinese Medicine
  Herbal Practitioner Training in progress

Intensive Seminars in:
  Chinese and Ayurvedic Herbology, Planetary Herbology
  Vitamin Therapy for Major Illnesses with Michael Murray, MD and ND

Specialized areas of independent study:
  Alternative Cancer and AIDS Treatment, Fasting, Macrobiotics, Life Extension, Tibetan Medicine, Homeopathy

RELEVANT ACCOMPLISHMENTS

HEALTH EDUCATOR

As Nutritional Consultant at Living Foods and at Vitamin City:

- Disseminated herbal and nutritional information to hundreds of people weekly.
- Developed trusting on-going relationships with dozens of customers and salespeople.
- Listened perceptively to identify customer's personal health needs.
- Clearly explained complex physiological systems and functions.
- Motivated people to think holistically and change habits for healthier living.

ORGANIZER

As Vitamin Buyer at Living Foods:

- Doubled vitamin department sales over two months through excellent customer service and product promotion.
- Effectively managed vitamin department by maintaining large inventory, supervising employees, and keeping organized records.

As Public Educator at Greenpeace:

- Increased awareness and motivated thousands of people to take action by speaking publicly to large groups and appearing on TV and radio.

WORK HISTORY

1993-present	VITAMIN BUYER & NUTRITIONAL CONSULTANT	Living Foods, San Rafael
1990-92	MANAGER & NUTRITIONIST	Vitamin City, San Francisco
1989-90	PUBLIC EDUCATOR	Greenpeace, San Francisco
1987-88	RETAIL SALESPERSON	Outback Clothing, San Francisco
1985-87	OWNER & OPERATOR	Starlight Clothing & Accessories, San Francisco

- Resume writer: Jenny Mish -

Matt Parker

Guitarist, electric and acoustic — Mandolin

Post Office Box 3289 • Berkeley CA 94703
(510) 658-9229

Looking to play lead and rhythm guitars with vocals and establish a versatile dance band with ...attitude ...good equipment ...playing a good mixture of blues, rock, original and cover tunes

★ Serious, committed musician who knows how to have a good time.
★ Over 20 years experience playing guitar in bands.
★ Contribute actively to making a band an exciting entity; good at working with a group to establish its unique sound.
★ Theatrically oriented — into lighting, mood, sweat, romance; dynamic and charismatic on stage; enjoy stimulating the crowd.
★ Extensive roadie work with other bands: driving, lighting, setup, teardown.
★ Own and provide sound reinforcement and recording equipment.

BAND EXPERIENCE

FEELIN' EASY BAND (1994) Star Club, San Pablo CA – country and blues standards
Alternate Lead Guitar, & Vocals   (clubs and country bars)

CROSSROADS (1993) Berkeley CA - with Sheila G. and Ginger – folk and old time blues
Acoustic Guitars, Mandolin, & Vocals   (street fairs, busking, and rest homes)

LOST HIGHWAY (1992) East Bay & Contra Costa – country with steel guitar, covers & originals
Lead Guitar, Vocals, and PA equipment   (clubs and country bars)

LOOSE DIAMONDS (1990-91) East Bay & Contra Costa – Bluegrass-oriented rock, cover & originals
Guitars, Mandolin, Vocals – cofounder   (parties, clubs, weddings, special events)

THE MERCURIES (1987-89) Oakland CA – original and cover rock & roll, '60s-'80s dance music (clubs)
Lead Guitar, Backup & Lead Vocals

ROADHOUSE (1986-87) Berkeley CA – country and rock club dance band (clubs, parties)
Lead Guitar, Backup Vocals – cofounder

BUZZARD MOUNTAIN (1980-81) Oneonta NY – southern rock, blues rock, kickass dance band (clubs)
Second Lead Guitar, Backup Vocals – cofounder

WHISKEY RIVER BAND (1979-80) Oneonta NY – southern blues, country rock, bluegrass (clubs)
Lead Guitar, Backup Vocal

SOUTHERN ADIRONDACK HARD TIME BAND (1978-79) Oneonta NY – rock country, bluegrass (clubs)
Lead Guitar, Backup Vocals

FIREHOUSE (1976) Oneonta NY – blues and hard rock (clubs)
Rhythm Guitar, Backup Vocal

IRON HORSE (1975-76) Cooperstown NY – early metal hardrock (very theatrical/showy)
Rhythm Guitar, Backup Vocals – cofounder

STORM (1974-75) Cooperstown NY – early metal hard rock (high schools)
Lead Singer, Lead Guitar – founder

EQUIPMENT OWNED

— Amplification & Sound Reinforcement —

- Yamaha MR-1642 mixing console
- Mackie 1604 Mixer
- ART Multiverb III Effects Processor
- Simetrix Compressor Gate
- Rane EQ
- Mesa Boogie Mark III combo amp
- GK bass amp
- Peavey Express 112
- Tascam 238 Syncaset 8-Track
- Alesis Microverb III
- Crest FA901 Power Amp
- QSC Mono-Monitor Amp
- JBL MR825 15" 2-way mains
- Community 12" 2-way monitors
- Shure microphones (one 58, one 57)
- AKG CS1000 Cond. Mike
- Audio Technica Vocal Mikes
- ADA Midi-Controller
- D'Armond Weeper
- 100-foot 16x4 snake

— Instruments —

- Fender Stratocaster
- Fender Telecaster
- Gibson Les Paul, custom
- Jackson Soloist solid body electric
- Gibson Firebird
- Yamaha APX-7 Electric Acoustic
- Guild D-40
- R.L. Givens Mandolin, A-style
- Spector Bass   Jazz/Precision
- Talk Box; Boss and Korg tuners

- Resume written by Matt Parker & Yana Parker -

Mixed Bag

Edward Q. Sanchez

1224 Colombus St., San Francisco, CA 94124
415-822-3123

OBJECTIVE: A position in airport security or police dispatch

SUMMARY OF QUALIFICATIONS

- Several years experience and training as a military security specialist.
- Experience and training in monitoring alarm systems; training in dispatch.
- Excellent leadership skills and training.
- Training in emergency response and police duties.
- Customer service and public relations skills and experience; bilingual (Spanish).

MILITARY SERVICE

1984-88 United States Air Force — Received Honorable Discharge
Security Specialist
- Provided security for priority resources vital to U.S. Defense.

   TRAINING & EXPERIENCE 1986-87

   - Rose in rank to *Security Controller* through training/experience as:
     - Response Team Member   – Response Team Leader
     - Assistant Alarm Monitor   – Alarm Monitor
     - Assistant Security Controller   – Security Controller
   - Also trained in air base ground defense and security dispersal.

   AWARDS & HONORS

   - Selected as a member of the Emergency Services Team. 1987
   - Received Good Conduct Medal.
   - Received Air Force Achievement Medal for outstanding leadership abilities, performance in duties, and for helping to establish a flight training program for security police.
   - Selected by Military Board for Sr. Airman for excelling above peers. 1986
   - Received Airman of the Month award for outstanding performance and presentation. 1985

CIVILIAN EXPERIENCE

1988 to   Speedy Shipping, San Francisco, CA
present   *Cargo Handler, Courier, Tractor-Trailer Driver*
- Loaded and unloaded containers of freight; delivered and picked up packages.
- Promoted to courier position after excellent performance in training.
- Selected for promotion to tractor-trailer driver.
- Requested to train incoming employees.
- Frequently praised by dispatch department for excellent and efficient service.
- Trained on own time in dispatching for future promotion.

EDUCATION

San Mateo College, 1989–90
Coursework in Administration of Justice

- Resume writer: Rhonda Findling -

WILLIAM NEIBERLAND

1434 Rose Street
Berkeley, CA 94705
Home (510) 858-5858
Work (510) 797-9797

William enjoys management in blue-collar settings. He started out working on a dock, and a few years after getting a degree, he returned to shipping to step into management.—S.I.

Objective: Management in NVOCC, marine supervision, freight forwarding, warehousing, or trucking.

SUMMARY OF QUALIFICATIONS

- Over 15 years management experience in the shipping industry.
- Experience in both warehousing and container freight operations.
- Proven ability to meet deadlines and generate profits under difficult conditions.
- Strong record of providing personable and professional customer service.
- Successful history of promoting productive labor relations with Teamsters and ILWU.

RELEVANT EXPERIENCE & ACCOMPLISHMENTS

1988-present   **General Manager**   QUINLAN CORPORATION, Oakland, CA
Managed a 30,000-square-foot container freight station, loading and unloading up to 150 TEU per week of containerized marine cargo.

- Maintained profit margin during recession by raising labor efficiency and controlling expenses.
- Increased productivity by establishing cooperative relations with ILWU dock personnel.
- Provided high-quality customer service for up to 10 steamship lines, each having different policies, procedures, and personalities.
- Consistently met shipping deadlines, even on short notice, while maintaining a record on no lost-time accidents during a five year period.
- Worked closely with U.S. Customs authorities to expedite cargo movement.
- Supervised administrative and dock employees: hired, trained, evaluated, and terminated.

1985-88   **Operations Manager**   QUINLAN CORPORATION, Oakland, CA
Oversaw day-to-day operations of the dock and office.

1982-85   **Assistant Terminal Manager** INTERNATIONAL FREIGHT TERMINAL, San Francisco
Directed container freight operations in a facility that handled cargo bound to and from a variety of overseas ports, involving diverse Customs requirements and language issues.

- Managed and directed up to 20 personnel in transloading of 300-400 TEUs per week from China.
- Provided warehousing for, and oversaw delivery to, Northern California Target stores.
- Supervised 35 Teamster employees, including hiring, scheduling, disciplining, and firing.

1979-81   **Architectural Model Maker** FREELANCE, Bay Area, CA
Designed and built commercial and marine models for clients throughout the country.

1975-78   **Dock Foreman**   SHIPPER'S TERMINAL, San Francisco
Promoted to Dock Foreman after only 10 months as Warehouseman.

EDUCATION & TRAINING

Management Training Course, Lawrence Community College

Resume writer: Susan Ireland

MARTIN S. NAGRABSKI

4429 S. Waterfront
San Francisco, CA 94444
415-454-4545

Objective: A position as casino dealer on board a cruise ship.

HIGHLIGHTS OF QUALIFICATIONS

- ♣ Eight years experience dealing in Las Vegas casinos.
- ♠ Recently completed dealing refresher course.
- ♥ Reliable, loyal, and hardworking.
- ♦ Thrive in casino atmosphere.
- ♣ Enjoy working with all kinds of people.

EXPERIENCE AND SPECIAL SKILLS

Games of Chance

- Developed thorough knowledge of rules of games of chance, and dealt thousands of hands of:
    - ♣ Blackjack   ♠ Roulette   ♥ Big 6 Wheel   ♦ Mini Baccarat.
- Supervised dealer trainees at Barbary Coast Casino and at the Las Vegas School of Dealing.
- Quickly and accurately calculated customer winnings.
- Kept the table active.

Customer Relations

- Greeted customers with a welcoming smile, encouraging them to play.
- Related well with all personalities, and handled difficult customers with diplomacy.
- Always enlisted the help of supervisors to handle exceptional situations.

Back House

- Currently bondable; always maintained a spotless record.
- Precisely tallied end of day intake, and computed appropriate taxes.
- Got along well with other dealers and casino employees.
- Worked for the same family-owned chain for seven years.

EMPLOYMENT HISTORY

Recycler	Self-employed	Reno, NV	1988-1993
Casino Dealer	Barbary Coast Hotel & Casino	Las Vegas NV	1982-1987
Casino Dealer	Royal Inn Casino	Las Vegas NV	1981
Casino Dealer	Western Hotel	Las Vegas NV	1980
Computer Operator	City of Waterbury	Waterbury CT	1978-1979

EDUCATION & SPECIALIZED TRAINING

Las Vegas School of Dealing, Las Vegas NV	Refresher Course	1994
Las Vegas School of Dealing, Las Vegas NV	Six-week Course	1979
Computer Processing Institute, East Hartford CT	Certificate	1977
University of Connecticut, Waterbury CT	Math	1972-1973

- Resume written by Roving Resume Writers -

Stephanie Maple

459 Sixty-fifth St.
Baton Rouge, Louisiana 70806
(504) 333-9870

Objective: Entry level position in the field of Cosmetology.

PROFILE

- Graduate of Lockworks Academie of Cosmetology.

- Chosen to open the Brocato International Fashion Show.

- Career-oriented. Dedicated to professionalism.

- Able to set and achieve goals. Punctual. Reliable.

- Special ability to communicate easily with clients.

EDUCATION

Graduate, 1994, LOCKWORKS ACADEMIE OF COSMETOLOGY, Baton Rouge, LA
Awarded "Student of the Month"
Graduate, 1993, Assumption High School, Napoleonville, LA

SKILLS & EXPERIENCE
acquired at Lockworks Academie of Cosmetology

- Haircutting and Hair Styling

- Shampoo/Sets • Hair Coloring • Highlighting

- Fingerwaves • Pincurling • Precision Roller Placement

- Permanent Waves/Relaxers/Soft Curls • Wax Depilatory

- Hair and Scalp Treatments • Skin Care

- Manicures • Facials • Pedicures

- Make-up Applications • Clinical Practicum

- Speech & Customer Relations

WORK HISTORY

Seafood Processor, Errol Cajun Foods, Pierre Part LA, two years
•Set highest productivity levels.
Student, Lockworks Academie of Cosmetology

- Resume writer: Jim Ledford -

SHERRY LYNN HILL
MANICURIST • ESTHETICIAN
*Specializing in therapeutic massage of face/hands/feet
to redirect energy flow, rejuvenate the skin and nails,
and restore an overall positive self-image.*
888 Denuba Street • Oakland CA 94612
(510) 123-4567

SUMMARY OF QUALIFICATIONS
- Over 8 years experience in the field of personal beauty services, working with a wide range of clients from all economic levels.
- Able to accurately assess the client's real needs and wants.
- Strong artistic and esthetic sense in fashion, color, and design.
- Easy to work with; well liked by both customers and co-workers.
- Willing to take the initiative and take on new responsibilities.

RELEVANT EXPERIENCE

SENSITIVE CUSTOMER SERVICE
- Developed uniquely **effective techniques for massaging clients'** face, hands and feet -- using oils, scrubs, and aromas.
- Able to **tune in sensitively** to customers' physical stresses, working with acupressure points to **ease pain** and **increase their self-awareness** of the body's condition.

CLIENTELE DEVELOPMENT
- **Developed a loyal following of repeat customers** through:
  - Expertise in **producing a fine end product** that is natural looking, beautiful, and durable.
  - **Responsible, trustworthy advice** on relevant health issues.

CREATIVE DESIGN
- **Won first place in two Nail Art competitions,** for unique, beautiful and tasteful designs.

PRODUCT EXPERTISE
- **Thoroughly familiar with product characteristics and applications:**
  - Sculptured nail products: glues, tips, wraps, hardeners.
  - Skin care products: creams, cleansers, scrubs, facial packs.

HEALTH KNOWLEDGE
- **Scrupulous in applying the principles of sanitary practices.**
- Recognize **problems requiring referral** to medical professionals.

EMPLOYMENT HISTORY
1988-present	Manicurist	Affiliated with IRENE SARGENT, Oakland
1987-88	Manicurist	FANCY FINGERS, FEET & FACES, Alameda
1987	Manicurist	Independent operator: THE ELEGANT NAIL
1982-86	Loan Dept.	WELLS FARGO BANK, Bay Area

EDUCATION & TRAINING
Manicuring, Physical Fitness, Art, Interior Design - Laney College
Skin Care - Alameda Beauty College

- Resume writer: Yana Parker -

Maxine Gordon

qualifications

- Experienced with a wide variety of makeup applications: weddings, portraits, portfolio shots, promotional literature & camouflage makeup.

- Demonstrated success in sales and customer relations -- achieved highest monthly cosmetic sales for 12 consecutive months.

- Broad-based knowledge of skin care, nutrition, exercise and stress reduction.

- Knowledge of special effects makeup including: aging, monsters, bald caps, limited prosthetics, character development and hair work.

- Experience training, hiring, supervising and scheduling personnel.

experience

ESTEE LAUDER SPA, I. MAGNIN, UNION SQUARE, S.F., CA **Esthetician** *Facials, body care, waxing and makeup*	1989 -1991
ESTEE LAUDER, I. MAGNIN, UNION SQUARE, S.F., CA **Beauty Advisor** *Sales and makeup*	1988 - 1989
DELOITTE HASKINS & SELLS, San Francisco, CA **Graphic Assistant** *Graphic assistance with promotional materials*	1987 - 1988
JUNGLE JIM'S, Bellevue, WA **Beverage Manager** *Purchasing, personnel and operations management*	1983 - 1986
HARRY'S, HANSON BAKING CO., Seattle, WA **General Manager** *Cost control, purchasing, banking, personnel and operations management*	1980 - 1983

> I decided to create a resume that would have the feel of a brochure while including all the vital information of a resume, since freelance and part-time work are common in Maxine's field. We created a contemporary and aesthetic "look" for her resume, which is fitting for work that emphasizes aesthetics and creativity. Since most of the responsibilities in her field are generic, and many of her jobs unrelated, I felt it was appropriate to use minimalist job descriptions, while emphasizing her uniqueness in the summary at the top. —L.A.

training

ESTEE LAUDER TRAINING STAFF, S.F., CA, Continued Training	1989 - 1991
ATARASHI DESIGN SCHOOL, Seattle, WA, Certification	1985
JOE BLASCO SCHOOL OF FILM MAKEUP, L.A., CA. Certification	1987

licenses

Licensed Esthetician, Washington & California

references

Available upon request.

Maxine Gordon   •   Esthetician   •   221 Alcatraz Avenue   •   Oakland, CA 94609   •   510/655/9928

- Resume writer: Laila Atallah -

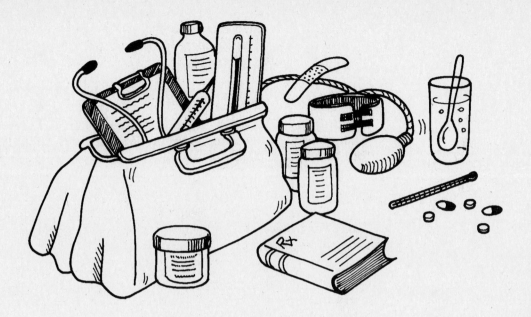

RESUME CLINIC

Tough Problems
& Creative Solutions

NOW . . . What if you are tripping over problems?

And what if you can't think of the right way to express yourself?

Check out the advice on the following pages, where we'll offer some creative solutions for each of the problems below:

PROBLEM #1: No clear job target. "I'm kind of vague about the job I'm looking for—so I don't know what to say for a 'Job Objective.'"

SOLUTION:

Getting clearer about your job direction is CRUCIAL, and it's not as impossible as you might think. You'll have to take a little time out to do some exploring and find out what you'd really LIKE to do and CAN do. One great way is called **information interviewing.** See page 175.

*(I can hear you muttering: "Don't DO this to me, Yana—**I don't have TIME for this stuff**." But without a clear focus on your goal, you can endlessly spin in circles. THAT'S what takes TIME.)*

PROBLEM #2: More than one job target. "I want to keep my options open, keep my resume general so I can use it to apply for LOTS of different jobs."

SOLUTION:

Don't do it. **Make a separate resume for EACH different type of job,** and modify each version at least a little, depending on the skills and experience called for. A generic resume is like generic anything else: weaker, less impressive, less effective.

▶ **TIP:** Write a resume targeted at the most APPEALING job possibility FIRST. It will probably bring out the skills you're most interested in using—and market you for job satisfaction based on your true creative spark.

PROBLEM #3: Lack of experience. "I think I could do the job, but I don't have much experience to put on my resume."

SOLUTIONS:

Here are several ways to deal with lack of experience (which could mean lack of ANY experience, lack of RECENT experience, lack of PAID experience, lack of RELEVANT experience):

a. **FIX it. Get some minimal experience** in the field before you apply for the REAL job you want—either through **short-term temporary employment, or briefly working for free** in a similar role, if at all possible.

b. **VIEW the source of your experience differently**. Make sure you are counting ALL your experience, whether it involved pay or not. Volunteer work, self-employment, or even a hobby, ALL COUNT AS EXPERIENCE. You can even **include this unpaid work in your Work History** to help prove you have skills and experience. Just think up a reasonable job title for the unpaid work (for example, "Freelance Guitarist" or "Coordinator of Volunteers" or "Owner/Manager") and be sure to label the "Employment" section "*Work* History" rather than "Employment History."

(continued on page 176)

ABOUT INFORMATION INTERVIEWING

"INFORMATION INTERVIEWING" is a rather fancy phrase for a very straightforward, logical, and extremely helpful NETWORKING idea. Here's what you do:

a. Think back on your most enjoyable days of work (or play), and **jot down some ideas about what you think you're best at and enjoy doing**—not actual job titles, but SKILLS and ABILITIES and TALENTS and INTERESTS—all the things you bring into your various jobs and hobbies.

b. **Ask around** among all your friends, relatives, friends of relatives, neighbors, people you used to work with, ANYBODY, and **get from them the names of people who are already at work using these same SKILLS and abilities that YOU most enjoy using**—somebody you could interview for information (NOT for a job, just for information about that line of work).

c. **Ask** each friend, relative, etc., **for permission to mention THEIR name** when you call the person they recommend.

d. **Call each of the people** they recommend and:

- mention the friend or relative's name;

- **ask for 15 or 20 minutes of their time** to visit with them and learn a bit more about THEIR line of work;

- **explain that you think you might be interested in that field** because it uses skills and abilities you have, BUT you're not sure yet, you're still checking things out and deciding your direction;

- **tell them you're not looking for a job,** just getting more info to help you get clear.

e. **Make an appointment to** visit them at their workplace for about 20 minutes.

f. **Make up a good list of questions** that you'd like to ask—for example: How did you get this kind of job? What are the requirements for this work? What's the best and the worst aspects of this work? What kind of pay range can be expected in this line of work? What chances are there for moving ahead in this field? Anything that would help you decide whether this is a good direction for you.

g. **Show up right on time** for the meeting, **ask all your questions,** and **take some brief notes** so you won't forget.

h. **Wrap up the meeting on time, thank the person**, and as you leave **ask them for the names of two OTHER people** who use those same skills that you want to use in your next job.

i. When you get home, sit down and **write that person a short thank-you note and mail it right away**.

j. Next day, **call the two people mentioned,** make appointments with THEM, and follow the same plan as above.

k. **Continue this process until you find yourself EXCITED and ENTHUSIASTIC about a particular line of work** and know that this is the direction you want. THEN you'll have a Job Objective you can happily pursue with all your energy.

l. Always keep in mind that **THIS PROCESS WORKS,** and admittedly it **SEEMS a bit scary**, but the fact is that **people ARE willing to share their information** when you show **respect** for their time, **interest** in their line of work, and **appreciation** for their help.

(continued from page 174)

c. **TRANSFORM the appearance of your experience.** Arrange your experience into groups of **SKILLS YOU USED** (this is called a functional format), zeroing in on those transferable skills most crucial to the new job you want. Show clearly, through specific examples, that some of your past experience was **EQUIVALENT to** or **SIMILAR to** the kind of experience called for in the job you want.

   For example: If you handled all the details for a fund-raising event for the Little League, this could translate into a skill called Marketing if you were now looking for a sales job. Or it could translate into a skill called Project Organizing if that fit your job target.

d. **If your most useful experience is way back in time, rearrange your work history**, putting it in chronological order beginning with the earliest job held. **Then your best experience will show up at the TOP of the resume** where it will get full attention.

e. **If you were recently in school and are just entering the work force** with no paid employment experience, **use a functional format** and include school activities where you gained skills. Here are some examples:

   • Working on a school paper or yearbook (researching, editing, writing, selling ads)

   • Coaching sports

   • Class projects in science, photography, marketing, etc.

   • Helping promote a concert or school event

   • Holding an office in a school club

PROBLEM #4: Long-term underemployment. "I've never had a decent job that used all my abilities—so my resume doesn't look very impressive."

OR

"I've always had low-paying jobs and unimpressive job titles, even though I had to accept a lot of responsibility."

SOLUTIONS:

Here are two ways to improve the LOOK of a resume and show that you deserve a higher-ranking position:

a. **Change the job titles so they are more accurate and fair.** For example, use "Office Manager" instead of "Administrative Assistant" IF that more reasonably reflects your level of skill and responsibility. If this makes you uneasy, you could try a compromise such as "Office Manager/Administrative Assistant." Or ask yourself if your (former) boss or co-workers would consider it accurate.

Other more accurate job titles for an Administrative Assistant might be:

- Client Liaison

- Scheduling Coordinator

- Contract Assistant

b. **Switch the focus to SKILLS and RESULTS,** rather than job titles and job descriptions, **by using a functional resume format.** Describe your most impressive accomplishments and show their full impact.

For example:

"Developed a greatly improved inventory-tracking system that sped up order processing, improved customer satisfaction, and saved the company thousands of dollars every month."

OMIT mentioning any menial tasks you did.

Here's the essential difference between a Functional resume format and a Chronological resume format:

CHRONOLOGICAL	FUNCTIONAL
JOB #1 something I did in that job something I did in that job	SKILL #1 something I did using that skill something I did using that skill
JOB #2 something I did in that job something I did in that job	SKILL #2 something I did using that skill something I did using that skill
JOB #3 something I did in that job something I did in that job	SKILL #3 something I did using that skill something I did using that skill Job #1 Job #2 Job #3

PROBLEM #5: No accomplishments to speak of. "I can't think of anything special to say; I just did the job."

SOLUTIONS:

a. **Learn to recognize your accomplishments,** because they are VERY important if you want your resume to stand out. Even if you don't have *measurable* accomplishments to put on your resume (such as "Increased sales 40%"), **look at ALL the other evidence of accomplishment** you may have overlooked, such as:

Recognition from your employer:

- Being asked to take on **more responsibility.**

   "Chosen out of a staff of 15 to train new employees in the clothing department."

   "Selected by my manager to handle special and rush assignments."

- Being **awarded an advancement,** a step up in rank.

"Promoted to senior cargo handler in 1994."

- **Earning a bonus** for bringing in a new customer or maintaining a difficult customer.

- Getting **good feedback on performance evaluations.** You can transform those comments into accomplishment statements, as shown on page 69.

Recognition from other sources:

- **Praise and acknowledgment from customers,** co-workers, outside agencies you contact for your company, union leaders, even competitors. Here's an example from a flight attendant's resume:

"Received over 100 personal letters of gratitude from passengers served over a 12-year period."

(The solutions above are by Rhonda Findling, a San Francisco area career counselor who works with job hunters in vocational rehabilitation.)

b. **The "P.A.R." approach** is one of my favorite ways to **discover accomplishments.** You look at your actions on the job in terms of **PROBLEMS, ACTIONS,** and **RESULTS.** In other words:

- what **PROBLEM** existed in your workplace?

- what **ACTION** did you take to resolve the problem?

- what were the beneficial **RESULTS** of your action?

"Transformed a disorganized, inefficient warehouse into a smooth-running operation by totally redesigning the layout; this saved the company $250,000 in recovered stock."

P.A.R. statements are powerful because they show clear examples of you *making money for your employer,* directly or indirectly, and this should look *very* interesting to your potential *new* employer.

c. **Talk to yourself!** If you can't think of anything great to say about yourself, **ask yourself the questions below.** Get a friend to listen in or to ask you the questions. This may get your creative juices flowing.

- **Do my co-workers or my boss always count on me** for certain things they know I'm good at? **What, specifically, do my co-workers think I'm good at?**

- Exactly what do I do on the job, that **I do in my own special way,** that gets good results?

- If one of my friends at work were to **brag about me** to somebody else, what would they brag about? What does that say about my skills?

- If I had to teach a new employee the tricks of the trade—that is, teach them how to do a GREAT job in my line of work—what would I teach them? **What do I do that's special, that I could teach a new employee?**

- If I suddenly had to leave the area—say, to take care of a dying relative—**what would my work buddies miss about me** while I'm gone? How would their jobs be tougher when I'm not there to help?

- If I became the boss, and I was looking to hire someone with the same skills and talents I now use on my job, **how would I describe the skills and abilities I wanted to see in this new employee?**

- If I had to put together a Training Manual for my job (or the job I'm now looking for), **how would I describe what it takes to excellently do this job?**

PROBLEM #6: Worry about age discrimination. "They'll think I'm too young" or "They'll think I'm too old."

SOLUTIONS:

a. **If you're a younger job seeker,** broaden your definition of work to include every possible way that you acquired knowledge and experience, and describe any accomplishments in a **functional format emphasizing skills related to the job,** rather than years of work experience.

If you started working in your early teens, **start your work history with those first lower-level entry jobs** and show how you've progressed over the years.

> *Example*: Sam, a new grad in his early twenties, worked in his father's business all through high school and beyond. When he included ALL that experience on his resume, he appeared to have the experience and maturity of a 30 year old.

b. **If you're an older job seeker,** you don't have to list ALL your work history on your resume. You could call the Work History section "Recent Work History," then **include only the last 10 to 15 years.** You could even add a line or two below that to cover the period left out. *For example:* "Additional earlier experience includes six years of retail sales."

Leave off the dates in the Education section rather than call attention to your age.

Notice other clever solutions for avoiding tell-tale years on pages 43, 65, 70, 132.

(The "too young" and "too old" solutions above were suggested by Susan Ireland, a Berkeley, California, resume writer.)

SOLUTIONS:

a. No problem. **Stick to YEARS** and the little gaps usually disappear. Here's how it looks:

WORK HISTORY

1990–present	Sales Associate	QuickTime Computers
1988–89	Marketing Rep	Trillium Products Inc.
1985–87	Math Teacher	Midline High School

▶ **TIP:** You can also COMBINE a couple of similar short jobs to minimize the choppy look, *for example:*

1985	Legal Secretary	Smith-Jones Attorneys, and Perry Larson, Esquire
1993–94	Teacher, ESL	College of Marin, Oakley, and City Community College, Kent

b. You could also **include unpaid work in your Work History** to fill in a small gap created by job hunting, as shown in Problem #3. This strategy works for BIG gaps too, such as years spent bringing up children, as shown below in Problem #13.

c. If you had any **training** during this period (even a LITTLE bit) **include that in your Work History** to help fill in the gap. In place of a job title for that period you could insert something like "Trainee" or "Student."

(If the training relates to your job goal, it **could** show up in two locations on your resume: under both Work History and Education/Training.)

SOLUTIONS:

What to Leave Out ...

- **Omit jobs that were very brief UNLESS** they are needed to show how you developed your skills—or to fill in a skimpy work history. Round off your employment dates to years, to avoid creating small gaps.

- **Eliminate the earliest jobs** if you're worried about **age discrimination.**

- **You COULD omit jobs that aren't important to your new goal**—or jobs that create a not-so-great impression—as long as dropping them doesn't leave a big hole in your work history.

What to Include . . .

- **Include ALL of your jobs**, however short-term they were, **IF you are very young or you have very little work experience.**

- **Include ALL of the jobs that show experience related to your job objective** even if they were short-term or unpaid.

- **Include jobs that are not particularly related** to your current job goal **IF** they help create a picture of stability, but don't describe them in detail.

- **Include unpaid work in your Work History** if it helps to prove you have skills and experience (see Problem #3) or it fills in a gap (see Problems #7, #12, and #13).

- You could **include a period of training or education** in your Work History if that helps fill in a gap, as shown in Problem #12.

> **PROBLEM #9: Confusion over education and training.**
> **"I'm not sure what to put IN and what to leave OUT in the sections on Education and Training."**

SOLUTION:

Training

- If you **completed the training, list just the certificate** you earned.

- If you **only completed PART of the training** (or you didn't get a certificate or diploma), **list every course you took** that is **directly related** to your current job target.

- If you are **new in the field, list every course you took** that is related to your current job target—even if you DID complete the training.

Education

- If your **education goes beyond high school, include any academic credentials and your degree,** even if they aren't directly related to your job goal.

- You can **mention your college work even if you don't plan to get a degree.** Here are some ways to show it:

  - Liberal Arts, Laney Community College, Oakland, CA

  - Accounting Major, 1991–92, Brooks College

  - Business Classes, Reno Community College, Reno

  - Business Classes, 1987, Reno Community College
    -Accounting -Financial Planning -Sales & Marketing

  - Correspondence Coursework in the military, equivalent to A.A. Degree in Electronics

- **Don't mention a high school diploma UNLESS** your new job specifically calls for it and you have no other schooling or job-related training to put on your resume.

- If you have **no job-related training,** and you recently left high school, **you could list any courses you took in school that show your interest** and commitment to this job goal. List the courses under a heading called "Related Education."

PROBLEM #10: No "mainstream" employment; just odd jobs. "I have hardly ever had a regular job where you get a paycheck. Mostly I've done odd jobs for cash. How can I list these jobs on a resume? Will anybody believe me?"

SOLUTIONS:

There are several ways to deal with this, depending on your situation:

a. **If you did roughly the same kind of odd job repeatedly,** or for a long period of time, you could **create your own job title and call yourself self-employed.** (In a sense you were, weren't you?) *For example:*

> *Mister Fix-It* (self-employed handyman), Chicago, 1991–present
> (Customer references available on request)

> *Household Repairman* (self-employed), Chicago, 1991–present
> (Customer references available on request)

> *A&S Hauling & Cleaning* (self-employed), Chicago, 1991–present
> (Customer references available on request)

> *Child Care* (self-employed), Chicago, 1991–present
> (Customer references available on request)

Since these **jobs can't be verified** through the normal channels, it will be very important to **find a few people you have worked for who can act as good references (see "Uses of Recommendation Letters" on the next page).**

b. **If you've done lots of very different odd jobs,** it will be more of a challenge, but the basic idea is the same: **create an appropriate job title (or titles) and list it just like a regular job.**

You should **pick the odd jobs that you did most often** and ignore the others, for simplicity and to make a better impression. Certainly don't mention any demeaning jobs or jobs you hated if you can possibly leave them out.

Remember, when you've been a self-employed person, creating an appropriate, reasonable, honest job title for yourself can be a big **boost to your self-esteem and self-confidence,** and contribute to the success of your job search. **Give yourself credit** for all the struggle and hard work it took to create your own work (and market your own skills), especially when jobs are hard to find.

c. **If you have been self-employed for quite a while,** then your work history can't be easily verified just by one phone call. BUT, **you can still prove to a new employer that you really DO have the experience,** and also a record of reliability, by **getting recommendation letters from past clients and customers—or** even others in the field who are familiar with your work. **Choose a few people you have worked for who can provide the most impressive references**—meaning they sound believable and you **know** they're willing to put in a good word for you.

It's very important to get GOOD recommendation letters! And very few people just naturally know how to write a great one, because they have no experience at it and don't know what to say. So even the *nicest* of people will just cop out and say, "YOU write it, I'll just sign it." That's NOT to your advantage, though; they're in a better position to brag about you than you are. But they need your help, which you give them by handing them a **WORKSHEET/GUIDE FOR A RECOMMENDATION LETTER** (see page 184) which **YOU** have filled out, along with a copy of your resume.

USES OF RECOMMENDATION LETTERS

Good recommendation letters are one route to credibility **when self-employed people can't otherwise document their work history.**

Here are some MORE problem situations where good recommendation letters would help:

- **When you left your last job under unfortunate circumstances**—say you quit, got fired, or left with a dispute unresolved—and you can't use your last employer as a reference. Or for some other reason your last employer won't give any meaningful reference.

- **When you have little or no employment history** and want to strengthen your job application with character references.

- **When you relocate a great distance away**—so far that it will be inconvenient or impossible for a potential employer to directly contact your past employers for references. Then, get the recommendation letters written BEFORE you move away.

PROBLEM #11: Employment history limited to temp jobs. "I've only worked through temporary help agencies, in assignments that lasted a day, a week, or a month, so I have 20 or more job assignments to list for just the past few years! **I need to list all these assignments** to document my work experience **but it makes me look like a job-hopper."**

SOLUTION:

List the TEMP AGENCY (or agencies) as the EMPLOYER on your resume, and pick one job title that covers *most* of the temp work. Then, under that, list the specific assignments, describing the accomplishments, the experience, and the skills gained. **Round off dates.**

(continued on page 185)

Worksheet/Guide for a Recommendation Letter

■ **INSTRUCTIONS for the job hunter:** Make some photocopies of this blank form so you'll have one for each person you ask to write a recommendation letter. **Then carefully <u>fill in the blanks</u> on the worksheet, attach a copy of your resume, and give the worksheet and resume to the person you asked to write a recommendation letter** (same as a "reference letter"). Once <u>you fill in the blanks,</u> this form will become a helpful GUIDE for your reference person for writing an <u>effective</u> recommendation letter for you.

<u>Remember</u>: if you request recommendation letters from several people, <u>each form you fill in will be a little different</u> because the information you write down depends on your relationship with that person.

■ **INSTRUCTIONS for the person writing the recommendation letter:**

Date the recommendation letter is needed: _____

Name, title and company of the potential employer who will get the recommendation letter:

_____

1. In the first paragraph, **state that this is a letter of recommendation for:**

   _____ (job hunter's name), who is seeking a position as:

   _____ (job title, or kind of work sought).

2. In the second paragraph, **state your relationship to the job hunter** (supervisor, colleague, long-time personal friend, teacher, etc.), **how LONG you've known the job hunter, and the nature of the work, projects or other experience that you shared.**

   Relationship: _____ Length of time known: _____

   Nature of the work or project: _____

   _____

3. In the third paragraph, **mention several of the job hunter's skills, talents, abilities, or personal qualities, and describe one or two primary accomplishments** that you believe would be interesting to the new employer because they demonstrate the skills needed for the work NOW being sought by the job hunter.

   A skill or ability important to the new job: _____

   A skill or ability important to the new job: _____

   A skill or ability important to the new job: _____

   An accomplishment that illustrates those skills: _____

   An accomplishment that illustrates those skills: _____

   (Note: The job hunter should point out the relevant skills and some accomplishments they'd like mentioned, but the reference person is the one who actually writes the letter.)

4. In the last paragraph, if you are willing to be called by the potential employer, **state how you can be reached for more information.**

Finally, please give the completed letter to the job hunter to deliver to the employer.

© 1995 Damn Good Resume Service

(continued from page 183)

It could look like this:

1991–92 **Administrative Asst./Secretary**, Kelly Services, Atlanta

Assignments & accomplishments:

- Typed business correspondence and routed incoming calls for several busy offices.

- Cleaned up a backlog of past due accounts receivable for Martinson Dry Cleaning.

- Conducted accurate year-end inventory for Graphic Design Studio.

If you think it would be impressive, you could mention the length of time you worked in each assignment, as shown on page 98.

- Filled in for the Executive Secretary of Claiborne Industries, quickly learning the office routines and successfully keeping projects on time. Earned a bonus and commendation from my supervisor (8 months).

  ▶ NOTE: I have worked for temp agencies myself, so I know that these positions can be VERY demanding (taking over during illness, crises, or overload). This experience can be a rich source of accomplishments that would favorably impress a new employer.

> **PROBLEM #12: Work history gap due to unemployment.** "I've been job hunting for a while and it's beginning to look bad on my resume—AND, there's all those OTHER times I was out of work."

SOLUTIONS:

a. If you are **CURRENTLY** unemployed, it would help a LOT to **find an immediate short-term opportunity to get some unpaid volunteer work experience**, preferably in your desired line of work, and **put that on your resume now** even if you don't start until next week. This will look better on your resume than being unemployed. But don't use the word "volunteer" to describe this position—work is work is work! (Rename the "Employment History" to read "Work History.")

b. For any **PREVIOUS periods of unemployment,** think back to what you were actually doing. If you can find **ANYTHING** that could be presented as "work," then create a job title alternative for it that will have the most credibility in the work world. Be realistic, and at the same time **don't buy the idea that certain work "doesn't count." Instead, present that work with dignity.** Here are some examples from several different people's resumes:

1990 **Self-employed Handyman** (4 months)
1991 **Electronics Trainee** – City Vocational Program (6 months)
1988 **Apprentice Painter** – Moe's Paint Shop, San Bruno
1988 **Full-time Student** – Carlsbad Community College
1983 **Full-time Caregiver** – Home care of elderly parent
1980 **Full-time Parent** – Three small children
1975–83 **Parenting and Community Work** – PTA, Scout Leader

SOLUTION:

Avoid the traditional chronological resume format and **create a functional style resume to emphasize your skills and knowledge.** Customize the Work History to fit your own circumstances. **If you DID do some volunteer work during this period** (even a LITTLE bit), include that in your "Work History" to help fill the gap.

For example: Vivian, a high school graduate, **hasn't had a *paid* job in 15 years** and is now looking for clerical work. All her work experience came from raising her children and doing volunteer community work, and could appear on her resume like this:

WORK HISTORY

1980–1995   Full-time Parent, plus community work involving Fund-raising, Voter Registration, and Community Service Committee work

Vivian would **choose a functional format,** and then draw out the "transferable skills" from her volunteer work that best support the kind of clerical job she is applying for. *For example:*

- Constantly updated an extensive mailing list of contributors, learning to accurately use a FileMaker database program.

- Successfully ran a phone bank to register voters, developing a confident and businesslike phone manner.

Vivian will **omit the Education section** until she has some training or schooling beyond high school.

> ▶ **NOTE:** Some advisors call for pulling out skills from parenting and homemaking. Unless you are *extremely* clever and sophisticated in doing this, I believe it is likely to backfire with most employers. **Unfortunately, we haven't yet arrived at a point in civilization where the work world honors parenting with the respect it deserves**. Until that happy day, dig hard for skills developed *outside* the home, in community work. (Of course, if you luck out and come across an *enlightened* employer, *why not go for it!)*

SOLUTION:

Avoid the traditional chronological resume format. **You need a customized resume to fit your circumstances.**

For example: Carol was **out of work for five years** healing from stress and a chemical imbalance. She has signed up for Dental Assistant training (which will start in a few weeks) and now she's applying for a part-time job as a clerk in a business office near the school, to help support herself while she studies. She has put together a **customized resume format** that looks like this:

RECENT WORK HISTORY

Student - Dental Assistant Training, to be completed 4/95
Legal Secretary (2 years)
    Smith-Barrow Atty. and Perry Larson Esq., Miami, OH
Advertising Sales Secretary (1 year)
    Trevor Peters & Co., Miami, OH
Executive Secretary (1 year)
    AT&T, Miami, OH

EDUCATION

Medical & Legal Secretarial Studies, and
Office Support Studies (shorthand, data processing)
    Harris Community College, Miami, OH

Notice these creative strategies that were used:

- She omitted dates and generalized about the total time in each job, under the heading, "<u>Recent</u> Work History."

  ▶ **NOTE: Only omit dates in a RARE case like this,** where the risk of omitting this crucial information is more than counterbalanced by the risk of calling attention to a substantial gap.

- She included "student" in her work history to help fill the gap and draw attention away from her current unemployment.

- She combined her two, short legal secretary jobs to create a larger-looking chunk of time. In fact, she could later combine ALL the secretarial jobs if she definitely decides to leave that field for Dental Assisting.

PROBLEM #15: Work history gap due to prison. "I have a big gap in my work history for some time I spent in prison. How do I explain this on a resume?"

SOLUTION:

The resume is not the place for explaining or admitting. Explanations can be offered at the INTERVIEW—AFTER you've had a chance to present your skills and show how you could benefit your employer. (Obviously you need to do some **very careful preparing and rehearsing for that interview,** where the tough questions will THEN have to be honestly talked about.)

Your resume is meant to GET the interview, so the information that might turn off the employer does NOT belong on the resume. (Most likely, the details WILL have to go on your formal job application—but try to postpone filling it out until you've had a chance to be interviewed and present your skills.)

You probably acquired some good work experience and marketable skills in prison. **You need to include that work experience on your resume to avoid creating a gap.** Just as shown in Problem #10 for the self-employed, this work probably has a job title similar to a job in the "outside world." And the words you use on your resume to refer to your "Employer" don't *have* to read "Folsom Prison"! You could simply use the name of the **foreman** and the **unit** you worked in, omitting the city if it's an obvious tip-off.

For example:

1989–91 ***Lathe Operator,*** CARPENTRY SHOP (John Riley, supervisor)

Here's an example from *The Ex-Inmate's Complete Guide to Successful Employment* by Errol Craig Sull:

> **BRICKLAYER**, State of Texas (Midland, TX) 1981–90. Began an apprenticeship program; worked up to certified Bricklayer. Duties: Mixed mortar, cleared and laid out site; assisted in building and repairing a variety of structures including floors, walls, fireplaces, curbs, and curing bins. **Complimented by supervisor for quality of work.**

> ▶ **NOTE**: If you have not yet been released, your Prerelease Counselor is the source of information about any legal restrictions on the kinds of jobs you apply for and the information you supply to the potential employer.

IDEA: Twelve-step Approach for Job-hunting Ex-drug Abusers

The Pacific Career Center in Santa Rosa, California, helps job hunters who are **looking for work after completing a drug rehab program.** Most of their clients have felony records, the staff says, and the felony is almost always related to drug abuse—like stealing to support their habit. So once the drug problem is resolved, there is no longer any felony problem.

The Center counselors use the Twelve-step Program's concept of "making amends" and have a client call their previous employer and say, "Here's what happened since I left." The job hunter explains that they've been in rehab, have dealt with their habit, and are ready to get back to their lives and their work.

Here's the good news about the success of this approach:

a) **Employers are happy to hear the report.**

b) **Several clients have actually gotten REHIRED** because the reason they lost the job was related to the drug abuse. Employers were willing to take them back ("they're a known quantity") now that the drug abuse was resolved.

c) **Almost all the employers agreed to at least be pleasant** when they are called for a job reference.

d) Even those who weren't able to give a reference have been **willing to limit the information they gave out** to a new employer, mentioning only the facts of the job.

Pacific Center clients who have been convicted are advised to **check "Yes" on application blanks when asked about a felony,** and add that the felony offense was drug related, that they have now successfully completed a drug rehab program and drugs are no longer an issue.

According to The Center's staff, **"It is not such a big deal anymore, as long as it can be shown that the problem has been handled and no longer affects their work."**

A NOTE ABOUT
Computer Scanning of Resumes

Most large companies are now using a computer program such as Resumix to copy hundreds or thousands of resumes into a computer database so they don't have to handle, sort, and store all those resumes by hand. This makes it faster and easier for employers to pick out the resumes of people they consider qualified for a particular job. They don't even have to LOOK at resumes that don't show the right qualifications because the computer does all the sorting once they've told the computer what to look for.

If you send your resume to one of those companies that scans them with a computer, you need to be sure your resume contains all the "magic words" that the computer is looking for. Exactly what it's looking for depends on the job opening, and **you can find out what the "magic words" are by looking carefully at the company's job description or classified advertisement** for that job. Take a red pencil and circle what looks like all the KEY WORDS that describe the qualifications, experience, skills and any other requirements that go with that job. THEN, **make sure that all those KEY WORDS show up on your resume**.

It's best to **work those KEY WORDS into your "juicy one-liners" that tell about your accomplishments.** But just to be SURE you've covered the bases, you could **add a paragraph at the bottom of your resume called "KEY WORDS"** and put in that section ALL the key words (and even the VARIATIONS of all the key words) that appear in the job description and ALSO are true about you and your experience. In this Key Word paragraph ONLY, you can apply a policy of "More Is Better," and list all the industry jargon. If in doubt, put it in! It won't hurt to have too many key words, but it *might* hurt to have too few.

Finally: To **be sure your resume is "scanner-friendly"** (meaning the computer has no trouble reading it) make these changes:

- Remove any italics, bold, underlines, and parentheses.

- Remove any shading, graphics, and horizontal lines.

- Remove anything on the first line other than your name.

- Use only one "plain vanilla" type font, and keep it at least 10 and no more than 14 points in size.

- Separate the key words with periods or commas.

- Make sure all the key words are nouns—for example:

> Purchasing. Raw Materials. Electronic Components. Manager. Amplifier Circuit. AAS Degree in Electronics Technology. Bookkeeper. General Accounting. Lotus 1-2-3. Drafting. Blueprints. Product Development. OSHA Training. Freight Operations. HVAC., etc.

These ideas adapted from Joyce Lain Kennedy's book, *The Electronic Resume Revolution*, John Wiley & Sons, Inc., 1994.

Index

Index

List of Contributors

*Resume writers whose work
appear in this book:*

Laila Atallah
Resumes for the Real World
69 Glen Avenue #304
Oakland, CA 94611
(510) 670-5738

Ron Bartlette
Winnipeg Transition Centre
1836 Main Street
Winnipeg, Manitoba,
Canada R2V 3H2
(204) 338-3899

Cory Beneker
Katannya van Tyler
Opportunities Campbell River
437 Tenth Ave., Room 201
Campbell River, B.C.,
Canada V9W 4E4
(604) 286-3436

Hinda Bodinger
Career Planning Techniques
69-16 229th Street
Bayside, NY 13364-3119
(718) 631-3635

Lauri Callen
Callen Computer Services
1279 West 24th, #2
San Pedro, CA 90731
(310) 519-8517

Kim Coats
A Better Resume Service
2127 Fifth Ave.
Moline, IL 61265
(309) 764-2470

Dislocated Workers Project
4510 NE 102nd Ave.
Portland, OR 97220
(503) 252-0758

Alina Ever
Higher-Powered Resumes
4095 Army Street, #3
San Francisco, CA 94131
(415) 647-7209

Rhonda Findling
7315 Elphick Road
Sebastopol, CA 95472
(707) 824-9142

Jan Hurley
J. Wolff Enterprises
P.O. Box 5158
Silver City, NM 88062
(505) 388-5834

Susan Ireland
Dynamite!! Resumes
46 Windsor Ave.
Kensington, CA 94708
(510) 524-5238

Wanda Jenkins
PreView Resume & Desktop
   Designs
11002 Captain's View Lane
Fort Washington, MD 20744
(301) 292-4967

Claudia Jordan
Work/Life Publications
2513 Yucca Street
Phoenix, AZ 85028
(602) 992-0144

Maurine Killough
Document Lab
1523 Judah Street
San Francisco, CA 94122
(415) 661-2323

Vicki Law-Miller
Scribbles to Script
820 South Tenth
Montrose, CO 81401
(303) 249-7451

Margaret Lawson
Professional Resume Writer
New York City, NY
(212) 862-4874

Jim Ledford
Power Resumes
14827 Colonel Allen Ct.
Baton Rouge, LA 70816
(504) 755-3894

Jenny Mish
Higher-Powered Resumes
P.O. Box 417
Tempe, AZ 85280-0147
(602) 966-1456

Yana Parker
Damn Good Resume Service
P.O. Box 3289
Berkeley, CA 94703
(510) 540-5876

Judi Robinovitz
Resumes That Work
999 U.S. Highway 1
Vero Beach, FL 32960
(407) 778-8001

Nancy Rosenberg
Resume Expert
4819 Balsam Drive
Land O'Lakes, FL 34639-5601
(813) 973-7181

Roving Resume Writers
c/o Henry Ostendorf
Episcopal Community Services
705 Natoma Street
San Francisco, CA 94103
(415) 487-3716

Karen Staggs
AccuWord Resume Writing Svcs.
26837 Contignac Dr.
Murrietta, CA 92562
(909) 698-6028

Bernie Stopfer
Resumes Plus
2855 West Cactus Rd, Ste. 28
Phoenix, AZ 85029
(602) 789-1200

Sallie Young
The Wordsmith
2797 LaJolla Ave.
San Jose, CA 95124
(408) 978-7278

Damn Good Resume Service

Publications • Products • Services

"Weird·Fred"

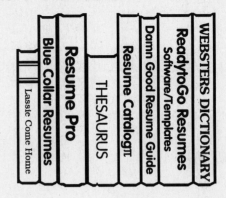

BOOKS

Available at bookstores everywhere, and ...

    ... through the publisher, Ten Speed Press, P.O. Box 7123, Berkeley CA 94707. Tel. 1-800-841-BOOK

- **Damn Good Resume Guide** – 80 pages $6.95. Half-million in print.
- **The Resume Catalog: 200 Damn Good Examples** – 320 pages, $15.95
- **Resume Pro: Make Money Writing Resumes** – 410 pages, $24.95 (see related newsletter below)
- **Blue Collar & Beyond: Resumes for Skilled Trades & Services** – 197 pages, $8.95   "

SOFTWARE

- Damn Good **ReadyToGo Resumes**

Self-Teaching Resume Templates – $39.95 (+ shipping)
THREE VERSIONS available:
• For Apple Macintosh, in Microsoft Word
• For IBM compatibles, in Microsoft Word & Word for Windows
• For IBM compatibles, in WordPerfect & WordPerfect for Windows
Includes comprehensive manual with hard copy, crash course, and resume clinic.
Available from publisher 1-800-841-BOOK OR from the author, Yana Parker, address below.

Available through the author ... P.O. Box 3289, Berkeley CA 94703 • Info Msg: (510) 540-5876 • FAX: (510) 658-9614

NEWSLETTERS

- **Resume Pro Newsletter** – Quarterly newsletter "exploring and promoting excellence in resumes."
  For professional resume writers and counselors. Subscription $20 per year ($25 USD outside the USA)
  Checks to Yana Parker, PO Box 3289, Berkeley CA 94703. Corporate Purchase Orders to FAX 510-658-9614.
  FREE sample Newsletter and detailed index to back issues sent on request.

- **Blue Collar & Beyond Newsletter** – Quarterly newsletter supplement to *Blue Collar & Beyond*.
  Additional "damn good" examples, plus ongoing Resume Clinic for tough problems. $20/year as above.

TRAINING

- Write for information on professional development workshops for entrepreneurs and agencies in the career
  field, held in Oakland, California ... and occasionally elsewhere in the US, on request.

INDIVIDUAL RESUME WRITING

- A team of professional *"damn good"* resume writers is available for one-on-one resume writing
  for clients anywhere in the USA, via mail, phone, or fax.
- Current detailed information recording: (510) 540-5876

What IS a Resume?

A good resume is a "self-marketing tool" that shows off your job skills and their value to a future employer, **for the purpose of getting a job interview.**

It starts off naming your job target and then describes your skills, experience, & accomplishments as they relate to that job target.

Front

Ten Steps in Creating a *Damn Good Resume*

1. **Choose a target job** (also called a "job objective"). An actual **job title** works best.

2. **Find out what skills, knowledge, and experience are needed** to do that target job.

3. **Make a list of your 2, 3, or 4 strongest skills or abilities or knowledge** that make you a good candidate for the target job.

4. **For each key skill, think of several accomplishments** from your past work history that illustrate that skill.

5. **Describe each accomplishment** in a simple, powerful, action statement that emphasizes the results that benefited your employer.

6. **Make a list of the primary jobs you've held, in chronological order.** Include any unpaid work that fills a gap or that shows you have the skills for the job.

7. **Make a list of your training and education** that's related to the new job you want.

8. **Choose a resume format that fits your situation**—either chronological or functional. (Functional works best if you're changing fields; chronological works well if you're moving up in the same field.)

9. **Arrange your action statements** according to the format you chose.

10. **Summarize your key points** at the top of your resume.

In REAL-LIFE resume writing, we DO skip around. So don't worry if YOUR resume comes together in some other sequence — as long as you do #1 and #2 first!

— Check out the OTHER side of this bookmark, too —

Back

– A Bookmark Mini-Guide –

No More B-o-r-i-n-g Resumes!

Five Key Concepts for powerful, effective resumes:

1. Your resume is YOUR marketing tool, not a personnel document.

2. It is about YOU the job hunter, not just about the jobs you've held.

3. It focuses on your *future*, not your past.

4. It emphasizes your *accomplishments*, not your past job duties or job descriptions.

5. It documents *skills you enjoy using*, not skills you used just because you *had to.*

A good resume makes you feel proud, makes you look your best, puts a smile on your face.

Taken from Yana Parker's books:
- **Damn Good Resume Guide**
- **Resume Catalog:** 200 Damn Good Examples
- **Resume Pro:** Make Money Writing Resumes
- **Blue Collar & Beyond:** Resumes for Skilled Trades and Services

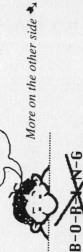

More on the other side ➤

z-z-z

B-0-R-I-N-G

Ten Speed Press, Berkeley (800) 841-BOOK

Damn Good Resume Svc (510) 540-5876 (info)
(510) 658-9614 (fax)

These bookmarks, in quantity, are available FREE to agencies and career centers.

Big Deal

FREE Bookmarks

- A handy giveaway for your students or clients.

- A provocative handout for your resume workshop.

- A nifty bookmark and reminder for you.

Shipped in bundles of 200 bookmarks. Just send postage:

☐ POSTAGE $1 (for each 200) if you want them sent by snail-mail.

☐ POSTAGE $3 (for each 200) if you want them in a hurry, first-class mail.

US stamps, US cash, or check made out to Yana Parker, Box 3289, Berkeley CA 94703

Ship to: _____

_____

_____

Date: _____

Two Damn Good
Newsletters

1. Resume Pro Newsletter
back issues

• Issue 1-2-3-4

(Special; BEST of first 4 issues)
-Guidelines, Starting a Resume Business
-Money Smarts
-New Client Intake Form
-Resumes for Ex-Military
-Hot Tips on Marketing
-Awful Truth About Resume Writing
-Resume Writing Ethics
-Counseling Inmates
-Systems Approach to Career Security
-Resume Clinic #1, on Work History

• Issue 5 *Special double issue*

-Business Woman's Resume
-Resume Clinic, student internship
-How To Write a Dreadful Resume
-Selecting a Copy Shop
-43 Marketing Ideas
-Myra's Marketing Sources
-Choosing Your Computer System
-Hinda's Career Dev't Resources

• Issue 6 *Special Large Issue*

-A New Resume Writer's Questions
-Getting Started With Your Client
-Clinic: No Experience? No Problem!
-A Job Hunter's Marketing Strategy
-Working with Soviet Emigres
-Resume for an Injured Worker
-How to Create a Good Newsletter
-Developing a Marketing Position
-Peeking Into Other Offices
-More on Resumes for Ex-Military
-Resume Writer or Resume Creator?

• Issue 7

-How Do Employers Really Think?
-Money Smarts
-Letters from Resume Writers
-Determining an Hourly Rate
-How Much Should I Charge?
-Profile of a Home Business
-Volunteering Pays Off
-LOVE that Functional Format!
-Cover Letters, Crimes, Confusion

• Issue 8

-Poor Counseling That Paid Off
-No More Boring Resumes
-Speaking of Money . . .
-Key to Excellence: Client Involvement
-Peeking Into Others' Offices
-Using Resume to Supplement a SF-272
-Inside Dope on Employers & Resumes
-Judi's Great Resume & Why It's Good

• Issue 9

-Transition: Employee to Entrepreneur
-Defining the Job Objective
-Working With Asian Populations
-Romancing the Employer
-THEN What Happens to a Resume ?
-Employer Salary Requests
-Prize Winning Resume of the Month
-The Evolution of the Cover Letter

• Issue 10

-How to Choose a Good Resume Writer
-Resume Clinic: Solutions to problems
-"Business is Great,"one writer reports
-Letters from readers: on pricing,
   competition, tracking results
-Marketing in THIS economy
-A Recruiter's Plug for Better Resumes
-Prize-Winning Resume of the Month
-Questions & Answers; Getting Started

• Issue 11

-Resume Scanning Software
-Developing Your Bag of Tricks
-Finding a Price Structure
-Letters From Readers
-Networking Cards
-Using the Library for Job Search
-Prize Winning Resume of the Month
-Broadcast Letters
-Value of Networking
-The Last Line Gets Attention

• Issue 12

Special double issue
-Resumes for Leaving the Military
-Eight Ex-military Resumes
-Lying on Resumes
-Clinic: No Job Experience; Now What?
-Letters From Around the Globe
-Re-Package the Job Hunter
-On-Line: JobPlace Bulletin Board
-What About Want Ads?
-Prize Winning Resume of the Month
-How Long, How Revealing?
-Measuring Effectiveness
-Business: Getting Started

• Issue 13

-Knock Their Sox Off
-Clinic: Legacy of Bad Relations
-Peeking Into (three) Other Offices
-Taming the (client) Shrew
-PowLitzer Prize: Russian job hunter
-Check List for Assessing a Resume
-Voicemail for Homeless Job Hunters

• Issue 14

Special Oversize Issue
-Co-mprehensive Pull-out Guide:
   Selecting a Resume Format
-On Resume Design:
   Nine Design Examples
- Make Friends w/Resume Scanning
-Clinic: Generic or not?
-Tale of a New Resume Pro
-PowLitzer Prize Winning Resume
-Short on Accomplishments? DIG!
-Letters: Customer Svc;
   Office on-the-run

• Issue 15

-Resumes on TV!
-Letters from Resume Writers
-Resume Clinic: Dates, How Far Back
-Online Career Center
-Prize Winning Resume of the Month
-Tips for Yellow Pages ads
-Helping Clients w/Emotional Blocks
-Kathleen's Marketing Tools
-Hinda's Marketing Tools
-Blue Collar Resume Packet Avlbl

• Issue 16

Special Double Issue
-Resume Clinic (3 full pages)
   11 tough questions answered
-International Networking
-Resume Scanning Technology (5 pg)
   examples of scanned resumes
   a higher-tech strategy
-Joyce Lain Kennedy's new book
-Resume Anxiety: dealing with it
-SFSU'S popular Student Job Line
-A Resume is About the Worker
-News of the Decade
-But I Just Have ONE Question ...
-Four Excellent Resumes
-Networking by Postcard-Resume

• Issue 17

Special Double Issue
-Ernie the Cat's Resume
-Job Objective: Keep it Focussed
-Twelve-Steps Help Ex-Drug Users
-Crash Course In Resume Writing
-Kids & Resumes: a Goal-Setting Tool
-Salary Requirements: what to do?
-Long-Distance Resume Writing
-Two Resume "Make-Overs"
-Letters: Resources for Resume Writers
-Two Great Resume Examples
-Resume Wizardry: Writing Tips
-Start-up Adventures in Resume Biz
-Help Wanted

• Issue 18

-Hiring Alternative: Mentorship
-Resume as Contract Proposal
-Networking With a Resume
-After Four Years in Business
-Success With Job Fairs
-Great Resume for a Chef
-Helping Homeless Job Hunters
-Using the Telephone for Job Search
-Business Start-Over Report
-Report from a Seattle Resume Service
-Darn Good Career Discovery Process
-Resume FAX-periment
-Help Wanted; October workshop flier

**Each BACK ISSUE of Resume Pro
Newsletter costs $5.
A standard issue is 12 pages.
Special issues are 16-24 pages.**

To subscribe to either newsletter:

Check or circle what you want:

1. Resume Pro Newsletter:

❑ $20 for one year (4 issues) within the U.S.A.

❑ $25 (US dollars) for one year, Canada & other countries

❑ $____ back issues #1,#5, #6, #7, #8, #9, #10,#11,#12,#13,#14,
   ($5 each)   #15,#16,#17,#18

2. BLUE COLLAR & BEYOND Newsletter/Supplement:

❑ $20 for one year (4 issues) within the U.S.A.

❑ $25 (US dollars) for one year, Canada & other countries

Date ——————————————

Name ————————————————————

Company/Title————————————————

Street ———————————————————

City/State/Zip ———————————————

Work phone ————————————————

Home phone ————————————————

Please make check payable to "Yana Parker" and send to: PO Box 3289, Berkeley CA 94703.

(or corporate P.O. to FAX (510) 658-9614)

Blue Collar & Beyond Newsletter

A Quarterly Supplement to BLUE COLLAR & BEYOND: MORE Resumes for Skilled Trades & Services

Summer 1995 • Editor/Publisher, Yana Parker • Issue #1

Subscribe to our Quarterly Newsletter
A Supplement to this Blue Collar Resume Book

Each 12 to 24 page issue includes:

◆ More **good examples of resumes** for skilled trades and services — sent in by readers. **SEND YOUR RESUME EXAMPLES NOW!** *Your subscription will be extended one issue each time one of your resumes is accepted for publication in the newsletter.*

◆ **Feature articles** on great resume writing and effective job hunting.

◆ **Problem-solving tips;** creative ways to write a good resume despite a less-than-perfect background.

◆ **Profiles** describing programs and projects around the country, that successfully serve ...
— blue collar workers
— displaced workers
— workers in military-to-civilian transition.

To subscribe...

Check or circle what you want:

❑ $20 for one year (4 issues) within the U.S.A.

❑ $25 (US dollars) for one year, Canada & other countries

**Please make check payable to "Yana Parker"
and send to: PO Box 3289, Berkeley CA 94703.**

Date _____

Name _____

Company/Title _____

Street _____

City/State/Zip _____

Work phone _____

Home phone _____